Native Performers in Wild West Shows

Native Performers in Wild West Shows

From Buffalo Bill to Euro Disney

Linda Scarangella McNenly

University of Oklahoma Press : Norman

Library of Congress Cataloging-in-Publication Data

McNenly, Linda Scarangella, 1970–
  Native performers in wild west shows : from Buffalo Bill to
Euro Disney / Linda Scarangella McNenly.
    p. cm.
  Includes bibliographical references and index.
  ISBN 978-0-8061-4281-4 (hardcover : alk. paper) 1. Indian cowboys—
West (U.S.)—History. 2. Circus performers—West (U.S.)—History.
3. Wild west shows—West (U.S.)—History. 4. Indians in popular
culture. I. Title.
  E78.W5M375 2012
  305.897—dc23

                                                              2012001794

The paper in this book meets the guidelines for permanence and
durability of the Committee on Production Guidelines for Book
Longevity of the Council on Library Resources, Inc. ∞

1 2 3 4 5 6 7 8 9 10

Contents

FIGURES

PREFACE

This book moves through space and time and delves into the complexity of Native participation in Wild West shows and spectacles by focusing on Native perspectives and experiences. It follows the stories of Native performers' experiences through the archival record and oral histories up to the voices of contemporary performers, revealing additional meanings and alternative interpretations of this experience: narratives of opportunity, success, pride, skill, and identity. The journey begins in the archives and ends at tourist sites.

The task of reading through the vast archival record in sixteen different depositories, even when it is concentrated on materials that referenced Native performers with Wild West shows, was both challenging and rewarding. Many finds ignited my curiosity: passport applications for Native performers to travel to Germany to work in the Sarrasani Circus; letters from Native people asking for employment in shows; a sixty-four-page program for Buffalo Bill's Wild West show. There were scrapbooks, newspaper clippings, correspondence, photographs, show programs and couriers, and more. Gaining access in the archives to specifically Native voices and perspectives was, however, challenging, given the nature of what is preserved in the record. "Central records" such as the ones I examined, that is, documents from the dominant society (created by, and then assembled in the archives by), present one perspective and tend to lend themselves to certain types of analyses. The experiences of Native performers through tourist and heritage sites were also overshadowed by the creations of non-Natives. Contemporary Wild West shows are produced for a particular (Euro-American white, maybe even western) audience, and analyses of the discourses and representations of Native peoples in this context tend to generate postcolonial critiques focused on the deconstruction of stereotypes and power. This is worthy project that has contributed much to the scholarship, but my goal was to complicate this picture.

One way I tackled interpretive challenges (and biases) and gained access to Native voices was to use multiple methods and sources of data: interviews with contemporary performers and oral histories from descendants of Mohawk performers from Kahnawake. There was, in fact, still much to be learned about Native peoples' experiences in Wild West shows; there were other stories to be told. Indeed, the strength of ethnographic research is its capacity to expose the experiences of people on the ground and discern how they create meaning. And the oral histories not only gave me insight into emic or "insider" perspectives but led to different interpretations of archival materials, photographs in particular. As Cruikshank observes, oral histories are valuable for "generating different kinds of social analysis, leading to different interpretations of a given event" (1992, 22). Thus, interviews and oral histories from performers' descendants and their interpretations of the archival record were crucial for revealing and substantiating alternative perspectives of Native experiences in Wild West shows and spectacles.

A second way to address these interpretive challenges is to apply different theoretical and analytical lenses that provide other ways of thinking about both historical and contemporary experience. The overarching framework of this book is the idea of a Wild West show contact zone (after Pratt 1992) to explore the complex encounters and negotiations that take place between non-Native people and Native performers. In the context of participating in Wild West shows, in fact, there has been more agency than first appears. Just how much agency Native performers have exerted and in what ways seems to be the question. Ortner's dual-modality view of agency as power *and* as intentions, or cultural projects, provides a productive approach to address this question because it offers another way of thinking about agency. Using these analytical lenses, I was able to trace and qualify the various forms of agency in a more nuanced way. These approaches (methodological and interpretive) may be applied more broadly to study other (post)colonial relationships to explore how indigenous peoples have exerted agency and expressed identity, as scholars such as the Comaroffs (1991, 1997), Ortner (1999), and Phillips (1998) have done. In this book, I explore one lens for examining Native peoples' negotiation of colonial encounters—the Wild West show contact zone.

Acknowledgments

This book was possible only through the generosity and cooperation of numerous people and funding agencies. During the course of my research I was fortunate enough to meet many wonderful people, who were generous with their time and knowledge. First and foremost, my sincerest thanks to all the research participants for their generosity, time, and openness, in particular Ferlyn Brass, Jeff Briley, Erin Brown, Ronny Brown, Tim Bruised-Head, Tammy Burr, Barbara Delisle, Kevin (Kave) Dust, Brian Hammill, Lane Jenkins, William Jim, Conway Jocks, Edre Maier, Kevin (Wiley) Mustus, Earnest Rangel, Silvia Trudeau, Billy Two-Rivers, Carter Yellowbird, Jimeno, Brad, and Paula. I also thank Morgan Phillips and Alex Rice for sharing their experiences and insightful comments.

There are so many librarians and archivists to thank for their patience with my endless questions about their collections and requests for photocopies. Thank you to the staff at the Denver Public Library (Western History) and the University of Oklahoma Libraries, Western History Collection, at the Norman campus. I also acknowledge the assistance of Steve Friesen from the Buffalo Bill Museum and Grave in Golden, Colorado. Mary Jane Warde and Judith Michener at the Oklahoma Historical Society went above and beyond, helping me sift through the archival records, and the librarians were always available to assist. Ronny and Erin Brown at the Pawnee Bill Museum and Ranch, as well as Jeff Briley, assistant director of the Oklahoma Museum of History, made time out of their busy schedules to talk Wild West. Librarian Mary Robinson at the McCraken Library, Buffalo Bill Historical Center in Cody, Wyoming, was efficient and kind, and Juti Winchester offered research assistance. Thank you also to Francois Cartier at the McCord Museum Archives and Documentation Centre and to Moira McCaffrey.

My warmest thanks to Edre Maier and all the wonderful people of Sheridan, especially Cate Ambrula, Deanna Dillon, Tammy Burr, Della Herbst, and Mr. Maier. Thanks to everyone at Euro Disney for an enjoyable experience, including Christel Grevy, Nick Rogers, and Karine Moral. My gratitude to the community members of Kahnawake and the staff at Kanien'kehá:ka Onkwawén:na Raotitióhkwa for their kindness and assistance, in particular Brian Deer, Donna Goodleaf, Martin Loft, Lisa Phillips, Alex Rice, Anna Mae Rice, Kara Dawne Zemel, Cory, Lynn, and Morgan.

This research has been an ongoing project over many years and has benefited from the direction and advice, as well as editorial suggestions, of other scholars and colleagues. I am grateful to have had a doctoral supervisor who supported me throughout this long process. I thank Dr. Trudy Nicks for her steady support, patience, advice, and editing skills as she reviewed draft after draft. Thank you for your excitement and the many lively discussions about this project. To my committee members Dr. William Rodman and Dr. Eva Mackey, I appreciate all your valuable insights, advice, comments, and support. Thanks also to the external examiners of my dissertation and the two reviews of my manuscript, who provided interesting and insightful comments. My thanks to Dr. Ruth Phillips for sharing her passion and scholarship, and for her inspiration and support. Thank you to the wonderful team at the University of Oklahoma Press for supporting this project and making the publication experience so enjoyable, especially Alessandra Jacobi Tamulevich, Alice Stanton, and Sandy See. Jean Middleton efficiently indexed the book, a task I gladly passed on. I would also like to thank the two anonymous reviewers, who provided constructive advice and ample ideas for improving the manuscript.

My gratitude goes to the many funding organizations that supported the research and writing phases of my work, which ultimately resulted in this book: the Social Science and Humanities Research Council Doctoral Fellowship and Postdoctoral Fellowship; the Royal Anthropological Institute of Great Britain and Ireland (RAI) Emslie Horniman Scholarship Fund and the RAI/Association of Social Anthropologists Radcliff-Brown Trust Fund; the McMaster University School of Graduate Studies Fieldwork Funding; and the Buffalo Bill Historical Center Garlow Fellowship.

I dedicate this book to my family, Domenico, Lucia, and Enza, my daughter Sofia, and my wonderful husband, Terry, for their unwavering love and support. Terry, your encouragement, patience, love, and support throughout this journey have made all the difference.

A Note on Terminology

I originally intended to use the term *Aboriginal* to refer to the indigenous people of North America; however, I found that performers at Euro Disney did not recognize or associate themselves with this term. I have chosen to use *Native* as opposed to more politically correct terms such as *First Nations, Native North American,* or *American Indian* because it is more intuitively inclusive of both First Nations from Canada and Native North Americans from the United States. I occasionally use *Indian* in reference to historical contexts and contemporary theoretical usage, as well as when employed by the people I interviewed. All these terms are problematic and have been criticized, but terminology is needed. When known, I include tribal and nation or band affiliations, which is the preferable terminology. Because I use the term *Native,* I use *Nativeness* as opposed to Indianness—used in the literature—for consistency. More recently, *indigeneity* has been used by scholars, but I have chosen not to introduce yet another term into this book. *Westernness* is shorthand for western culture, history, and identity—a complex that defines what is "western." Some may disagree with this usage and suggest that "western heritage" may be a more appropriate term. However, the term *Westernness* more closely parallels my usage of the term *Nativeness.*

Another question was what to call non-Natives. I use *non-Native* and *white* interchangeably. When applicable, I use more specific terms such as *European, Euro-American,* and *white settler.*

One more qualification: the words *tradition* and *traditional.* These terms are problematic, for they denote some sort of static, unchanging culture. This is not what I mean to convey. I use these word to mean community (First Nation or tribe) or locally produced cultural expressions, recognizing that these are in fact multiple and diverse as well as adaptive, creative, and ever-changing. At times I also use *local* or *tribal,* but these terms are not always adequate because of the multiplicity of expressions. In some cases I use *traditional* in reference to the Office of Indian Affairs' and public's view of cultural expressions.

Native Performers in Wild West Shows

Buffalo Bill's Wild West Show Program

⟶ THE COWBOYS ⟶
Auguste Durand-Ruel, the famous French impresario, welcomes
the troop of Western riders – the cowboys! – as they race in
on their horses.

⟶ BUFFALO BILL'S ENTRANCE ⟶
Buffalo Bill welcomes the cowboys who carry the colours
of the four ranches.

⟶ PRESENTATION OF ANNIE OAKLEY ⟶
The legendary rider and crack shot

⟶ PRESENTATION OF SITTING BULL ⟶
AND OF AMERICAN INDIANS
Buffalo Bill introduces the man who beat Colonel Custer
at the Battle of Little Big Horn, the great chief of
the Sioux nation and members of his tribe.

⟶ THE HERD ⟶
Image of the cowboys' daily life, as they drove their herds
from the Texas plains to the cities of the North.
We can see with what skill the cowboys capture the cattle. . . .

⟶ BUFFALO HUNTING ⟶
Dances and rituals – on the theme of the visionary quest –
that helped them hunt the legendary animals.
A real buffalo chase . . . authentic Indian dances and songs

⟶ ANNIE OAKLEY ⟶
Returns to the arena and overwhelms the public
with her shooting demonstrations

⟶ RODEO GAMES ⟶
Teams of cowboys and Indians compete

⟶ THE DEADWOOD STAGECOACH ⟶
Arrives, but just as it is crossing the arena,
something unexpected happens!

⟶ THE FINAL REVIEW ⟶
Auguste presents the whole team for a last farewell to
the public. . . . Buffalo Bill pays a last tribute
to the American West.

Introduction

The Wild West Lives On

The program with which this chapter opens could describe a Wild West show from the late 1800s. In fact, it is a program for the 2005 Euro Disney reproduction of Buffalo Bill's Wild West show in France, still in production as of 2011.[1] The 2004 brochure entices the public to "Imagine wild buffalo, Indians and cowboys together in an arena right before your eyes! With stagecoach attacks, gunfight showdowns, shooting demonstrations, horse-riding displays. . . . this will be a night to remember."[2] Why has North America's Wild West continued to fascinate audiences for over a century? And, more important in terms of this book, why would Native people wish to perform in a Wild West show, a genre of spectacle which, scholars have convincingly argued, has contributed to the production and dissemination of stereotypes and images of an "Imaginary Indian"?[3]

The more I investigated the popularity of Wild West shows, the more shows I found, not only throughout North America but in Europe as well. Contemporary spectacular traveling productions such as the Great American Wild West Show from Branson, Montana, promise "action, history and thrills" for audiences all over the world. Montie Montana, Jr., based in Springville, California, states that "the tradition continues" with his one and only Buffalo Bill's Wild West Show, touted as the best reenactment show around. People all across the United States imagine their history through Wild West shows in Greenbush, Wisconsin; Pawnee, Oklahoma; and Cody and Sheridan, Wyoming. Or they may attend a reenactment of Buffalo Bill's funeral at the Buffalo Bill Museum and Grave in Golden, Colorado. Canadian equivalents include a Native-run Wild West at Pat Provost's Wild Horse Show and Buffalo Chase in Brocket, Alberta, and the Indian Village at the Calgary Stampede.[4] First Nations from British Columbia perform at a Wild West theme park and reenact traditional life at a living history site in Sweden.[5] There are rodeos, teepees, and mining camps at Pullman City theme park in southern Germany.[6] The Buffalo Bill's Wild West show reincarnation at Euro Disney is certainly the most spectacular re-creation, aimed to please even the most demanding spectator. All of these spectacles showcase "the West" to some extent, but Indians are the stars of the shows.

International fascination with Indians today is a continuation of historical narratives and processes. Contemporary Wild West shows emerged from a historical trajectory of the display of indigenous peoples. In the nineteenth century, displays and live performances featuring Native peoples were an established part of world's fairs, exhibitions, pageants, and a variety of Wild West shows.[7] Natives were represented as the bottom of the savage–civilized scale, a position that justified the evolutionary views and nationalistic aspirations of Europeans and Americans at the time. Images of Natives as exotic, noble savages were also fabricated and are still widely reproduced around the world today in different media forms and spaces. In these ways, the participation of Native peoples historically in these contexts (and the stereotypical representations that ensued) may be viewed as another form of colonization or, at the very least, another type of colonial relationship (e.g., Bank 2002; Jasen 1993–94; Mathur 2000; Nash 1989; Parezo and Troutman 2001). Even though Wild West shows produced stereotypes and reproduced colonial relationships, this does not mean that Native people did not willingly participate in some cases. The nature of Native participation in Wild West shows, past and present, is the subject of this book.

With its demonstrations of frontier cowboy skills and Indian life and proclaimed authentic reenactments of history, the Wild West show became an internationally acclaimed phenomenon that dominated public entertainment for approximately thirty years from the late 1800s to the early 1900s. Russell's seminal work (1970) was one of the first studies to outline the scope of Wild West shows systematically. The most famous and successful Wild West show was undoubtedly Buffalo Bill's Wild West, which existed from 1883 to 1913.[8] A vast literature deals specifically with Colonel William F. Cody (also known as Buffalo Bill) and his famous show. Comprehensive biographies of Cody provide insight on his life and his American tours, as well as the successes of his Wild West show business (e.g., Blackstone 1986; Wilson and Martin 1998). But Wild West shows were not simply forms of entertainment; they reflected and formed ideologies of the time. Thorough histories (e.g., Kasson 2000; Moses 1996; Russell 1970; Warren 2005) demonstrate how Wild West shows contributed to the frontier myth and the making of American nationalism and identity, as situated within a particular social, cultural, and political context (see also Brooklyn Museum 1981; Slotkin 1981, 1992; and White 1994). This historical context is explored in some detail by Warren (2005, xi), who shows how Buffalo Bill's Wild West is related to the development of theater, the rise of industrialization, and the growth of the upper class and an ethnically diverse settler culture in America; he further interprets the meaning of the show's performances in terms of the settlement and urbanization of America, what he calls "domestication," and increasing racial tensions in America.[9]

With such excellent histories about Buffalo Bill's Wild West show, there is no need to write another, although chapter 1 does outline briefly the scope and content of the top three Wild West shows. This book offers a "revisionist history" of sorts by focusing on Native performers' experiences and perspectives, following other scholars who have begun to tease out the complexities of the Wild West show experience. Maddra (2006), for example, explores in more detail the experiences of ghost dance prisoners who traveled with Buffalo Bill's Wild West in 1891/92 in order to critique interpretations of the ghost dance as "hostile." Moses's (1996) important book examines the tensions between the images of Native people created in Wild West shows and those promoted by Indian agencies and the struggle of one image to prevail over the other—the traditional, uncivilized Indian versus the civilized, educated Indian, respectively (see also Deloria 1981). His understanding of federal government policies and deep historical research shed light on Native experiences in this context. Building on this line of research, this book investigates Native–non-Native encounters in the context of Wild West shows through time and offers additional interpretations of Native performers' experiences.

Buffalo Bill's Wild West show is perhaps the best known, but other Wild West shows existed. Reddin (1999), Shirley (1993), and Wallis (1999) explore contemporaries of Cody's show, with similar attention to the entrepreneurs and their shows. Reddin investigates the "Wild West show phenomenon" over a hundred years, from Catlin's tour of his "Indian Gallery" of paintings, which was animated by Native performers in the 1830s to '40s, to Buffalo Bill's Wild West and the Miller Brothers' show, and concluding with Tom Mix, a star of Wild West shows and movies in the 1930s. His book explores the evolution of the phenomenon and the "changing perceptions of the Plains and its people" through time (Reddin 1999, xvi). This begs the question, are contemporary Wild West shows simply reproductions of historical shows, or have Native representations and performances changed? Have Native performers' experiences changed?

Why do they participate? An examination of contemporary Wild West show reincarnations is overdue, and this study moves forward into the twenty-first century to address these questions, based on fieldwork observations, interviews, and content and discourse analysis of related media at two contemporary Wild West shows.[10]

The performances themselves (past and present) are also of concern in this book. Wild West show performances produced meanings that resonated with American audiences. As Kasson observes, historic Wild West shows involved a process of myth making and "memory showmanship." Her study illustrates the link between "Americans' understanding of their history and their consumption of spectacularized versions of it," illuminating the connections between performance, memory, and national identity (Kasson 2000, 8). In particular, the performance of the conquest of "savage" lands and peoples supported America's nation-building project, based on the notion of western expansion and progress (Slotkin 1981; 1992; White 1994). But did these performances have any meaning for the Native participants? A reexamination of archival materials sheds light on how performances in Wild West shows connected with Native performers' sociocultural, political, and economic lives and with expressions of Native identity.[11]

Wild West shows were an international sensation and well received by European audiences overall.[12] In addition, Native performers received the attention of the press (see Scarangella 2008). Some excellent studies provide details on European tours and audiences' reception of the shows and perception of Native performers.[13] One question that remains is whether the Canadian experience was different, and if so, how? With the exception of brief discussions from Baillargeon and Tepper (1998), Bara (1996), Lounsberry (2000), and Skidmore (2003), there is a lack of in-depth studies on American Wild West show tours in Canada and Canadian Wild West show counterparts. How did Native people in Canada engage with

Wild West shows, and what did performing in these shows mean to them? What were the implications of participating in Wild West shows for Canadian Native people's political, economic, and cultural lives? Blanchard's synopsis (1984) of Mohawk showmen and Nicks's overview (n.d.) of Algonquian and Iroquois performers begin to examine the Canadian context, with a focus on Native people's experiences in various public performance spaces. These First Nation groups in particular have been active in public performances throughout history. I was intrigued by the fact that some Native people in Canada organized their own performance troupes and wondered if oral histories about these experiences existed in the communities.[14] Although more research is needed, this book begins to investigate the Canadian experience in more detail on the basis of oral histories, interviews, archival research, and content analysis of historical photographs. A case study of some Mohawk performances from Kahnawake (Quebec) offers a glimpse into Canadian Native participation in a variety of performance spaces historically. In addition, interviews with contemporary performers at Disneyland Paris provide insight on the experiences of some Canadian Native performers today.

Throughout history, Native peoples, cultures, and identities have been appropriated and commercialized by whites for the consumption of mainly white European and American audiences (Meyer and Royer 2001). Television, films, literature, tourist sites, and hobby groups, even museums and art, are all sites for the construction of cultural myths and images of the Indian (Bataille 2001; Bird 1996; Doxtator 1992; Francis 1992). Perhaps it should not have been surprising, then, to discover that Wild West shows still exist, given the persistence of images of Indians in popular culture. Sites of cultural representation such as these are complex, dynamic spaces for the construction of histories and identities (Deloria 1998).[15] These sites represent and misrepresent Native peoples, and Wild West shows are no exception.[16] This book contemplates the representation of Native people in Wild West shows. However, whereas much of the scholarship focuses on the construction of stereotypes and the commercialization of Nativeness, I investigate how Native performers negotiate representations and narratives produced in Wild West shows.

How Native peoples are depicted by non-Natives is an important topic because sites of cultural representation and performance are ideological and political arenas.[17] These sites are not neutral; they reflect and form ideas about Native peoples. Scholars have examined the construction of social meaning and portrayal of indigenous peoples in various spaces of public display and performance, such as museums (Karp and Lavine 1991; Phillips 2004a), world's fairs and exhibitions (Parezo and Troutman 2001; Raibmon 2000; Rydell 1984), film (Germunden 2002; Lischke and McNab 2005, 281–303), and tourism (Hendry 2005; Johnson and Underiner 2001; Nicks 1999; Stanley 1998). This scholarship has been central to our understanding of colonial relationships and dominate society's construction of images of indigenous peoples, revealing the ideological and political uses of such representations as well as how these images have been contested. Although I also consider these issues, the goal is to highlight how Native participants have interacted with dominant society and produced their own social meanings in the context of Wild West shows.

This book engages with anthropological debates of the representation of Native people and questions of agency through a series of comparative case studies that investigate Native people's participation in Wild West shows through time.[18] I examine the experiences of Native performers with the top Wild West shows historically (1885–1930), of three Mohawk families from Kahnawake who performed in a variety of spectacles in the early twentieth century, and of contemporary Native performers in Wild West show recreations at Disneyland Paris and Buffalo Bill Days (Sheridan,

Wyoming). The impact of the colonial project and the legacy
of Wild West shows in terms of perpetuating stereotypes
are certain. However, with this book I move away from a
focus on exploitation to one of encounters and negotiation.
I show how Native performers have actively engaged with
non-Native society and individuals in what I am calling a
Wild West show "contact zone" (after Pratt 1992). I follow
the work of other scholars who have examined Native–non-
Native encounters as a two-way engagement; examples are
Ortner's (1999) investigation of Sherpas' involvement in
mountaineering; Maddra's (2006) critique of interpretations
of the ghost dance as "hostile" in the context of assimilation
and Wild West shows, revealing the "accommodation" of the
Lakotas; Troutman's (2009) exploration of the politics of "Indian" music; Phillip's (1998) study on Iroquois beadwork and
tourist arts; and Nicks's (1999) exploration of "Indianness" at
Indian Villages and other performance spaces. I propose that
Native people's experiences in Wild West shows are a site for
the investigation of agency and of the negotiation of social
meanings and representations of Native identity.

WILD WEST SHOW AS "CONTACT ZONE"

In her book on the history of imperial narratives in travel
writing, Pratt employs the concept of a "contact zone" to
refer to "the space of colonial encounters, the space in which
peoples geographically and historically separated come into
contact with each other and establish ongoing relations, usually involving conditions of coercion, radical inequality, and
intractable conflict" (1992, 6). This definition highlights asymmetrical power relationships but does not preclude the possibility of resistance or agency. Pratt explains: "By using the
term 'contact,' I aim to foreground the interactive, improvisa-
tional dimensions of colonial encounters so easily ignored or

suppressed by diffusionist accounts of conquest and domination. A 'contact' perspective emphasizes how subjects are constituted in and by their relations to each other" (1992, 6). She further argues that this interactive contact zone is a place of transculturation, a process whereby marginal groups selectively incorporate dominant culture to varying degrees for their own use (1992, 6, 228).[19] Others have similarly noted that transculturation occurs in spaces of intense cultural contact, such as tourism, suggesting that it involves a two-way process of interaction and cultural production (Nicks 1999; Phillips 1998). In short, contact zones are (post)colonial spaces of interaction by multiple participants with various agendas involving unequal power relationships, but with the possibility of agency by the marginal groups.

The idea of a "contact zone" as an arena for the encounter of previously separated groups of people has been applied to various sites of contact and interaction. For example, museums are contact zones in that they are spaces of interaction between communities and involve the negotiation of power and agency (Clifford 1997, 204, 212). Furthermore, the production of museum exhibits is a complex process involving many people with varying interests (Clifford 1997, 206–7).[20] Fairs and powwows are also examples of contact zones, where individuals unite in their common interests or gather to engage in sociopolitical action (Buddle 2004; Ellis 1999; Ellis et al. 2005; Herle 1994; Lerch 1992). At powwows Native participants have the opportunity to imagine themselves as part of a larger community based on their shared experiences and history—poverty, discrimination, alienation (Herle 1994, 79). They are also sites of face-to-face interactions where Native people make connections, advance political claims, and assert their own indigenous identity in a contemporary world (Buddle 2004, 5, 31). Buddle's examination of Native-run fairs suggests that Native participants have "reframed or indigenized the zone of contact" (2004, 40). Have Native performers similarly "indigenized" Wild West shows, and to what extent? One thing is certain: the Wild West show is also an arena of encounters and negotiations.

In the late 1800s and early 1900s, Wild West shows, exhibitions, pageants, and other public performances were one of the few sites of contact in which non-Natives could see Native people and culture (Buddle 2004; Herle 1994; Maddox 2002; Patterson 2002). Wild West shows, therefore, may be conceptualized as a space where normally separated groups come together—a Wild West show contact zone—where Natives and non-Natives meet, interact, and create meaning. In this contact zone, multiple encounters involve the negotiation of representations, performances, and social meanings; that is, representations and meanings are actively constructed. Maddox (2002, 9) claims that Native people could represent themselves in various performance spaces in the late 1800s to the early 1900s. Have Wild West shows provided Native performers a space to experience and express their own social meanings of Nativeness? To what extent, if at all, have Native performers negotiated representation and performances in Wild West shows through time?

In the nineteenth century, entrepreneurs recruited Native performers for a variety of shows and exhibitions. Like the colonial encounter Pratt described as being characterized by coercion and inequality, Wild West shows have involved control, exploitation, appropriation, and commodification of Native peoples and culture. Reports of ill treatment and complaints from Native performers, as well as performances of the superiority of white society and the savagery of Indians in shows, reflect the unequal power relationships at Wild West shows. Contemporary Wild West show re-creations continue to be motivated by market demands for the exotic Indian and the profits to be made by selling Nativeness.

Still, though Wild West shows have produced stereotypical representations of Native people and power relationships have been unequal, there is evidence that Native performers have found ways to use this encounter for their benefit and to experience identity in their own ways, both in the past and in the present. In short, in spite of exploitation and commercialization, there has also been agency. This is where Pratt's notion of a contact zone is useful for my analysis, because it considers both power and agency, highlighting how Native performers participated in these encounters for their own reasons.

So now comes the task of identifying and qualifying the varying degrees and forms of agency that Native performers have possibly exerted in Wild West shows through time. A practice theory approach to agency opens up ways to think about, analyze, and explain Native performers' experiences because it considers the dialogical relationships between sociocultural structures and human action (Ortner 1994, 2006). Practice theory attempts to "restore the actor to the social processes without losing sight of the larger structures that constrain" and is based on examining cultural processes such as discourse and representation with social actors on the ground, opening up a space for questions of power and agency (Ortner 2006, 3). Such an approach to agency complements a Wild West show contact zone framework, and this study draws heavily on Ortner's work. Still, the notion of agency itself remains contentious. Ahearn's (2001, 112) definition of agency as "the socioculturally mediated capacity to act," in which social action is mediated in both its production and interpretation, is a good starting point. But this definition leaves open some questions about intention, power, and forms of agency.

Scholars vary on the centrality of intention. Ortner (2006, 132, 136) argues that intention is central (it differentiates "agency from routine practices") while recognizing the importance of unintended consequences. Conversely, Asad critiques anthropologists' overemphasis of conscious intention (2003, 69 n. 6). Asad's critique is related to anthropologists' concern over the tendency to discuss agency in terms of free will, or "responsibility" (Ahearn 2001, 114). Although agency "calls to mind the autonomous, individualistic, Western actor" (Ortner 2006, 130), I do not view agency as solely the exertion of free will or individualistic experience. As Ortner (2006, 130–31) argues, social agents are embedded in "the multiplicity of social relations in which they are enmeshed," including power relationships. Native performers' have their own intentions and reasons for participation in Wild West shows, but their participation is nonetheless embedded in a complex web of (unequal power) relationships with show entrepreneurs, government agents, and the public, to name a few.

Scholars also give varying weight to power as cultural and institutional order (i.e., structure) and as social relationship (Ortner 2006, 5). Bourdieu (1977), like Foucault, focuses on the structural power that shapes people's action, which in turn reproduces structure; this is the crux of his notion of habitus (Ortner 2006, 5). I take a more middle-of-the-road position, leaving room for the possibility of agency by social actors beyond solely the reproduction of structure.[21] As Sewell contends, although structure consists of asymmetrical power relations, "agency [is] not opposed to, but . . . constituent of, structure." He argues that social agents have knowledge of cultural schemata and access to resources (which are controlled by all members of society) and can be empowered by this access to resources; therefore, social agents are able to exert "some degree of control over the social relations in which [they] are enmeshed" (1992, 20). Still, power differentials and the sociocultural milieu affect social actors' capacity for agency, which differs in kind and extent (Sewell 1992, 20). Agency is culturally and historically constructed; the form it takes varies in different times, places, and contexts (Ortner 2006, 136). This book traces the various forms and degrees of agency in the context of participation in Wild West shows, as it is shaped by different sociopolitical and economic structures ranging from the Office of Indian Affairs and Indian schools to Wild West show entrepreneurs and contemporary heritage and tourism sites.

Finally, scholars consider the form of agency: what does agency look like? An important question for this book is how to identify agency in the Wild West show contact zone. Ortner (2006, 134) discusses agency in terms of intention, the cultural construction of agency, and the relationship between agency and power. Following Ortner, I view agency in terms of (a) power negotiations and (b) intentions—what she calls "cultural projects" (or in her earlier work, "serious games"). She writes that agency as power "is organized around the axis of domination and resistance, and thus defined to a great extent by the terms of the dominant party, while [agency as the pursuit of projects] is defined by local logics of the good and the desirable and how to pursue them" (2006, 145). Power and agency are inexorably linked, and, although power is often thought of in terms of domination and resistance, agency is not necessarily equated with resistance. I heed Abu-Lughod's caution (1990) against the "romance of resistance." As Ahearn (2001, 115–16) points out, oppositional agency (i.e., resistance), is only one form of agency. Ortner concludes that domination and resistance are not irrelevant, but "questions of agency within relations of power and inequality are always complex and contradictory" (Ortner 2006, 137; see also Asad 2003). Throughout this book, I trace agency in terms of the negotiation of power and as *intentions, or cultural projects*. I identify specific forms of agency that Native performers exert, always situated within the cultural, political, economic, and performative structures that constrain them. At times I refer to different specific forms of agency—expressive or performative—in order to qualify the extent of agency that exists, rather than claim a large-scale, all-encompassing form of agency. In other words, I trace Native performers' agency in its specific and limited forms and degrees.

WILD WEST SHOW PROGRAM:
ORGANIZATION OF THE BOOK

This study is not about one group of Native peoples from one community; rather, it explores the experiences of Native performers from various tribes and First Nations in Wild West shows through time. This "unrooted," multisited approach to fieldwork has been increasingly necessary in anthropology and other disciplines in response to an increasingly mobile, transnational, and globalized world.[22] Scholars such as Appadurai (1990) and Marcus (1995) have conceptualized this new field site as consisting of "pathways" or "flows" where people, stories, objects, technology, capital, media, and ideas and images, for example, circulate.[23] My research pathway is an experience—Native participation in Wild West shows—that cuts across different locations and Native groups. I trace the story of Native performers' experiences through the archival record and oral histories up to the voices of present-day performers.

Between June 2004 and August 2005, I conducted multisited ethnographic and ethnohistorical research across Canada, the United States, and France. There are limits to this study. I do not purport to have a complete picture of the entire field of Wild West shows, past and present. There have been countless Wild West shows throughout history. Moreover, contemporary Wild West shows also come and go; some exist only for a short time but are annual, while a few others, like Euro Disney's, continue throughout the year. This spatial and temporal ephemerality characterizes Wild West shows and certainly multisited research in general (Hannerz 2003, 210; Kurotani 2004, 207). Indeed, multisited research cannot have an "ethnographic grasp of the entire field" for *each locality*; rather, it permits the examination of processes that traverse linked localities (Hannerz 2003, 207). This book thus provides a series of case studies that examine processes, encounters, and relationships through time and space.

The organization of the individual chapters requires some explanation. Chapters 2 through 6 are organized into two main parts. The first part of each chapter explains the context of Native participation in Wild West shows, as demonstrated in archival materials and popular media. It describes and analyzes dominant society's power to shape representations in the show, as well as the nature of encounters between Native and non-Native peoples. The second part of each chapter builds on this analysis with the aim of complicating our understanding of Native participation in Wild West shows and other performance spaces and spectacles. Drawing on archival sources, interviews with Native performers, and oral histories, this section brings forward Native performers' perspectives and experiences and explores how they have engaged with and negotiated these encounters. It points to additional ways of thinking about and analyzing what we know about Native participation in Wild West shows. Chapter 4 is the exception to this format; it focuses predominately on Native experiences and perspectives, aided by oral histories and archival sources from Kahnawake, Quebec.

Chapter 1 provides background on the Wild West show phenomenon from the 1880s to the 1930s and establishes the context of Native experiences and representations in these shows. It outlines the origin, content, and format of the top three Wild West shows in which Native people participated: Buffalo Bill's Wild West, Pawnee Bill's Wild West Show, and Miller Brothers' 101 Ranch Real Wild West Show.

Chapters 2 and 3 examine historic Wild West shows with a focus on Native performers from reservations in the United States and the American context. Chapter 2 explores Native performers' experiences as employees of Wild West shows. The focus is on the recruitment and hiring of Native people as well as working conditions, encounters characterized by unequal relationships among a variety of parties. Although it is a story of control, exploitation, and commercialization to a certain degree, this chapter also draws attention to the fact that some Native performers considered working in Wild West shows an opportunity. Native performers had their own goals and intentions and actively pursued the opportunities and benefits of working in Wild West shows, including the chance to travel freely and procure much-needed income while maintaining traditional activities and the family unit, during a time of forced relocation and the reservation period.

Chapter 3 focuses on the performances in Wild West shows themselves as another form of encounter—a performance encounter. Wild West shows claimed to be authentic representations of history and identity. Performances perpetuated myths of the frontier and American progress as they invoked images of exotic warrior savages. Though the shows produced stereotypical images of exotic noble savages, Native participants also experienced performances in their own way and created their own meanings. Specifically, they experienced Nativeness by expressing their "warrior identity" and by maintaining traditional dance and dress. This represents another form of agency in that they adopted and modified this encounter, as well as the performances themselves, to express their Native identity.

Chapter 4 is based on the rich history available in archives and oral histories from Kahnawake (Mohawk Territory in Quebec, Canada). It provides a case-study analysis of some Mohawk performers who participated in Wild West shows and a variety of exhibitions, commemorative events, pageants, and vaudeville from the late nineteenth to early twentieth century. Many of these performance contexts share a Wild West theme or depend on images of a noble savage. However, oral histories from the descendants of Native performers offer additional interpretations of the archival record and thus of Native performers' experiences. Rather than stereotypes, statements of identity, pride, and success imbue these oral histories. These statements are evidence of agency because they reveal Native performers' own goals and intentions. This chapter also reevaluates Native performers' regalia, which were diverse rather than simply "stereotypical Plains." Some performers expressed their identity through the incorporation of local Iroquoian designs; others also used their Nativeness to their advantage to advance their careers, which again demonstrates agency. Finally, this chapter illustrates how an investigation of archival materials that incorporates oral histories and Native interpretations may bring us closer to understanding Native perspectives of this experience. It also lends support to the conclusions about the historical American context in chapters 2 and 3.

The last two chapters of this book move ahead into the twenty-first century to investigate contemporary reproductions of Wild West shows in France and the United States. Chapter 5 examines the construction of Westernness and Nativeness at an international, spectacular performance site— Buffalo Bill's Wild West Show at Disneyland Resorts, Paris. Studies of the representation of the Other provide a useful lens for deconstructing "Disneyfied" histories and identities but do not offer much insight into Native experiences. In this chapter, interviews with Native performers address questions of stereotypical representations, identity, and agency. Although chances for Native performers to challenge representations of the show itself are limited, the opportunities working at Euro Disney provide and the pride Native performers feel as a result of their professional accomplishments are forms of agency. Interestingly, these narratives of opportunity and pride mirror those found in the archives in chapter 2 and those expressed in oral histories in chapter 4.

In the next case study, Native performers have more control over their participation. Chapter 6 considers the (non) recognition of Nativeness at an American Wild West show that is part of Buffalo Bill Days in Sheridan, Wyoming. This encounter occurs in relation to a heritage site, the Sheridan Inn. The construction of "heritage" at Buffalo Bill Days involves a complex process of inclusion and exclusion in which selected histories and identities are commemorated. While

Buffalo Bill Days generates "official" histories and representations of Westernness, Native performers offer alternative representations and narratives of Nativeness through their powwow music, dance, and dress. I argue that this reflects their agency in that they use (and control) performances of Native identity to negotiate interactions, contest stereotypes, and make statements of cultural continuity. The Pawnee Bill Wild West Show in Pawnee, Oklahoma, provides another brief example of an American Wild West show reenactment at a heritage site and museum that similarly struggles with the inclusion of Native participation and representations; in this case, Native participation has declined. Besides the obvious economic reasons, I suggest that perhaps this "absence" is another way of contesting representations.

The Conclusion brings to light how a multisited, multimethod research approach that draws on different theoretical lenses enriches our understanding of Native experiences in Wild West shows. It revisits the two main objectives of this book: to identify the form and extent of Native performers' agency, and to illuminate the negotiation of Native identity in this context. In sum, this book reveals narratives of opportunity, success, pride, and skill as it also offers a glimpse into understanding Wild West show "contact zone" encounters from the perspective of Native performers.

CHAPTER ONE

Where the Wild West Began

Buffalo Bill, Pawnee Bill, and the Miller Brothers

In 1905 there were many opportunities to see Native people performing in Wild West shows and exhibitions. The Cummins Indian Congress and Wild West Show was touring in the United States, and the Miller brothers were organizing their first Wild West show at the famed 101 Ranch in Oklahoma. Native people from Kahnawake (Mohawk Territory, Quebec) were performing at the Indian Village at Earl's Court, London, as part of the Naval and Fisheries Exhibition. And Buffalo Bill's Wild West, on its second European tour, was now playing in France. Other entrepreneurs attempted to imitate Buffalo Bill's Wild West, but none could match William F. Cody, whose show career spanned three decades. After Cody's show, the two most successful Wild West shows were the Miller Brothers 101 Ranch Real Wild West Show and Pawnee Bill's Historic Wild West.

LIVE DISPLAY, EXHIBITS, AND THE EMERGENCE OF WILD WEST SHOWS

Wild West shows emerged in the nineteenth century as part of a larger context of spectacle that blurred the line between education and entertainment in the display of Others. In the 1840s, for example, American painter George Catlin toured the Great Britain and France with a troupe of Native performers.[1] Catlin combined his exhibition of paintings of Native Americans, called "The Indian Gallery," with lectures meant to educate the public on Native American life; his book *Letters and Notes* was very much like a Plains ethnology (Truettner 1979, 43). But it was Native performers who provided the entertainment value. Native dancers animated Catlin's paintings by performing "the mock ritual of the *Tableaux Vivants*" and spectacular war dances (Truettner 1979, 44). Large exhibitions and world's fairs began in the mid-1800s and also influenced the content and form of Wild West shows.[2] While world's fairs encouraged trade and industry, they also reinforced national identities and notions of progress based on material and economic growth (Rydell et al. 2000).[3] The fairs displayed people as well as goods (Benedict 1983, 13, 43), and Others were put on show in anthropological exhibits and villages arranged to illustrate the hierarchy of racial types as well as the progress and civilization of the Euro-American, white world. Midway and entertainment zones similarly displayed Others as representative of races lower on the evolutionary scale. These displays of colonial and imperial power popularized discourses about race and progress that were premised on notions of evolution (Rydell 1984, 5).

Other entertainments would similarly create and disseminate popular images of race and progress. In the nineteenth and twentieth centuries, historical pageantry was another popular expression of nationalism and identity (Glassberg 1990). In fact, the years from 1870 to 1910 witnessed the greatest growth in virtually all forms of outdoor and variety entertainment (Wilmeth 1982, 3). Wilmeth (1982) discusses the growth of theater, variety and vaudeville, minstrel shows, medicine shows, and dime museums, many of which often included Native performers. These forms of entertainment and public display and performance thrived in the decades leading up to the birth and growth of Wild West shows. These entertainments were not immune to displays of gender, race, and ethnicity; in fact, they were prime sites for the construction of narratives based on these attributes and categories. At the same time, dime novels told stories about the frontier and America's conquest and progress. The frontier was expanding, and the tension between settlers and Native people was growing. It was a time of unrest and confrontation competing with the desire to settle the West and fulfill manifest destiny. Wild West shows grew out of this context of colonialism and progress as well as this history of the cultural display of Others.

Combining elements of theater, circuses, and pageants along with the didactic goals of exhibitions, Wild West shows became a sensational phenomenon. In essence, the Wild West show was "an exhibition illustrating scenes and events characteristic of the American Far West frontier" (Wilmeth 1982, 77). Typically a two- to three-hour extravaganza, Wild West shows consisted of a series of spectacular acts that fall into roughly seven major categories:

Grand entry: introductions of the heroes (and enemies) of the West, who rowdily rode in on horseback.[1]

Cowboy pastimes: demonstrations of frontier and cowboy skills of horsemanship and marksmanship, such as trick shooting, fancy riding, lassoing, and racing.

Indian vignettes: reenactments of Indian ceremonies and life, such as a thrilling buffalo hunt or "savage" war dance.

Historical reenactments: reenactments of significant battles or famous attacks, such as the Battle of Little Bighorn or the attack on the Deadwood stagecoach; at the very least, an attack on an emigrant train or settler's cabin.

Military displays: military drills or shooting, often including representatives of U.S. Army units demonstrating their techniques and sometimes representatives from other countries such as Britain or Japan or Devlin's Zouaves.[5]

Ethnic Others: other international acts that exhibited the diversity of the "races," such as Russian Cossacks or Bedouin bandits.

Circus acts: variety acts such as dancing elephants and Arabian acrobats.

These categories are not exclusive and could overlap thematically. The top three Wild West shows incorporated these themes to various degrees.

COLONEL WILLIAM F. CODY AND BUFFALO BILL'S WILD WEST

William F. Cody, frontiersman, buffalo hunter, Pony Express rider, and army scout, was born in 1846.[6] Dime novels immortalized his legendary adventures, but Wild West shows brought them to life.[7] Cody's theater debut was in an 1872 stage production called *The Scouts of the Prairie,* followed by *Buffalo Bill Combination* in 1873, written by dime novelist Ned Buntline. The combination featured three frontiersmen: William Fredrick "Buffalo Bill" Cody, John "Texas Jack" Omohundro, and "Wild Bill" Hickok. The stage productions received a lukewarm reception from the press (Kasson 2000, 21), but Cody's experiences as a buffalo hunter and scout, combined with his charisma, made him popular with audiences. Cody continued to alternate between theater and scout work for the next decade (Kasson 2000). In 1882 he celebrated America's progress with a nationalistic display for the Fourth of July in North Platte, Nebraska (Reddin 1999, 59; Russell 1970). His recognition of the public's desire to see myths of the West live, together with his success as marshal of the Fourth of July celebration and encouragement from Nate Salsbury to move beyond "dime novel thrillers" (Reddin 1999, 59), eventually led Cody to produce a form of live entertainment that became extremely popular with international mass audiences—the Wild West show.

Cody toured with Wild West shows from 1883 to 1916, making two grand tours of Europe with his own Buffalo Bill's Wild West shows in 1889–92 and 1903–1906. His first Wild West show production in 1883—The Wild West, Hon. W. F. Cody and Dr. W. F. Carver's Rocky Mountain and Prairie Exhibition—brought recognition to Cody and to this form of entertainment. But it was not until 1884, when the show was reorganized according to the vision of theater businessman Nate Salsbury as Buffalo Bill's Wild West, that Cody achieved true stardom. That was not a record year in terms of profits, because of an accident and persistent rain (Kasson 2000; Shirley 1993, 110), but the Wild West formula proved successful. What the show needed now was a draw, something that would bring in audiences and thrill them. In 1885, Cody engaged Annie Oakley, known for her skill as a trick shooter, but it was Sitting Bull, the "killer of Custer," who drew in the crowds. A camp of Cheyennes, Arapahoes, Sioux, and Pawnees created an atmosphere of impending danger, and from that point on Native peoples continued to be an essential component of the show.

The 1885 program included an array of acts, mainly in the category of cowboy pastimes, Indian vignettes, and historical reenactments, and closed with the dramatic "Attack on Settler's Cabin."[8] In 1886 the show played at Erastina, on Staten Island, New York, for six months. The Oglala Sioux American Horse Jr. replaced Sitting Bull as the Indian star. Cody also added a Canadian hero, Gabriel Dumont, "the Hero of the Half Breed Rebellion" (the Riel Rebellion of 1885).[9] The winter show at Madison Square Garden was reorganized for an indoor arena and included a new feature, a pageant "History of American Civilization" in four epochs, or "The Drama of Civilization," produced in collaboration with Steel Mackay (Reddin 1999, 83).[10] The show progressed as a coherent narrative rather than as a series of acts.[11] Historical reenactments and vignettes of life in the West such as these would become standard features of Buffalo Bill's Wild West shows and other Wild West shows.

Buffalo Bill's Wild West show went on its first European tour from 1889 to 1892, bringing the production prestigious recognition from overseas. Cody's first overseas trip, however, was in 1887, to participate in the American Exhibition at Earl's Court in London, England. His show opened on May 9, but Cody held a command performance for the Prince of Wales on May 5 (Moses 1996, 50). On May 12 the arena was again closed to the public for a command performance for Queen Victoria (Moses 1996, 52). Reporters praised the show for its realistic portrayal of western life and authentic displays of horsemanship.[12] One reporter wrote of the London show, "the most realistic and dramatic representations of pony expresses, the postmen of the prairies, pursued by Indians, of stage-coaches stopped and rifled, of sleeping camps stormed in the night, of shooting, scalping, burning (of huts), and a score of other wild adventures."[13] The framework of the show was based on discourses of the savage and vanishing Indian, the frontier, heroic individualism, and progress. But more important, in terms of success of the show, Cody promoted his show as an authentic portrayal of life in the West, which distinguished it from other outdoor entertainments like the circus.

The press was obsessed with the Native performers, reporting on their appearance and their every move in stereotypical ways, both romantic and derogatory. In particular, Red Shirt was the "pampered favourite of European sovereigns."[14] Red Shirt's meeting with former prime minister William Gladstone, as well as his opinions and comments, was covered extensively by the British and American press, complete with sketches of his encounters with white society and his performances.[15] Other Native people with Wild West shows became well known, such as Sitting Bull, Black Heart,

Iron Tail, Black Elk, Luther Standing Bear, No Neck, Rocky Bear, Short Bull, and Kicking Bear, to name a few. The public's fascination with Native people never wavered, and they continued to draw curious audiences.

After a year of performances in the United States, Cody returned to Europe. Buffalo Bill's Wild West opened in Paris on May 19, 1889, at the Exposition Universale and the grand opening of the Tour Eiffel. The European tour covered France, Spain, Italy, Germany, Wales, Scotland, and England, including a return visit to Earl's Court in 1892.[16] The addition of ghost dance prisoners to the 1891/92 season following the "Wounded Knee Massacre" generated much interest and attracted crowds (Maddra 2006). Cody continued to enjoy the patronage of royalty, politicians, and well-known members of the elite, who all praised the show. The program consistently thrilled audiences with displays of horsemanship and marksmanship, races, Pony Express reenactments, emigrant trains, attacks on the Deadwood coach and settler's cabin, a buffalo hunt, Indians, and famous cowboys.[17] Also in 1892, "Rough Riders" were added to the show.[18] Cody subsequently added Cossacks, Mexicans, and Riffian Arabs and expanded military displays to include drill teams from the United States, Germany, and Russia, giving the show an international flavor—in 1893 advertised as a "Congress of Rough Riders."[19] In 1893 the show played next to the Columbian Exhibition in Chicago to record crowds, and from 1893 to 1901 the show toured North America.[20]

Cody proved triumphant in matters of showmanship but was less successful at managing financial matters, and James Bailey, of circus moguls Barnum and Bailey, took financial control of the show in 1895 (Russell 1970, 61). The basic show format and content continued along similar lines; however, Cody continuously added acts based on current events, such as the Battle of Tien-Tsin act in 1901 and the Battle of San Juan Hill (1898) act in 1902. Cody returned to Europe in 1903 for his second grand tour, which closed in Ghent, Belgium, in 1906 (Reddin 1999, 150).[21] The expanded program for this tour included twenty-three acts with a wide array of cowboy pastimes, historical reenactments, and Indian vignettes.[22] The show maintained its international flavor and military displays, but the Battle of Tien-Tsin and the Battle of San Juan Hill acts were replaced with the European crowd pleaser, the "Battle of Custer."

In 1907, Cody approached another successful entrepreneur, Gordon Lillie, for financial assistance. Their two Wild West shows combined in 1908 when Lillie bought one-third of Cody's show and became an equal financial partner with Cody, although he did not share in the recognition (Reddin 1999, 152). Buffalo Bill's Wild West and Pawnee Bill's Great Far East Combined, also known as the "Two Bills" show, toured North America. With Cody's reputation and fame and Lillie's financial backing and business sense, the Two Bills show continued to impress audiences in North America. The show format changed little, except for the addition of a Far Eastern component, which was condensed into one large act of "genuine Natives who enact the characters which they represent."[23] The 1909 version consisted of the full array of thematic acts: cowboy pastimes, Indian vignettes, historical reenactments, extensive military displays, different "races," and circus acts.[24] The show maintained its claims of realism and educational value: "The intent and purport of the allied exhibition is to entertain while educating the spectator, through the medium of animated pictures and scenes typical of the Wild West and Far East."[25] Even though the show continued to draw in significant crowds, it was coming to a close.

In 1910, Cody announced his retirement from show business with a series of "farewell" performances that stretched over two years.[26] In the end, it was competition from other Wild West shows, circuses, and an emerging film industry, as well as poor financial management on Cody's part, that led to the demise of the Two Bills show in 1913. Reportedly the Two Bills owed its printing company $40,000; Lillie could pay his part of the debt, but Cody could not, and Lillie would not transfer the mortgages secured from Cody in order for him to pay his share.[27] Cody lived out the last four years of his life in debt, touring with the Sells-Floto circus in 1914/15 and the Millers' Wild West show in 1916.[28] He died in Denver, Colorado, on January 10, 1917, at the age of seventy.

MAJOR GORDON LILLIE'S WILD WEST SHOW AND ETHNOLOGICAL CONGRESS

Frontiersman, scout, teacher, interpreter, and Oklahoma "boomer" Gordon Lillie's knowledge and experiences in the West formed the foundation for his show business career. As with Cody, his experience was his claim to authority and authenticity. Born in 1860, Lillie grew up reading dime novels; years later, as Pawnee Bill, he would become the inspiration for dime novels. In his teen years Lillie became acquainted with some Pawnees near Wellington, Oklahoma, who had been relocated from Kansas.[29] He eventually formed a friendship with the elder Blue Hawk, learned the Pawnee language, and went on buffalo hunts. He also joined a cattle drive and worked in the fur trade with "Trapper Tom." Lillie became a teacher to the Natives and an interpreter and secretary for the Indian agent Major Bowman at the Pawnee Indian Agency until 1881 (Shirley 1993, 73, 81).

Lillie entered the Wild West show business indirectly. He first provided Pawnees for Cody's Wild West show in 1883/84 and then took some on tour with the Healy and Bigelow Medicine Show in 1885 (Russell 1970, 32; Shirley 1993, 94, 105). In 1886 he worked as an interpreter with Buffalo Bill's Wild West (Russell 1970, 32). With his experience and connections with Natives and the Office of Indian Affairs, Lillie decided he could produce his own show rather than work for others (Shirley 1993, 115). In 1888 he went

on tour with Pawnee Bill's Historical Wild West Exhibition
and Indian Encampment (Russell 1970, 32), and from 1890
to 1893 he toured the United States and Canada with a new
and improved show.[30] Lillie also targeted the European market, going on tour in 1894 to Belgium, Holland, and France,
among other countries (Blanchard 1983; Russell 1970, 52).[31]
While in Europe he held a command performance for Queen
Wilhelmina I of Holland in honor of Princess Victoria of England (Shirley 1993, 143).

The Pawnee Bill's Historical Wild West show had all the
features of Buffalo Bill's Wild West and more. Major Gordon
Lillie billed himself as the "White Chief of the Pawnees"
and "famed guide, government interpreter and Oklahoma
hero."[32] Lillie and his wife May—"Champion Girl Horseback
Shot of the West"—were the central characters of the show
and demonstrated the usual array of cowboy pastimes. However, Native people and vignettes remained an important
feature attraction. The show also featured several historical
reenactments such as "Trapper Tom's Cabin," "Mountain
Meadows Massacre," "Horse Thief" acts as well as an attack on a stagecoach.[33] In later years Lillie's show consisted
of some military-themed acts, but not to the degree Cody's
show did. For example, one act presented a "Grand Military
Tournament—Introducing the cavalry tactics of the great nations of the world," with Americans, Cubans, English, Indians, and Arabians.[34]

As with Buffalo Bill's Wild West shows, Native performers
camped in an Indian village outside the performance arena.
But Lillie more explicitly advertised his encampment as part
of the show than Cody did. Certainly the encampment was a
draw because it afforded an opportunity to see Native people
going about their daily lives. In addition, Lillie traveled with
a museum of Native North American items he had collected
in the United States and Canada, such as garments, headdresses, beadwork and quillwork, wampum belts, scalps,

instruments of war, bows and arrows, and farming tools (Russell 1970, 52; Shirley 1993, 135).

Lillie's ethnic component was quite expansive in comparison with Cody's show. Pawnee Bill's Historical Wild West and Mexican Hippodrome of 1893 added a large Mexican segment, with vaqueros demonstrating their riding and roping skills, a Mexican contra dance, and a twelve-piece Mexican band.[35] By 1898, Lillie had expanded his show to include even more ethnic Others and circus acts, including mind readers, magicians, and snake enchanters.[36] His 1901 show contained Mexicans, "bushmen," Arab Bedouins from Africa, Russians, South American gauchos, Singhalese artists from Ceylon, Hindus, Japanese, and more.[37]

By the beginning of the 1900s, Wild West shows were no longer a novelty. According to Russell, Lillie's "Far East" component added much-needed interest in order to keep the show competitive (1970, 54). In the 1904 program Lillie states that not many are familiar with his travels to the East, and this feature "will be equally instructive, elevating and entertaining." Lillie promoted three main components—the Wild West, the Far East, and the Mexican Hippodrome—as unique, not-to-be-missed features: "All three will present . . . a living, picturesque and consummate history of the entire world."[38] Thus, the show drew in the public with an incredible mixture of cowboys and Indians, Eastern exotics, ethnic diversity, circus-type acts, an array of animals, museum-like displays, and an Indian encampment.

In 1908, Lillie bought out one-third of Cody's show (Mrs. Bailey's share) to form the Two Bills show. His wife, May Lillie, was against the merger and did not travel with the combined show; she argued that the Pawnee Bill show had made good money and that the Pawnee Bill name was well established (Shirley 1993, 180). But Lillie envisioned combining the top two Wild West shows into a megaproduction with him as manager. Despite Cody's intention to leave the show to Lillie after his retirement, Lillie did not continue with the Two Bills show after Cody could not pay his share of the debts.

At the age of seventy, Lillie attempted to recapture the West one last time. In 1930 he established the Old Town and Indian Trading Post near Pawnee, Oklahoma. The trading post sold items made by local Pawnees and Poncas, and a museum displayed Lillie's collection of curios. The west side of the Old Town contained a model of Southwest cliff dwellings; the east side featured a Native village with replicas of Pawnee dwellings and "towering tepees of the Cheyennes, Comanches and Kiowas, the bark houses of the Seminoles and Pottawatomies, and the historical Pawnee Council House and mud lodges" (Shirley 1993, 228). Tourists could visit for the day or stay in one of fifteen cabins for the full experience. Former employees and Native friends from Lillie's show served as custodians of the Old Town until it burned down in 1939 (Shirley 1993, 228). Lillie died on his ranch in 1942. Today, a visit to the Pawnee Bill Ranch and Museum leaves no question about Lillie's success and the mark he left on Oklahoma as one of the participants in the "winning of the West."

THE MILLER BROTHERS' 101 RANCH
REAL WILD WEST SHOW

Colonel George W. Miller founded the 101 Ranch in Oklahoma on land leased from the Poncas (Reddin 1999, 159). The Miller "empire" grew to 110,000 acres of farming and ranching, and afterward oil investments (Reddin 1999, 159; see also Collings 1971). After the death of the colonel in 1903, his three sons took over. Zack took care of the ranch and livestock; George was in charge of the finances, management, and the oil and gas business; and Joe would become director of their Wild West show ventures.[39] The Millers staged their first Wild West show in 1905 to entertain convention goers from the National Editorial Press, the National Association of Millers, and the National Association of Cattlemen, as well as a crowd of other spectators (Reddin 1999, 160). They presented an awe-inspiring spectacle that included a buffalo hunt, an Indian attack on a wagon train, Indian dancing, bull-dogging, and bucking broncos, as well as five hundred cow-boys and a thousand Indians, including the famed Apache leader Geronimo (Reddin 1999, 161).[40] The show engrossed the public and press alike.

After the success of their Wild West shows in 1905 and at the 1907 Jamestown Tercentenary Exhibition in Norfolk, Vir-ginia, the Miller brothers decided to make their Wild West show a permanent business enterprise.[41] A joint venture with showman Edward Arlington of Ringling Brothers, the Miller Brothers' & Arlington 101 Ranch Real Wild West Show toured Mexico, North and South America, and Europe from 1908 to 1916. They often had more than one show travel-ing at the same time. For example, in 1913 the Millers had a show touring North America as well as a contract with the Sarrasani Circus in Germany. Zack also took their Wild West show to London for the Anglo-American Exposition of 1914. The four-act production consisted of a western vignette with settlers building a cabin and displaying cowboy skills followed by an attack by Indians who burned the cabin; an Indian vignette with Indians setting up camp, complete with a war dance followed by an attack on a stagecoach; a pioneer vignette of the Santa Fe Trail; and finally another Indian am-bush on settlers in the Grand Canyon (Reddin 1999, 173–74).

From 1905 to 1916, the Millers' Wild West show followed a formula reminiscent of Buffalo Bill's Wild West. It consisted of displays of cowboy pastimes, Indian vignettes, and his-torical reenactments with "real Indians, real cowboys, real scouts, real cowgirls" from the 101 Ranch.[42] A unique aspect of the Miller brothers' show was the large cowgirl contingent; the fifty-cowgirl entourage attracted the attention of the pub-lic and received much publicity in the press (Reddin 1999, 170). The 1912 show featured a Pony Express demonstration, a buffalo hunt, a stagecoach holdup by bandits, and the "Indians' thrilling attack on an old-time pioneer's camp"— standard Wild West show fare.[43]

The Millers attempted to redefine Wild West shows by presenting a new view of the West based on ranchers rather than celebrating the "conquest of the Plains," as was the case with the Buffalo Bill and Pawnee Bill shows (Reddin 1999, 162–63). They promoted their show as a reproduction of ranch life in Oklahoma, with the 101 Ranch epitomizing the "American era of ranching." Programs described the 101 Ranch "empire" and the Millers' success. Detailed descriptions of the founding of the 101 Ranch and in-depth biographies of the three brothers established the Millers and their ranch as representative of the West. A 1911 program stated: "The 101 Ranch is to-day a monument to the enterprise and industry of the owners. . . . Each one has contributed their best to the accomplishment of the ambition of all; to carry out the purpose of the father and husband, George W. Miller, to make the 101 the largest, the best and the most famous ranch in the United States. In this they have been successful."[44] An advertisement for the 1912 tour similarly publicized the show as an opportunity to see "heart-stirring events of the old days" and "sports and pastimes of the modern ranch."[45]

Reddin maintains that this new narrative did not resonate with audiences because no "imaginative literature" about ranchers existed, as it did with frontiersmen such as Buffalo Bill. Furthermore, their narrative was too narrowly restricted to the Millers' experience, and audiences "would not accept the Millers and the 101 as the sole embodiment of the West" (Reddin 1999, 162, 164). The Millers may not have been completely successful in transforming the narrative of the West to one of ranching, but their show proved interesting to audiences and fairly successful because it offered something more. Moses suggests that the success of the show was due in part to the Millers' emphasis on "real ranching" rather than "marauding Indians" (1996, 183). In addition, although some of the acts were similar to those in Cody's show, such as fancy riding and shooting, the Millers' show was closer to rodeo, featuring rough-riding of mules and steers, bronco riding, bulldogging, bucking horses, and lassoing events, and it emphasized competition between the performers.[46] It may be that the Millers' Wild West show was successful in part because it incorporated more rodeo events, which certainly brought a different kind of excitement to the show.[47]

Reddin also suggests that the role of Native Americans and Native performances was less prominent in the Millers' shows because of their focus on the ranch as representative of the Plains (1999, 163–64). Based on show programs, advertisements, and newspaper clippings, it would be fair to conclude that the Millers' show did follow a primarily western theme, focusing on the skills of the cowboy and ranching life. Out of twenty-one displays described in the 1911 program of events, for example, only two explicitly included Native participation: Indian war dances and an attack on an emigrant train crossing the Plains.[48] However, the number of Indian vignettes and reenactments with Native participation in the Millers' production in general did not differ greatly from the other shows. There were three or four Indian vignettes out of twenty or more scenes in Buffalo Bill's and Pawnee Bill's shows as well, the main difference being that Cody and Lillie more explicitly highlighted the Native components of their shows. I agree with Roth (1965–66, 423, 425) on this point, who states that Native people continued to play an important role in historical reenactments and vignettes in the Millers' Wild West show. A portion of their program invariably featured Indian dances or a buffalo hunt. Most important, the Millers' programs featured pictures and stories about Native people and their cultures, and their posters and advertisements almost always included Natives.[49] The Millers hired Native people from various tribes and agencies, including Ogalala, Brulé, Cheyenne, Ponca, Sac and Fox, Comanche, and Kiowa (Moses 1996, 179). And in terms of numbers, the

Millers' show included just as many Native performers as Cody's and Lillie's.[50]

Military displays were also a part of the Millers' show. The 1916 version in particular followed a militaristic theme, adding patriotic displays of military power in their military pageant "Preparedness" and capitalizing on current events with a reproduction of the Battle of Columbus (Reddin 1999, 175).[51] In 1926 the Millers invited Swift's Zouaves to display their skills and Russian Cossacks to demonstrate their daring horsemanship.[52] The 1929 program and daily review magazine stated that the show would offer a "gathering of crack cavalry troops of the world powers," including English, Germans, Italians, Mexicans, and Americans, but the section that outlined the show's acts listed only the Zouaves and Cossacks.[53]

The Millers reentered show business in 1925 after a nine-year hiatus and attempted to keep the Wild West show alive into 1930, with little success.[54] Reddin writes: "In this time when circuses often included a western segment and the Millers' entertainment contained a circus, Wild West shows lost their identity as a distinctive form of entertainment" (1999, 180). In response to growing competition, the Millers incorporated more circus acts and Eastern themes in the 1920s. Now called the Miller Brothers' 101 Ranch Real Wild West and Great Far East, their "Far East" component included Eastern dances, circus acts, elephants, and camels to meet the public's demand for novelty and to compete with a growing circus business.[55] In fact, one-third of the show consisted of a Far East spectacle. The Millers even experimented with ancient history themes such as "Julius Caesar" (Reddin 1999, 178, 180).

Still, the Millers' Wild West show maintained some traditional western acts. The 1926/27 and 1929 seasons featured more than twenty acts demonstrating cowboy pastimes, Indian vignettes, ethnic Others, circus acts, and historical reenactments.[56] According to the 1929 courier program, cowboy pastimes featuring cowboy skills and rodeo events continued to be an important part of the show.[57] A section in this program explicitly links early roundups on the 101 Ranch with the development of Wild West shows and western rodeos. Eight of the acts contained a cowboy sports component, in addition to the Pony Express display. Possibly because of the show's identity crisis in later years, business declined. By 1931, competition from Western films and the emergence of rodeo contests, coupled with the Depression and the Millers' financial troubles on the ranch, finally put an end to their Real Wild West show; the demise of the 101 Ranch "empire" soon followed in 1932.

FILMS: THE END OF LIVE WILD WEST SHOWS?

Perhaps in an effort to sustain the Wild West show as a form of entertainment, all three of these prominent show entrepreneurs produced films. The contribution of their films and Wild West shows to the development of the Western film genre requires further investigation, but for the purposes of this book it is worth mentioning their attempts to move into the film industry.[58] Cody stated that his goal had always been the preservation of history.[59] In 1914 he embarked on a film venture that sought to immortalize the Indian Wars and the stirring events of American history in moving pictures.[60] Produced by the Essanay Film Company, *Indian Wars* presented "realistic portrayals" of significant battles of the Indian Wars from 1876 to 1891.[61] Filmed at the Pine Ridge Reservation, the motion picture provided a visual record of progress—the winning of the West and Indians' progress toward civilization.[62]

Whereas Cody sought to preserve historical events on film, Lillie's main goal was to provide "educational entertainment." In fact, Lillie reproduced his Wild West show in his film *Pioneer Days*, or *Pawnee Bill in Frontier Days*.[63] Unlike

Cody, Lillie produced numerous films: *The Buffalo Hunters;
May Lillie, Queen of the Buffalo Ranch*, a classic story of robbery and ransom; and *Pawnee Bill, the Frontier Detective*.[64] His
film *Pawnee Bill, the White Chief* presented a more biographical storyline, portraying his life as a guide and trapper and
early life in Oklahoma.[65]

The Miller brothers also produced several film reels of
their Wild West show and ranching life.[66] Moviemakers came
to the ranch to film as early as 1908 (Reddin 1999, 186; Wallis
1999, 342, 377). The Millers had a contract with the New York
Moving Picture Company to use their Wild West show outfit in film projects during the 1911 and 1912 winter seasons
in California.[67] This quickly turned into a partnership as the
Bison 101 Film Company, which produced four epic two-reel
movies: *War on the Plains; The Indian Massacre; The Battle of
the Red Men*; and *The Deserter* (Wallis 1999, 372). Descendants
of the Millers claim that they did not receive the recognition
they deserved for their contribution to the Western film genre
(Wallis 1999, 349–50).[68] Perhaps this is so. But despite their
success with their outdoor spectacles, Cody, Lillie, and the
Millers all failed to make the transition into Western films.
The live outdoor Wild West show had become a thing of the
past, or so it seemed.

CHAPTER TWO

Working in Wild West Shows
Pursuing Opportunities

Wild West shows brought Native peoples, government officials, reformers, and show entrepreneurs into contact through the employment of Native performers. Power relationships among these different individuals were unequal. The Office of Indian Affairs (OIA) dominated this encounter because it had the power to regulate recruitment and employment. OIA policies discouraged the hiring of Native performers because officials believed that working in Wild West shows was potentially harmful. Nevertheless, show entrepreneurs still purportedly profited from, and sometimes exploited, Native performers. OIA restrictions for employment were in place to protect Native performers, but these restrictions also coincided with government assimilation policies. An examination of Indian school newsletters provides telling examples of these policies and ideologies, as well as of reformers' agendas, to "assimilate the Indian." In general, newsletters highlighted the opinion that working in Wild West shows inhibited the civilizing process. I suggest, however, that some Native people considered working in Wild West shows an opportunity. Native people had their own goals and intentions and were therefore also active agents in this encounter. They pursued opportunities available to them within the constraints of OIA regulation and the existing political and ideological context. In fact, employment in Wild West shows provided Native people with opportunities outside of reservation life and benefits that made this a desirable prospect.

"ENGAGING INDIAN ACTORS": RECRUITMENT, THE OIA, AND INDIAN SCHOOLS

The hiring of Native performers was situated within the larger political and ideological colonial context of the time—the assimilation of the Indian. Power relationships are made visible in the OIA's ability to regulate employment and the Indian schools' aim to define Nativeness in terms of civilized or uncivilized in the context of Wild West shows. Despite the OIA's attempt to regulate employment and protect Native people, working conditions varied.

Recruiting Native Performers

"Public interest in the Indian never lags. Savage or civilized, he is always picturesque and always mysterious."[1] Quoted in a 1908 newspaper article titled "Engaging Indian Actors and How the Shows Secure Them," theatrical manager and recruiter William McCune recognized the appeal of the Indian. Show entrepreneurs, managers, agents, and local businesses hired Native people to perform in Wild West shows, exhibitions, fairs, and other entertainments. In the 1880s and '90s, the OIA received many requests for Native people to appear in a variety of local entertainments and exhibition venues.[2] Sometimes theater managers and show agents hired Native people on behalf of organizers of local events or for larger show entrepreneurs. For example, McCune recruited Natives for shows for more than twenty years, drawing mostly on the

Sioux tribe at Pine Ridge, South Dakota.[3] Although Moses (1996, 170) maintains that William F. Cody hired mainly Oglala Lakotas (Sioux) from Pine Ridge, archival correspondence from Indian agents, as well as show programs, indicates that he and other show entrepreneurs also hired people from other tribes and reservations, including Brulés, Pawnees, Poncas, Cheyennes, Cherokees, Arapahoes, Sacs and Foxes, and Kiowas, to work in public entertainments.[4] Moses also correctly points out that Lakotas were hired to play other tribes (1996, 170). Nonetheless, performing in shows and exhibitions was not solely a Lakota-Sioux experience.

The three major Wild West shows had long-standing agreements with the OIA, and other large companies such as the Thompson Exhibit and the Doc Carver show also applied to the OIA to hire Native people.[5] Indeed, Native performers were in high demand; by the late 1800s and early 1900s competition to recruit appropriate (read "authentic, traditional"), good (read "disciplined and skilled"), and famous Native people as performers was fierce. Lillie wrote in his unpublished autobiography: "You also know, that during all this time the 'Buffalo Bill show' did all in their power to stop us. Even hiring our best performers, also stopped us from getting a permit from Washington, D.C. to legally take the Indians off ther [sic] reservation. I had to steal them, thereby, taking a chance of going to jail. We would have been lost without them, as the 'Pawnee Bill's Show' featured Indians, and we would have had to stop showing without them."[6] Lillie's comments clearly illustrate the demand for Native performers, who were essential to the success of Wild West shows.

Employment was regulated by the OIA, which gave permission to recruit Native people for Wild West shows, exhibitions, and other entertainments only under certain conditions. One of the earliest references to these conditions is in an 1884 letter from Cody to Captain Penny about arranging bonds and contracts in order to secure Native people for his show.[7] In general, the OIA required security bonds of up to $10,000, transportation from and back to the reservation, a fair wage for Native performers, and provision for food and medical care.[8] Employment contracts varied from a few weeks, for local events, to one or two years with larger Wild West shows. Recruiters were also required to sign individual contracts with those they hired that stipulated the length of employment and confirmed the performer's understanding of the terms. That the OIA was able to regulate the hiring of Native people in shows and establish the terms of contracts demonstrates that the power over how Native people participated in Wild West shows lay with the OIA. This does not mean there was no agency for Native performers in this context, a point I address shortly.

The archival record does not reveal a clear pattern of reasons why requests for Natives were either denied or accepted. One possible explanation for the inconsistencies is that, in many cases, the requests went through the various individual Indian agents rather than directly to the OIA.[9] Also, smaller companies and fairs often had difficulty meeting the conditions of employment, in particular the large security bonds and the requirement to provide transportation. Consequently, these smaller operations sometimes hired Natives without contracts or permission from agents (Greci Green 2001, 114). Indian agents might deny requests if they were not satisfied with the credentials of the entrepreneur, recruiter, or entertainment company.[10] For the most part, the big three Wild West shows had no problem hiring Native performers, because they had the resources and reputation (Deloria 1981, 52). Generally the OIA trusted them and considered them reliable entrepreneurs because of their background: Lillie's experiences as an interpreter and teacher, the Millers' reputation as successful ranchers, and Cody's authority as a scout and frontiersman, as well as his connections with certain army and government officials.

OIA Policies: Protecting Native People from Harm

As a matter of official policy, the OIA did not support the hiring of Native people for Wild West shows, exhibitions, or any other performance venue. Native employment in Wild West shows presented challenges to assimilation, or the so-called civilizing project. As guardians of Native peoples, the OIA expressed concern in their memos and letters to Indian agents about the potential harms of working in Wild West shows and exhibitions and therefore discouraged the hiring of Native people. Their concern about the consequences of working in Wild West shows appears as early as 1887, when OIA commissioner Atkins sent a letter to Kiowa Indian agent Jesse Lee Hall outlining some of the negative consequences. He wrote: "Experience has shown that where irresponsible persons have taken Indians away for exhibition, or other purposes, they have sometimes abandoned them, without clothing, subsistence, or means of returning to their reservation."[11] On March 8, 1890, OIA commissioner Thomas Jefferson Morgan sent a memo to all Indian agents clearly outlining the department's position on Native participation in Wild West shows and any other form of entertainment, exhibition, or fair: "The replies of agents to Office circular of November 1, 1889, fully confirmed the previous impression of this Office that the influence of 'Wild West' and other similar shows has been harmful both to the Indians individually participating in the 'shows' and also to the Indians generally. Therefore, in the interest of Indian civilization and advancement, I deem it the duty of this Office to use all its influence to prevent Indians from joining such exhibitions."[12]

In these and other memos and letters, the main argument against the hiring of Native people for Wild West shows was that it would be harmful. Traveling with Wild West shows, among other things, exposed Natives to the worst aspects of white society, tempted them with many vices such as alcohol and gambling, and encouraged idleness and waste. OIA officials also discouraged the hiring of Native people for shows because it took them away from more "civilized" activities such as educational programs, tending their crops, or ranching.[13] Government officials further argued that wearing traditional clothing, dancing, and riding around like warriors only encouraged traditional ways. Finally, employment was harmful because it exposed Native people to mistreatment and illness.

The opportunity to make a strong case against the employment of Native performers in Wild West shows occurred in 1890, when General O'Beirne charged Cody with mistreatment of seventy-five Indians with Buffalo Bill's Wild West after the reported deaths of five Native performers in Europe, which were well publicized in the press.[14] These deaths and others were mainly due to infectious illness or disease, but reports of negligence also existed; there was also a concern about the performers' access to medical care and adequate living conditions. A group of Native performers who returned from Europe claimed that Chief Rocky Bear and interpreter Bronco Bill had treated them cruelly (Maddra 2006, 67). But after positive testimonies from other Native performers, including No Neck, and an unsuccessful (from the OIA's perspective) investigation into the charges, the case was dismissed, and Cody and his show manager-promoter John Burke returned to Europe with more Natives.

What exactly does the archival record tell us about the harms of working in Wild West shows? Were cases of mistreatment and illness rampant? The correspondence between Indian agents and show entrepreneurs, plus occasional letters from Native performers, does reveal cases of exploitation by show entrepreneurs and a lack of Native agency in regard to controlling hiring policies and working conditions. Aside from the 1890 charge, however, few archival records suggest mistreatment of Native performers with the Buffalo Bill's Wild West show. This is not to say that cases of mistreatment did not occur with other Wild West shows and exhibitions.

For one thing, Native performers with other Wild West shows sometimes complained about unpaid wages. This was the case for Native performers with the Cummins Wild West Show in 1905—Herbert Walker, Ida Walker, Margarite Walker, Starving Elk, Wolf Robe, and William Howling Wolf—who complained to their Indian agent that they were anxious to receive their pay.[15] Sometimes Native performers wrote to Indian agents about breach of contract, requesting assistance to return home.[16] For example, Mack Hay, Coyote Red Cloud, and Frank Hill wrote to their Indian agent in 1910 that fifteen Indians, most of whom were women, had been stranded by Mr. McNeill of El Reno, Oklahoma, and were owed more than one month's wages.[17] Sam Mayson, himself a Native, also wrote on their behalf: "As is usual in taking Indians off of reservations for show purposes, the parties so doing are required to give bond for their safe return. . . . I hope it is so in this case . . . [and] that you will take such actions as may relief to these people."[18] The main concern with Native employment in Wild West shows was the frequent reports of illness, which led to the assumption that Native performers were not well cared for. Cases of illness did occur, but archival evidence demonstrates that Cody showed respect and concern for Native performers with his show and honored the terms of his contracts; he sent home performers who were themselves ill or who needed to take care of ill family members back on the reservation.[19]

In short, some Native performers complained of unpaid wages or breach of contract and suffered from infectious ailments.[20] Given such evidence, one could easily make an argument for the exploitation and mistreatment of Native performers. However, the negative letters discussed above may also be a reflection of the nature of the material that has been preserved in the archival record. That is not to say that some Native performers were not exploited—real harms did exist, as outlined above—only that what is preserved in the record affects how experiences in this encounter might be interpreted. Native performers sought assistance from Indian agents if the terms of their contracts were not met, whereas contracts that were fulfilled did not generate letters, with few exceptions.[21] This is an inherent bias of such sources. In addition, most of these letters were in regard to smaller companies or the Miller Brothers' 101 Ranch Wild West Show. These materials also need to be considered within the context of government assimilation policies; the OIA collected these reports because it was continually building its case against Native employment in Wild West shows and seeking to gain public support on the issue.

Furthermore, it is important to note that, even though illness, injuries, disputes over pay, and drunkenness did occur, these conditions were not restricted to Wild West shows. Problems with illness, alcohol, gambling, and other harms also existed on reservations, so the argument that working in Wild West shows caused unusual harm to Natives was a simplification of their complex living conditions. Reservation life was plagued with similar problems because of a breakdown in traditional lifeways caused by relocation, fragmentation of traditional family and kinship ties, and disintegration of subsistence patterns.[22] In addition, similar diseases existed on reservations and in Indian schools; many died of tuberculosis, influenza, or smallpox, and children sent to Indian schools in the East also became sick because of "climate change and new diseases" (Starita 1995, 161). Sadly, an estimation based on available data from 1890 suggests that the number and types of deaths were comparable in both contexts. In 1890, approximately forty-five people died every month out of 5,500 living on the Pine Ridge reservation, a shocking 9.8 percent of the population.[23] In comparison, five of seventy-five performers (6.7 percent) with Buffalo Bill's Wild West died in 1890 (Moses 1996, 92–98).

The above estimate is for only one year and the statistics on illnesses and deaths require further investigation, but the point is that Native people's deplorable living conditions were not restricted to the Wild West show context. Many died from illness and disease, both on and off the reservation. These "Wild West show problems" also occurred on reservations, but it is possible that the OIA found it convenient to shift the focus away from reservations by targeting Wild West shows and exhibitions. By condemning the shows, the OIA may have been attempting to deflect criticisms about the failure of and problems in the reservation system. Maddra (2006, 82) comes to a comparable conclusion in her investigation of ghost dance prisoners with Cody's show, stating that similar allegations of mistreatment could "have been laid against the government itself." Ironically, the desperate conditions on reservations may have influenced some Native people to explore the Wild West show opportunity.

Indian Schools' Support of OIA Policies and the "Civilizing Project"

OIA policies on Native employment in Wild West shows re flect broader government policies and the political milieu of the era. As stated previously, government policies in the late 1800s focused on "civilizing" and assimilating Native people, which involved prohibition of ceremonies and dances and settlement onto reservations.[24] Reservations were meant to encourage a sedentary life based on farming or ranching— productive and civilized industries that would lead to Native people's self-sufficiency. Therefore, besides concern about the well-being of Native performers, the underlying worry was that participating in Wild West shows would undermine government policies of assimilation, which sought to extinguish, not reinforce, traditional ways. Indeed, Moses

effectively demonstrates that images of "traditional" Natives presented in Wild West shows conflicted with images of
"progressive" Natives disseminated by government officials
and Indian schools: "The major conflict between Wild West
shows and Indian-policy reformers became largely a struggle to determine whose image of the Indian would prevail"
(1996, 5). This tension between civilized and uncivilized (or
progressive and traditional) Native images represents the negotiation of multiple interests and power. The desire to present images of "progressive" Natives is also evident in Indian
school newsletters, such as *The Arrow* and *Indian Helper* from
the Carlisle Indian Industrial School in Pennsylvania, established by William Henry Pratt in 1879. Building on Moses's
analysis, an examination of these newsletters reveals how
Indian schools attempted to promote a particular vision of
Nativeness in relation to Wild West shows.

Indian school officials, who aimed to civilize Native peoples through education, supported the OIA's position against
Native employment in Wild West shows. Indian school officials were white; therefore, these newsletters were written
by whites and reflect not only their agendas but also Euro-
American paternalistic views of Native people at the time.
Many articles expressed the opinion that Wild West shows
promoted images of "old Indians" as savages and did not
represent "today's new Indians" and the progress they had
made toward civilized existence. An 1888 article in the *Indian Helper* criticized British audiences for their enthusiasm
for the Buffalo Bill's Wild West show's "overdrawn pictures
of our western life . . . thinking that the Indians are savage
beasts." School officials rightly recognized the stereotypes
produced in Wild West shows. But more important, Wild
West shows undermined the goals of the OIA and the work
of Indian schools to civilize and assimilate the Indian: "This
disgraceful show can do more in six months, to drag the Indian down and give a wrong impression of his real character,
than forty Carlisle's could do in six years to build the Indian

up and help him to stand on his own feet. . . . Buffalo Bill is rapidly tearing down what all good schools for the Indian are building up."[25]

Indian school officials also argued that Wild West shows encouraged Natives to act in these "old" uncivilized ways, hence preserving tradition rather than progressing in the white world. In particular, Native dress, long hair, use of war paint, and performance of traditional dances in Wild West shows marked Native performers as uncivilized. For example, an 1897 article in the *Indian Helper* described Iron Tail wearing "braided hair" and "all sorts of toggery" such as beaded necklaces, blankets, leggings, moccasins, and beaver skin.[26] Native people such as Iron Tail were paid to appear in "wild dress" and perform the "most blood-thirsty savage dance known." The contrast between civilized and uncivilized was exemplified in the difference between father and son. The article stated that, while Philip Iron Tail "was out on a New Jersey farm, gaining manhood and experience that will fit him for useful, civilized life," his father, Iron Tail, was "a perfect picture of ignorance and superstition!" Son and father represented opposite poles of the civilized/uncivilized Indian.

Indian schools banded together with other reformers, agencies, and authorities to support their position against Native participation in Wild West shows, encouraging Native participation in productive "civilized" industry: "Let the American Indian Association and other agencies, together with the authorities in Indian Schools, tell the Indian of the dangers which lurk in the practice of Indian youth wasting their days in such activities. Help these young people see that it is their part to settle down to some kind of productive industry which will lead to larger happiness and greater contentment, and to turn away permanently from the activities which though exciting are short-lived and harmful."[27]

Many of the newsletters, like the correspondence from the OIA and Indian agents, emphasized the exploitation of vulnerable Native people, who were portrayed as helpless victims incapable of making decisions of their own. A 1911 article in *The Arrow* stated that the American Indian Association vowed to use its influence against the "luring" of Indians into shows and circuses, where they would "squander" their money and become "engulfed in viciousness and vice."[28] According to another Indian school newsletter, not only did spectacles such as Buffalo Bill's Wild West present degrading images and encourage Native participants to act in old savage ways, they also exploited Native people: "The hope is . . . that those who should witness the disgraceful exhibition of the so-called savagery of their kin, would have the intelligence enough to see that the whole thing is only a bold scheme to get money out of portraying in a exaggerated and distorted manner the lowest and most degraded side of the Indian nature. Only the SAVAGE in the Indian does Buffalo Bill care to keep constantly before the public gaze."[29]

This was a complex issue, not simply a contest between Indian schools' goals (and OIA control) and Native performers' right to employment. As Maddra (2006, 46–47) observes, Native people could be progressivists, traditionalists, or somewhere in between. The right to employment was a contentious issue, especially after the attempted hiring ban in 1890. Some Native people, like performer Black Heart, supported their right to choose employment: "If Indian wants to work at any place and earn money, he wants to do so; white man got privilege to do same—any kind of work he wants." He also stated that the pay was good and the work was well suited to them (Maddra 2006, 79, 9).

Other Native people subscribed to the Indian schools' views of progress through education. Chauncey Yellow Robe, a Sioux from the Rosebud reservation and an 1895 graduate of the Carlisle Indian School, delivered a forceful critique of the "commercializing of Indians" in Wild West shows, moving pictures, and fairs in a speech at the Society of the American Indian conference in 1914. He argued passionately that the commercialization of Indians was "the greatest hindrance, injustice, and detriment to the present progress of the American Indians toward civilization" and that showmen manufactured these shows to entertain and instruct the public but were "teaching them that the Indian is only a savage being" (Yellow Robe 1914, 225). In reference to battle reenactments in shows, and specifically in the film *The Last Great Battle of the Sioux*, Yellow Robe criticized claims of historical accuracy, stating that "the whole production of the field was misrepresented and yet approved by the Government." Ironically, Yellow Robe costarred in the 1930 movie *The Silent Enemy* (Francis 1992, 127); perhaps the draw for him was that the film was offered as a "corrective" Native history narrative. The goal of the writer/producer, Douglas Burden, to present an "authentic picture of primitive Indian life to counter inaccurate and demeaning portrays of Indians as wild savages" (McBride 1995, 98), may have influenced Yellow Robe's decision. In fact, however, the film substitutes one stereotype for another. Clearly, the opinions and actions of Native peoples were by no means homogenous.

Indian schools were not the only ones to promote the notion of civilizing through education. Cody spoke (not surprisingly) in favor of employment of Native people by arguing that working in Wild West shows would be educational. It would provide them an opportunity to see the wonders and successes of the white world, and, in consequence, Indians would set themselves on the path to becoming civilized. Cody also stated that working in Wild West shows did not encourage idleness; rather, it provided Native people an opportunity to earn an honest living.[30] He went so far as to say that working in Wild West shows in fact supported the goals of the OIA because it made Indians self-sufficient.[31] On rare occasions, even Indian agents endorsed the idea that Native people would benefit from working in Wild West shows; Commissioner Browning stated that such employment gave "Indians a chance to earn money and to see something of civilization."[32] Thus, the OIA and Indian agents were not a homogenous group either. General Miles and Secretary Noble were also pro-employment in 1890, believing that it would be educational, and that Indians would see and experience the power of the whites (Maddra 2006, 96, 100). Using his reputation and connections, Cody worked to establish good relationships with both Native performers and the OIA early in his career as a Wild West show entrepreneur, but he also used the language of the colonials to promote his own interests. He emphasized the educational value of employment as leading to the "civilizing of the Indian." Ironically, Wild West shows still depended on images of the "traditional, uncivilized" Indian.

NATIVE EXPERIENCES WORKING IN WILD WEST SHOWS

The OIA and Indian schools attempted to advance a certain vision of Native people—civilized, industrious, sedentary, and assimilated into white society—representing the broader political agendas of the time as well as the negotiation of power in this encounter. Despite the OIA's insistence that Native people stay on reservations and its vigilant monitoring of Native recruitment and movements, hundreds of Native people left the reservations every year, with and without permission, to work with Wild West shows and exhibitions. Given what the archival record reveals about the exploitation and regulation surrounding the hiring of Native performers, why did some Native people opt to work in Wild West shows? What were their experiences like, and what agency could they exercise in their employment?

The OIA may have controlled recruitment and some entrepreneurs may have exploited Native employees, but Native performers were also active social agents in their employment. I argue that Native people adopted, or "indigenized"

(Buddle 2004, 39–42), this encounter for their own reasons. Other scholars have similarly suggested that Native people joined Wild West shows for good reasons: the possibility of continuing with "old ways" while avoiding forced assimilation and opportunities to travel freely without passes, to see and learn about the world, and to make some money (Deloria 1981, 54; Napier 1999, 385, 6; Warren 2005, 358, 361). Archival records support this hypothesis and reveal how, and to what degree, Native performers wielded agency in their employment.

There are two related facets of agency: power (involving domination and resistance) and intention, or what Ortner calls cultural projects (see Ortner 2006, 177; 2001). Intention, or cultural projects, refers to Native peoples' goals and interests guided by the social and political relationships that structure their lives. In other words, Native people's goals and lives are not limited by, or simply a response to, their relationships with dominant society and structures of power. (In this case, structures of power include colonialism and the OIA's control of hiring processes as well as entrepreneur exploitation). This view of agency does not deny the fact that power was unequal or that Native performers were exploited. Rather, it complicates an oversimplified view of Native–non-Native encounters, as other scholars have done for other contact situations (e.g., Comaroff and Comaroff 1991; Maddra 2006; Nicks 1999; Ortner 1999; Phillips 1998; Troutman 2009). In addition, it highlights the fact that agency can be something other than resistance.

Native performers approached this employment encounter as one of *opportunity*. They recognized the benefits of working in Wild West shows and took advantage of those opportunities; this, and the fact that they consciously and actively pursued those opportunities and benefits, represents their agency. Furthermore, they had their own reason for working in Wild West shows: survival during an era characterized by assimilation policies. Native performers had self-conscious intention and pursued opportunities and the benefits that came with working in the shows. Their intention is demonstrated by the fact that a large number of Native people worked for Wild West shows, even established careers, and that some sought employment on their own initiative. The benefits of this opportunity included economic rewards, independence, the freedom to travel, and the chance to maintain the family unit.

Opportunity and Benefits as Agency of Intention: Prevalence, Economics, and Family

The archival record supports the fact that many Native people were eager to work in Wild West shows and other performance venues. From the late 1800s to the early 1900s, hundreds of Native people worked as performers in public entertainments ranging from Wild West shows and exhibitions to circuses and, later, Western films. "Buffalo Bill" Cody employed hundreds of Natives every year,[33] and more than a hundred Wild West shows existed from 1884 to 1938, which does not even take into account other forms of spectacle.[34] The archival record is incomplete and does not account for every performer in every year, so the number of Native people working in Wild West shows and other exhibitions is certainly underestimated.[35]

The table below is just a sample. It lists the number of Wild West shows per year based on Russell (1970) and does not include other exhibitions or local spectacles. Given these figures, the number of Native people working in shows or exhibitions at one time or another in their lifetime probably numbered in the thousands, an estimate that Warren (2005) supports in his historiography.[36] Moses (1996, 174) suggests, and I agree, that the maintenance and even lowering of wages by show entrepreneurs in the 1900s are indications of the large number of Native people available for employment.

Estimated Number of Native People Hired

Year	1890	1904	1905	1907
Buffalo Bill's Wild West Show	75+	110	75	
Miller Brothers' 101 Ranch Wild West Show			1,000	100–165
Cummins' Wild West Show		500	500	
Earl's Court Indian Village			42	
Total Number Employed	**75+**	**610**	**1,617**	**165**
Number of known Wild West shows that year	3	6	4	3

Estimates are based on programs and correspondences in the archival record: *Cummins Indian Spectacular Congress and Life on the Plains. Wild West Indian Congress and Rough Riders of the World,* 1904 program, DPL, Series 6, Copies box 5, FF14; *Naval, Shipping and Fisheries Exhibition, 1905, Earl's Court: Daily Programme* (London: Gale and Polden), Smithsonian Institution, National Museum of American History, microform 003107.163.6; and *Official Review and History of the Great Wild West. Miller Bros. 101 Ranch Wild West,* official program, 1926, WHC, M-407, Box 95, FF16. See also Russell (1970, 72).

The record also confirms that some Native people actively sought these employment opportunities on their own initiative.[37] In 1880 the Sells Brothers wrote to Indian agent D. B. Dryer that they had hired several Indians at Columbus, Kansas, "at their own solicitation *not* in the Indian nation nor knowing they belonged on a reservation."[38] The Miller brothers received numerous inquiries for employment on the ranch and in their Wild West show from both "cowboys" and "Indians."[39] One of them was Black Horse Sr., who wrote a letter to Joe Miller asking if he would be going out on the road again in the spring. An experienced performer, having worked for Buffalo Bill, Pawnee Bill, circuses, and the

Bigelow Medicine Company, Black Horse sent his inquiry on personalized letterhead that highlighted his riding, roping, and bronco riding skills, complete with a picture of himself.[40] Performing in Wild West shows, and in particular display-ing their superior horsemanship, was work that Native people knew how to do, and how to do well. Black Heart as-serted: "We were raised on horseback; that is the way we had to work. These men furnished us the same work we were raised for; that is the reason we want to work for these kind of men" (Kasson 2000, 186). Impresarios may have recruited Native people, but Native people also pursued employment possibilities.

Though not every Native person who appeared in shows made a career out of performing, many were employed more than once or in more than one show. A few of them, such as Black Elk and Luther Standing Bear, have written memoirs, but descriptions about their Wild West show experience in these memoirs are scarce. However, their opinions and expe-riences have been documented in newspaper reports to some degree. Red Shirt, Black Elk, Standing Bear, Ghost Dog, Little Iron, Samuel Lone Bear, Black Heart, Long Wolf, Rocky Bear, and No Neck, to name a few, worked more than one season with Cody's show. In particular, Lakotas from Pine Ridge and Standing Rock have a history of working as performers and gained professional status as "show Indians" (Moses 1996, 171). One such performer was George Dull Knife from Pine Ridge, who started with Cody in 1893 and worked as part of the large troupe of Lakota entertainers off and on for fifteen years (Starita 1995, 138). According to his grandson, employ-ment with Wild West shows could last a long time, from one to three years (Starita 1995, 145). Both Gordon Lillie and the Millers also had return performers. For example, Creeping Bear wrote to Joe Miller in 1926 seeking employment: "I am Creeping Bear, one of the Indians who went with you to Ger-many last year. I want to go with your show again this year, and hear that you are going to start sometime next month. I have a friend, Watan, who also went with you last year who wants to go with you again this time."[41] Working in Wild West shows was not the only job opportunity available, but it appears to have been appealing, given that some Native performers returned year after year. Although performing did not become a career for every participant, it was a bona fide occupation choice. On returning from their European tour with Cody, some performers who signed the agency register wrote as their occupation "Showman" (Moses 1996, 128).

Native performers were free to travel while employed in Wild West shows. Cody's jaunts in the city with Native performers, whether to promote the show or to keep them occupied and relieved from boredom, were followed by the press.[42] Examples of Native travels and sightseeing abroad are documented in photographs: at Land's End in England; at Caffe Greco in Rome; visiting Cliff House in San Francisco; along roadways and on riverboats in England.[43] On rare occasions, this freedom of mobility led to performers being accidentally left stranded. The performers left behind, such as Black Elk, usually found employment in other shows or exhibitions and worked in the performance circuit abroad.[44] In addition, performers joined or left the show as they chose. Some Native performers quit the show because they were tired of performing or were homesick.[45] Show manager Henry P. wrote that some of the Comanches liked the show, others did not and went home even before they were paid.[46] Even Cody had his share of Native performers leave the show for unspecified reasons. It seems that Native performers also broke contracts on occasion.

Working in Wild West shows also provided income for Native people beyond the jobs available on the reservation at a comparable rate. Luther Standing Bear wrote that he earned $300 in 1884 to teach, or about $25 a month. He was also paid $2.50 a day for a man and his team to fence in the reservation, work he considered degrading (Standing Bear 1975, xiv, 242). Based on archival evidence, the average pay for Native performers was about $1 per day, or $30 per month.[47] In 1890, for example, No Neck claimed that Native performers on average were paid $25 per month, but that his wage was $30 (Maddra 2006, 69).

Thus, Native people did not have to stay on the reservations to earn income; some found employment in Wild West shows, believing it offered a better opportunity. In part, working in Wild West shows was a response to the reservation system and living conditions. Employment prospects for Native people, even for those who, like Luther Standing Bear, were educated in Indian schools, were few. Many Native performers agreed with entrepreneurs that they were better off working in shows than on reservations. Short Boy, a performer with Buffalo Bill's Wild West, was quoted as saying: "I wouldn't go back to the reservation for a new rifle and cartridges enough to last me the rest of my life. . . . There's no more hunting for the Indian and there's no use fighting against the hopeless odds, and so we take a great pleasure in going up against a fair fight with the American soldiers even with blank cartridges." Then he shook his head in disgust. "But even there we don't get a square deal; we are always licked—always licked."[48] According to the reporter, Short Boy was echoing the sentiments of the entire band. Despite the satisfaction of performing a fight against whites, he recognized the irony of appearing in Wild West shows. Native performers were in effect reenacting their perceived fate as the conquered and defeated.

Wages were not equal among all performers and shows. An examination of the wages at the Millers' 101 Ranch Wild West Show, for example, draws attention to an obvious gender and ethnic or racial pay hierarchy.[49] Women performers, both cowgirls and Indians, were generally paid lower wages than men, and children were paid considerably less.[50] In most cases Native performers were paid less than cowboys and other ethnic groups such as the Cossacks.[51] There was also a pay hierarchy among the Native performers. The

Miller's 1928 payroll report notes that the Native superintendent of the "Indian troupe" received $35. But performers Red Bird, his wife, and child were paid a total of $19.75, and Fools Crow, his wife, and two girls were paid only $14.75; the highest-paid performer, Indian Eye, received $15, and Clinton Pawpaw received a mere $7.50. It is not known whether these wages were weekly or monthly; however, as Moses (1996, 174) observes, wages decreased in the 1900s. According to Reddin (1999, 163), the Miller brothers did not see the Indians as the main attraction of the show. Yet lower wages meant that the Millers could hire more Natives for less money, hence increasing the size of their cast without decreasing their profits. Even though Reddin claims that Native peoples were not the main attraction, Native performers actually formed an equal, if not larger, part of the Millers' show in terms of numbers. This implies a certain degree of exploitation of these performers. Still, the wages were decent in comparison with other job opportunities, and they received higher wages than non-Natives who were employed in the cookhouse or tending ring stock, for example. On average, Native performers with Cody's show faired better than those with the Miller brothers.

In fact, the pay differential among and between Native employees and cowboys was also based on the type of job (superintendent, interpreter, head performer, performer, or extra), skill level, and status (including fame or age). Those who had a special position, such as interpreter, superintendent, Indian police, or head Indian, earned higher wages than the cowboys. In addition, some Native performers were paid a higher rate because of their reputation (status, fame, or notoriety) and experience. For example, Yankton Charley, Short Bull, and Kicking Bear—ghost dance prisoners with Buffalo Bill's Wild West—earned $50 per month while Blackheart received $35 per month. Star performers or elders who had more experience generally commanded higher wages. Such pay differentiation may have led to tensions among the Native performers with the Millers' show. In 1925, thirty-eight "young Indians" wrote to the Miller brothers asking for equal pay for equal work: "We are aware that some of the older Indians are drawing about twice as much as we are; it is no wonder that they are perfectly contented."[52] Sitting Bull was paid $50 a week for his short stint with Cody in 1885. He also negotiated a $125 bonus and the right to sell his photographs and autographs (Kasson 2000, 174).

Although OIA and Indian school officials accused Native people of squandering their money, some Native people did, in fact, manage to accumulate savings. During his visit with the commissioner of Indian Affairs in Washington, Young Spotted Tail, a performer with the Pawnee Bill show, stated that "he not only had a good time, but he could go home with some money in his pockets and some fine clothes on."[53] Cody stated that Little Chief, who worked for him for two years, never gambled—rather, he saved his money.[54] Reportedly, Fast Thunder put aside enough money to acquire four thousand cattle and a comfortable cabin (Warren 2005, 409). Show wages paid for cattle, horses, and farm equipment as well as food and clothing (Warren 2005, 408). Many Native performers with Cody's show sent some of their pay home to their families as well. Cody claims that Native performers sent home 15 to 20 dollars every month.[55] Rocky Bear, for example, "continually sent money home" (Moses 1996, 101). Ghost dancers and performers Short Bull and Kicking Bear continued to send money to their families from Fort Sheridan prison, where they were returned after their 1890–92 British tour (Maddra 2006, 183). Their earnings may have been redistributed in a feasting system rather than "squandered" away.

It is important to point out that entire families worked and traveled together in Wild West shows. Scholars have focused mainly on the employment of male Native performers, and it is true that the more famous performers were males who had status as warriors and had participated in battle. The visual record is also skewed toward portraits of the male warrior, or "exotic" male. But women and children also traveled and performed in these spaces of public performance, and often family members traveled together. In her article on engaging Indian actors, Quimby wrote that Indians were often recruited as family units who could enjoy a "unique outing with pay"; men, women, and children alike were anxious to hand in their applications for the Buffalo Bill's Wild West winter recruitment in 1908.[56] Lillie employed "Indian Princesses," women and children for his Pawnee Bill's Wild West show.[57] The Miller brothers also hired families; one of their employees, High Chief Cheyenne, wrote to Superintendent Shell asking him to send his daughter to the Jamestown Exhibition, since his wife and some of his children were already there.[58] The Sarrasani Circus in Germany also recruited Native performers through the Miller brothers; Ghost Dog went with his wife and three children.[59]

In addition to the evidence mentioned above, photographs show women and children in Wild West show cast pictures and in the associated encampments, as well as city excursions (figures 1–4).[60] A group picture from the Red Man Golden West Exhibition at Earl's Court dated 1909 includes Mr. and Mrs. Spotted Weasel, Frank C. Goings and family, and Mr. and Mrs. Owns Many Horses (figure 2). In another example, women and children pose in front of a "western" backdrop for Cody's show (figure 3).[61] Many photographs illustrate women in the arena, suggesting that they were paid performers, not simply traveling with their husbands and kin, as in figure 4.[62] In another example, a photograph of a rehearsal for the "Battle of Summit Springs" for Buffalo Bill's Wild West, depicts women and children along with men singing and drumming; another from the same album shows two women and a child setting up teepees, perhaps as part of an Indian vignette.[63] In addition to performing in the Indian vignettes, dances, and reenactments, women engaged in everyday activities in the encampment outside the arena,

Figure 1. Women and children walking around tepees at Wild West show. Courtesy Western History Collections, University of Oklahoma Libraries, item 611.

Figure 2. Group of Native performers at Earl's Court, 1909. Courtesy Denver Public Library Western History Collection, X-32148.

Figure 3. Women and children at Buffalo Bill's Wild West show.
Courtesy Buffalo Bill's Historical Center, Cody, Wyoming, P.69.897.

Figure 4. Women performing at Buffalo Bill's Wild West show.
Courtesy Buffalo Bill's Historical Center, Cody, Wyoming, P.69.894.

which was promoted by show entrepreneurs and seen by the public as part of the show.

Women also brought in additional income by selling their beadwork and other handmade items such as moccasins and purses (Maddra 2006, 147–48; Warren 2005, 409). In terms of popularity, women and children drew as much public interest as the "brave savage" warriors. Standing Bear recounts the birth of his daughter while on tour with Cody in Birmingham. He writes that the birth was headline news in the papers and became a big draw (Standing Bear 1975, 265). Visitors lined up long before the show to catch a glimpse of his wife and daughter. "My wife sat on a raised platform, with the little one in the cradle before her. The people filed past, many of them dropping money in a box for her. Nearly every one had some sort of little gift for her also. It was a great drawing card for the show; the work was very light for my wife, and as for the baby, before she was twenty-four hours old she was making more money than my wife and I together" (Standing Bear 1975, 266). Standing Bear's account reveals his pride in his family and also the (in this case indirect) economic benefits of having women and children traveling with the family.

It seems that so many women and children were employed that letters were sent out to discourage this practice, particularly so for the Millers' Wild West show in the 1900s. Mr. Freer informed Joe Miller in 1911 that Indian families were considering joining the show next season, including the Prentiss family: Noble Prentiss and his wife, Julia, daughter Nellie, son Stewart, and an infant. In this letter, Freer asked Miller not to hire a "promising Indian girl" (Julia) from the Carlisle School.[64] In 1912, Freer received another letter about children employed with the 101 Ranch show in Venice, California, as well as in the Millers' film project.[65] There is, in short, ample evidence that families, both nuclear and extended, were part of Wild West shows. The participation of families is significant because it points to other possible benefits of working in Wild West shows.

Beyond the economic gains, there were sociocultural benefits to pursuing employment in Wild West shows. On the one hand, the fact that women and children traveled and worked in Wild West shows may be viewed by some scholars as exploitive; yet this is a very western view, one that privileges a certain perspective on family. On the other hand, some Native participants may have seen maintaining the family unit as one possible benefit of employment, in addition to economic benefits. It is possible that participating in public performance, therefore, "facilitated social cohesion" (Nicks n.d., 10). The opportunity to travel together as a family, and at times with kin from the community or other reservations, must have attracted Native people. To illustrate, Plains tribes lived together in extended family groups or bands. The *tiospayes* ("those who live together") was the fundamental social unit of Lakota society, for example (Starita 1995, 155–56). Guy Dull Knife, Jr., recalls stories that his grandfather George Dull Knife told him about his travels with Buffalo Bill's show. He said that Native performers lived together in a camp that "began to resemble the camps they had always lived in on the Plains," with campfires, children running, women beading, men smoking and talking, and occasionally fresh buffalo to eat, just like an Indian village (Starita 1995, 150–51). Thus, Wild West show encampments were spaces where Native participants could maintain certain aspects of "village life" (Starita 1995, 142–43; Warren 2005, 362). From this perspective, working in Wild West shows may have facilitated the sociocultural well-being of Native performers' families.

Cultural Projects/Intentions and Native Agency in Employment

The OIA, Indian schools and reformers, show entrepreneurs, and Native performers were all active (though unequal) social actors in this employment encounter with varying interests. The OIA was concerned with regulating and limiting recruitment as well as safeguarding Native performers, Indian schools sought to civilize Native people, and show entrepreneurs were interested in profit and sometimes failed to meet contractual obligations. Overall, the OIA and entrepreneurs dominated this encounter, with Native performers lacking control over hiring processes or working conditions. If we measure agency only in terms of power—Native performers' ability to control or resist employment policies and conditions—then Native people did not wield agency. As mentioned earlier, this approach to identifying agency centers on analyzing power in terms of domination and resistance. However, if we also recognize agency in terms of intentions, or cultural projects, then Native performers wielded agency. Native people sought to meet their own goals and needs. Specifically, their agency may be identified in terms of their conscious intention (and action) to pursue the opportunities and benefits of working in Wild West shows. Native performers worked within the constraints of OIA control and a political milieu characterized by assimilation policies (rather than transformed it), signifying an identifiable form of agency.

Even though power was unequal, Native performers had their own reasons for working in Wild West shows. They were not passive victims lured away from the reservations, as the OIA or Indian schools claimed. In fact, Native participants capitalized on opportunities to their advantage; some even established careers as "show Indians." That Native people wrote explicit requests for employment and worked for more than one show over extended periods indicates that they were treated satisfactorily, despite the evidence collected by the OIA, or, at the very least, treated well enough that they would return for another season. In 1890, Rocky Bear was quoted as saying "If [the show] did not suit me, I would not remain any longer" (Moses 1996, 101). In addition, Native performers exercised a fair degree of freedom within the context of working with Wild West shows: they joined and left shows as they pleased; they enjoyed the freedom to travel; and once on location they were free to wander the cities and take in the sights without passes. Show entrepreneurs such as Cody were not as diligent in restricting Native performers' movements as was the OIA (Warren 2005, 362), and this benefit may have led some Native people to work in Wild West shows. In short, some Native people pursued employment opportunities and the benefits of working in Wild West shows; and this represents their agency.

There were definite economic benefits to working in Wild West shows as well. Even though a hierarchical pay structure existed, Native performers were paid well in comparison to other opportunities available on or off reservations. Because Native people were now part of the cash economy, working in Wild West shows provided much-needed income to purchase necessities and feed their families, offering them independence from insufficient rations.[66] It is worth mentioning that income from working in Wild West shows was also welcome in Canada, where "wage labour was often paid in ration tickets and scrip" rather than cash (Baillargeon and Tepper 1998, 160).

Women were also active agents in this encounter. Employment in Wild West shows afforded occasions for women to sell their beadwork and other handmade items, providing additional income. The selling of beadwork is an example of Native people's "initiative and their efforts to take some control of their situation" (Maddra 2006, 148). That Native people, including women, demonstrated "the motivated capacity to act creatively" is also consistent with Sewell's (1992) interpretation of agency of intention; everyone has *access* to resources even if all people do not have *control* over these resources.[67] Specifically, even though Native people did not control the regulation of employment or working conditions, they accessed the opportunities and benefits that working in Wild West shows presented.

Money was likely a draw for Native performers; however, money is also an indication of Native people's own desires and intentions. As Ortner (1999, 65–66) found with the Sherpas' engagement in mountaineering, their desire for money represents the Sherpas' cultural projects: freedom from poverty and dependence. Money may be simply financial, but it may also be used to support kin, to travel, or to sponsor religious rituals or the monastery. In the present case, economic motivations may have driven Native people to work in Wild West shows, but money represented more than purely material wealth. It also meant independence from rations, freedom from the reservation, some status related to being a performer and traveling, and, finally, the ability to provide for and sustain one's family (economically and socioculturally). That employment opportunities were also a matter of survival does not diminish the fact that Native performers had their own agenda, their own intentions. In fact, it is their very engagement with and adaptation of this employment encounter for their survival that is of significance.

Working in Wild West shows was a family affair. While the OIA sought to dismantle Lakota society, kinship groups, and traditions through assimilation policies (Starita 1995, 153, 155), the Wild West show encampment was a place where Native participants could maintain their extended family unit, mobility, and traditions. As Warren notes, "travel away from the reservation allowed Lakotas to better retain proscribed spiritual and cultural traditions" (2005, 362).[68] Native participants freely socialized with relatives, wore traditional clothing, and continued traditional activities at the Wild West show encampment, away from the watchful eye of the OIA. Other studies similarly found that agricultural-turned-tribal fairs were opportunities to visit relatives (e.g., Buddle 2004; Troutman 2009, 32–33; Young Bear and Theisz 1994). I suggest, therefore, that these freedoms may be read as benefits of working in Wild West shows.

Viewed from this perspective, working in Wild West shows may also be seen as a subtle form of resistance. That performers would choose to travel with their families rather than send their children to Indian schools suggests another case of subverting OIA policies. Commissioner Morgan certainly thought that Native people who left the reservations and care of the government to purse employment in exhibitions were in "defiance of regulation" (Maddra 2006, 98). From the data collected, it is possible to suggest that Native performers consciously sought to evade OIA policies by working in Wild West shows. Still, I am careful here to emphasize that such resistance was subtle in degree and form; it was evasive rather than oppositional. Troutman's (2009, 37–48) study on music, in particular after the 1900s, similarly shows an increasing ability to circumvent OIA policies that banned dance, demonstrated by the revival of old and new dances by youths returning from residential schools, ultimately resulting in political change. There is no question that some Native people actively sought employment opportunities and, as a result of their employment, subverted government goals of assimilation as well as the reorganization of Lakota society into a European family model by engaging in traditional activities and maintaining the family unit. In this respect, the participation of women and children in Wild West shows is significant, for they contributed to both their economic and cultural survival. In fact, the employment of Native people in Wild West shows may have contributed to the continuation of Native culture at a time when government policies sought to extinguish it. This line of argument is explored further in the next chapter.

CHAPTER THREE

Performing in
Wild West Shows

Representing and Experiencing
Native Identity

"For many white Americans, their only contact with Indian people was through the medium of performance, and
for many American Indians, their only way of representing
themselves to white Americans was through performance"
(Maddox 2002, 9). The Wild West show, in essence, was a
performance. As Maddox notes, performance was a medium
for self-representation and facilitated contact between Native
peoples and whites. But how exactly did Wild West show performances represent Native peoples? A perusal of imagery
found in programs, advertisements, and newspapers reveals
how this performance encounter produced stereotypical images of exotic, savage warriors.

Although Native performers did not transform the meanings of arena performances, neither were they simply taken
over by them. The Wild West show contact zone is a complex and incongruous space in that it is both a performance
and a living space (Bruner and Kirshenblatt-Gimblett 1994).
Therefore, although they may be viewed as an exploitive
space where Native participants are asked to perform savageness and exoticism, this does not preclude the possibility

that Native participants experienced Nativeness in other ways—that is, that performances have other meanings besides those produced for the show. This chapter explores how Native participants adopted this context and modified performances, as well as how they experienced Native identity in the context of Wild West shows. Specifically, it considers the alternative, coexisting production of Native identity in this space. Native performers adopted this encounter as a space to experience their identity for themselves—as expressed through (new and modified) warrior songs, dances, and dress—which demonstrates their agency. In short, this performance encounter illustrates the process of transculturation that occurs in contact zones.

SPECTACLES OF THE "REAL AND AUTHENTIC" WILD WEST SHOW

Wild West shows are spectacles in every sense (sensu MacAloon 1984; Manning 1992). They are visual treats of dramatic action bordering on over-the-top entertainment. Such spectacles often involved the dramatization of culture and historical events (Kasson 2000; Martin 1996; Nelles 1999; Whissel 2002). Even though entrepreneurs promoted their shows as authentic reproductions of the West, Wild West shows were not true historical re-creations but rather "mythical histories" that both reduced and conflated complex historical moments into typical scenes that were ritually reenacted (Slotkin 1981, 33, 34). Wild West shows were also nation-building projects in that they shaped the construction of American identity and attempted to define, situate, and justify the place of Native peoples in America.[1] The production of Native peoples supported evolutionary views of race based on opposing tropes of civilization and savagery (Martin 1996, 95). The imagery produced in Wild West shows and related print media thus depicted Native people as exotic, savage (sometimes noble) warriors. More than images, these tropes reflect the capacity of performances to construct social meanings such as progress and form the public's view of Native peoples. But how exactly did Wild West shows attain this status of authenticity in the public's mind?

First, show programs and newspaper reviews stressed that Wild West shows were authentic representations of life in the West with real cowboys and Indians, not mere actors. In 1889 the *Gazette* stated: "These 'noble red men' are the genuine article."[2] Yet authenticity demanded more than real cowboys and genuine Indians. Wild West shows gained status as realistic representations of history by engaging people who participated in significant historical events to perform reenactments, what Whissel (2002, 227) calls "spectator position." In other words, not only were most performers "real people" from the frontier, they had also *experienced* the frontier firsthand. For example, several Wild West shows hired famous Native people such as Sitting Bull, Kicking Bear, Short Bull, No Neck, Spotted Tail, Chief Bull Bear, Standing Cloud, and Long Bull, in addition to veterans of the U.S. Cavalry, all of whom had participated in actual battles.[3] Cody, Lillie, and the Miller brothers also claimed firsthand knowledge of life in the West.[4] Not every performer had been "at the scene" or participated in the historical events reenacted, but the presence of a few representative individuals who had been there confirmed that these reproductions were based on firsthand knowledge and experience.

Given that performers were "real" individuals from the frontier, it is easy to imagine how audiences came to believe that what they witnessed in Wild West shows were authentic representations of life (and events) on the frontier. It is important to note, though, that in the case of Wild West shows this "spectator position" presents a partial view. Certain representations of history, culture, and identity are valued over others (cf. Conquergood 1991). Native people "from the scene" were essential for establishing the authenticity of

Wild West shows, but their views of life in the West were not equally valued. Wild West show performances legitimized the *elite's* vision of America; they sustained ideas of industrialization and progress and demonstrated the social order of civilization (Martin 1996, 96–97). In short, performances privileged the knowledge and experiences of frontiersmen and cowboys, that is, of dominant white society.

Second, performances gained status as authentic representations because they supposedly presented "living pictures" of cultures.[5] Wild West shows consisted of a series of performances and spectacles that reduced history and culture to a display form that Mitchell (1992) calls "world-as-exhibition." Characteristic of nineteenth-century imperial culture, the world-as-exhibition model entailed the framing of realistic scenes of life in wax museums (e.g., Schwartz 1998), fairs and exhibitions, landscape paintings, and dioramas that evoked cultural myths, values, and ideologies such as progress (Whissel 2002, 228). Similarly, Wild West shows framed scenes of life from the frontier in the form of historical re-enactments, cowboy pastimes or settler vignettes, and Indian vignettes. Again, these living pictures of life on the frontier privileged American (white) ideologies. They consisted of a series of "object lessons" that promoted a particular vision of America as well as a story of the discovery of the "savage" and America's conquest of the West (Martin 1996, 94, 96; Slotkin 1981; Whissel 2002, 227). Through historical re-enactments, military displays, and demonstrations of cowboy pastimes, for example, Wild West shows celebrated the admirable deeds of frontiersmen and cowboys, demonstrating the skills of horsemanship and marksmanship that they employed in order to conquer the West (Deahl 1975, 151).[6] European and American audiences alike witnessed "the hard work, the skill and the heroism of the cowboys ... whose relentless march forward [has] ensured their compatriots of the possession of a land they have often drenched with blood."[7] On the other hand, Indian vignettes demonstrated the savageness of Indians; every Wild West show included at least one scene with a war dance and a dramatic attack by Indians.[8]

This world-as-exhibition model was not limited to performances in the arena. The Indian village and encampments were crucial for connecting reenactment with "real," everyday life. A newspaper article on Buffalo Bill's Wild West show at the American Exhibition commented that the Indians of romance novels were there at the show, and that visitors could come to the village, enter teepees, chuck the chins of babies, and watch women at work.[9] The opportunity to gaze upon Indian and cowboy participants enhanced the realism and authenticity of Wild West show performances.[10]

Finally, Wild West show programs and couriers authorized the authenticity of historical reenactments and vignettes by employing educational, ethnological-like discourses.[11] Programs and couriers read like a cross between an anthropological monograph and a dime novel about the Old West. They were essentially promotional tools, often distributed or sold to the public before the show arrived in town. As Slotkin (1981, 33–34) notes, however, programs provided "historical and ideological rationale for the show," not just descriptions of the show.[12] These quasi-anthropological illustrated booklets provided detailed summaries of historical events as well as biographies of individuals and tribes of the West. For instance, feature articles recounted historical events such as the Custer battle, the attack at Deadwood, or the battle at Summit Springs.[13] Biographical sketches of Buffalo Bill Cody, Johnny Baker, Annie Oakley, and the Miller brothers described the deeds of western heroes, and detailed stories about "Indians at Home" and the "Ghost Dance" illustrated Native culture.[14] Programs, as well as other print media, described Native people's "weird" dances and "savage" attacks. These accounts are, of course, incomplete, distorted, and biased. Filled with romanticized vignettes and stereotypical images of noble savages, programs reflect how Nativeness was perceived and constructed by white society. In sum, the performance encounter was central for constructing, and authenticating, a particular view of America and of Nativeness.

Imagery of Native people in the context of Wild West shows were, however, ambiguous and contradictory. These contradictory images epitomize the "noble savage" dichotomy, which represents the simultaneous perceptions of Indians as noble children of Eden, close to nature, and as backward, uncivilized, and savage.[15] Deloria writes of this dichotomy: "the familiar contradiction we have come to label noble savagery, a term that both juxtaposes and conflates an urge to idealize and desire Indians and a need to despise and dispossess them" (1998, 4). Newspaper reviews of Wild West shows, which included descriptions of the Indians, clearly constructed and perpetuated this dichotomy.

On one hand stood the noble Indian. Almost every newspaper article included some description of Native people's physical appearance and stature, sometimes emphasizing the more "romantic" noble character.[16] The print media were rich with adjectives describing Native people as "statuesque" or "a picture from nature."[17] One article described Native performers in the 1903 Buffalo Bill show as "picturesque" and "half naked" yet spectacular in their Indian garb, displaying "all the lurid glory of war paint and native attire."[18] Another described the "strong lines" of Native performers' faces as indicating "thoughtful men."[19] Red Shirt was portrayed as "dignified, placid," with a "handsome face" and generally described as having a "bright appearance and intelligent face," even though the reporter considered him to have been one of "the most troublesome Indian[s] in the US."[20]

Notably, these physical descriptions often highlight the differences between the "Red Man" and whites. For example, one reporter wrote that Sitting Bull had a "face of massive proportions . . . [that was a] deep reddish brick tinge [and] copper colored."[21] A French newspaper more explicitly implied that the contrast between the Indians and cowboys was based on racial superiority: "These Indians are strapping fellows with a skin that is truly red, tattooed, and sporting other colorful markings. . . . The white cowboys contrast strangely in physique to the Indians. They are magnificent; they are pioneers as much as due to their physical strength as by their agility, and after seeing them, we can more easily understand how they are able to engage in the daily conquest of the American continent."[22]

On the other hand stood the savage Indian. In fact, the most pervasive image was that of the savage. According to one reporter, for example, Crow Eagle's countenance "indicates more of the savage and less intelligence" compared with Sitting Bull.[23] Yet another article described Sitting Bull as a powerful warrior who burned a fort to the ground and dealt with captives cruelly, tying them to a tree, tearing out their tongues, and cutting their sinews.[24] Moreover, one cannot read a program or newspaper article without coming across references to "wild war whoops" or "blood-curdling yells," attacks by Indians, and "wild" or "primitive" dances, all which are said to be representative of "the savage life and customs" of Native people.[25] In addition, references to "warriors" and "braves" were ubiquitous. Wild West show posters depicted Indians on horseback ready to attack or engaged in battle, and all Wild West shows contained at least one re-enactment of an Indian attack; all featured a war dance by "savage Indians."[26] These narratives and descriptions highlight the perceived savageness of Native people.

Somewhere in between the noble and savage Indian was the image of Native people as exotic, an image that was prevalent in both newspapers and programs. Native dances and ceremonies in particular were called "exotic and wild," "weird and peculiar," "superstitious," and "mysterious."[27] For instance, reporters described the Mojave cremation as "an interesting and somewhat weird feature" of the Pawnee Bill Wild West show.[28] The 101 Ranch Wild West show advertised the opportunity to see Indian war dances and their "weird rites," ceremonies, and pastimes.[29] Programs also offered detailed descriptions of tribal ceremonies and dances that the public did not necessarily see in the show, such as the sun dance and the ghost dance, which equally contributed to the image of an exotic Indian.[30] An 1893 program for Buffalo Bill's Wild West show, for instance, referred to the ghost dance as a "series of frenzied dances and incantations . . . a dance which is so weird and peculiar, so superstitious and spirit-like, as to rival the far famed Sun Dance."[31] Ceremonies that took place outside of the context of the show (but often in the encampments) were also reported in newspapers; the Dog Feast fell into the category of weird and peculiar: reporters called this annual ceremony a "strange rite," and the English were outraged at the idea of roasting a dog.[32] These dances and ceremonies, whether performed inside the arena for the public or celebrated outside the arena for themselves, were considered markers of an uncivilized society and an illustration of Native people's exoticism.

In sum, Wild West show performances were deemed authentic representations of life on the frontier, represented by real people with firsthand experiences, and promoted ideas of Euro-American progress as well as the savagery of Indians. Performances constructed and reinforced existing ideas and images of Indians as exotic, noble savages. The question is, could such performances have had other meanings?

NATIVE PERFORMANCES OF CULTURE AND IDENTITY

Did Native performers construct social meaning in this performance encounter? Did a space for agency exist? In what ways and to what extent? At first it may appear that Native performers were engaging in what Bhabha (1994, 96) has called "colonial mimicry." Although Bhabha (1994, 88) emphasizes the ambivalence of colonial mimicry, he ultimately considers it a power strategy of colonial power in which the Other appropriates colonial discourses, but only to reproduce them. So, in the case of Wild West shows, this would mean that Native participants perform the exotic, savage warrior, thus reproducing stereotypes.

Although not discounting this explanation entirely, in this section I present another interpretation of performances based on the idea of transculturation. Transculturation, in contrast to "colonial mimicry," emphasizes how Others adopt colonial relationships in a dialogical process, not only to reproduce them, thereby negotiating power and agency (Phillips 1998; Pratt 1992). This means that Native performers were not simply reproducing stereotypes in Wild West show performances (although performances did do this); they also constructed their own social meaning in this context. Most important for this study is the fact that Others have intentions and social relationships of their own beyond those created as a result of contact with white colonials. Ortner critiqued the Comaroffs' later work in *Of Revolution and Revelation* (volume 2) as lacking attention to this type of agency.[33] She writes that the Tswana react "but do not appear to have lives, as it were, outside of their relationships to the missionaries, lives with their own forms of intentionality" (2001, 81).

With this critique in mind, I consider Native performers' own intentions and forms of relationships beyond those formed as a result of their employment in Wild West shows. I argue that Native performers experienced their own so-cial meanings of Native identity as they adapted the per-formance encounter for their own ends, representing their agency in this context. I further qualify the form and extent of agency by suggesting that Native performers exerted *expressive* agency—the ability to express and experience personal meanings of Native identity—of which I provide three examples: the modification of warrior songs, the experience of dance, and the expression of identity through dress.

Warrior Dance, Warrior Identity

Native performers may have performed the savage warrior in Wild West shows, but they also used the performance encounter for their own ends. Government policies sought to assimilate Native people and eliminate their "savage" ways; accordingly, warrior societies and their songs and dances, in addition to other ceremonial dances, were prohibited. Wild West shows (among other American occasions and events that included performances) hence gave Native performers socially viable ways of maintaining and expressing their culture and identity—in this example, their warrior identity. Ethnographic information on the Lakotas informs this interpretation of the possible significance of performing a warrior identity in the context of Wild West shows. The Lakota example is relevant because many performers came from that tribe. In her study on Lakota performances and identity in the 1800s and 1900s, Greci Green (2001, 123) argues that participation in Wild West shows "reflected and expressed well-established Lakota standards of achievement and self-worth." Building on this insight, I maintain that performing the "war dance" at Wild West shows honored the warrior tradition and kept the songs and dances alive in a new context. Native performers adopted the performance encounter in response to their new living conditions as a space for the continuation of song and dance associated with a *modified* warrior identity.

In nineteenth-century Lakota society, a warrior had status and a position of honor. Two distinct honor traditions came together in a warrior: spiritualism and that of the fighter. Warriors' bravery was marked by the fact that they were always ready to face death. After the reservation period, the Native warrior identity lost strength. This occurred in part because of deliberate attempts by the OIA to "break the power of the chiefs and their *akicita*, or warrior societies," by disrupting

gatherings and outlawing warrior dances and sacred ceremonies (Young Bear and Theisz 1994, 79, 86).

In response, some dances were adapted for patriotic holidays as a way to circumvent these laws (or they went under-
ground). "Our warrior society parades and ceremonies were
adapted to fit white American patriotic holidays like George
Washington's or Abraham Lincoln's birthday, or Memorial
Day, or Flag Day in June, or July Fourth so the BIA agent
would allow us to dance" (Young Bear and Theisz 1994, 86;
see also Greci Green 2001). Not only were songs adapted, the
Lakotas also developed special new songs and dances for
holidays, American celebrations, fairs, and rodeos: "For New
Year's there would be lots of masquerade songs and honor-
ing songs, and for the patriotic days we would have many
veterans' and warrior songs, while for the fairs we would
have race-horse songs or bronco-riding songs and honor
songs too" (Young Bear and Theisz 1994, 55).

Lakota warriors found honor in other contexts as well.
They were ready to fight and face death during World War
I and in other wars as a way of maintaining their status and
"honored place" in society, for example (Young Bear and
Theisz 1994, 82). Warrior songs were adopted and adapted
for these contexts as well. For instance, victory songs such as
the one about the Battle of the Greasy Grass (Battle at Little
Bighorn) highlighted the bravery, honor, and duty of the warriors; "After [the] 1880s those old victory songs over other
tribes or against Custer and his cavalry survived and were
used as World War I victory songs" (Young Bear and Theisz
1994, 83). Young Bear and Theisz convincingly argue that the
Lakotas changed the wording of traditional warrior and victory songs to fit these new contexts, "but the meanings of the
songs were kept alive" (1994, 83). Even though World War I
is at the tail end of the height of Wild West shows, and of this
study, these examples are significant. They demonstrate how,
despite laws outlawing cultural expressions and ceremonies,

the Lakotas continuously found social meaning as warriors in new contexts.

Along with songs for patriotic holidays, fairs, and World War I, there is evidence that some Native people also adapted and created new songs specifically for Wild West shows. Traditional warrior songs are "high-spirited songs" that tell stories of battles and the way of life of the warrior. Such songs, in modified forms, would have been well suited for Wild West show performances. For instance, the "Sneak Up Song," a warrior honor song, tells the story of a fallen warrior and his rescue by his friends. This song started out as a *hunka bloka olowan* (honored warrior song), then changed names, Young Bear posits, as part of a show (Young Bear and Theisz 1994, 79, 80).

It is possible that the song was modified, on the one hand, because of the restrictive context of assimilation and laws prohibiting ceremonies, and on the other, to take advantage of the opportunity to perform the song in a new context, as was the case in the examples of songs adapted for American holidays or wars. We do know that the *oskate,* or "show tradition" songs and dances, emerged in the 1890s, and that special songs for show performers existed. Young Bear and Theisz (1994, 97) recount two songs:

> White Buffalo Man—his name was Sam Stabber—be brave. There's a big Wild West show coming for you. When you hear the sound of the boat, your heart will beat faster.

> There will be a Wild West show that will start soon, so I got my war bonnet ready and I'm ready to go. This is what (name the person) White Buffalo Man said, and then he went to the Wild West show.

In these ways, the Lakotas found social meaning as warriors in new contexts, including Wild West shows, merging expressions of a warrior identity with performance and the "show tradition."

When government assimilation policies forbade ceremonies and dances on reservations, patriotic events, holidays, fairs, and Wild West shows provided a context in which warrior songs and dances could hide in plain sight. The personal meaning and significance of these modified war dances probably escaped the viewing public. Ironically, war dances presented in Wild West shows could have been victory songs about the battle against Custer at Little Bighorn, for example. In fact, although Native performers were presented as savages who ultimately lost the battle, some historical reenactments—such as Custer's Last Stand, Pat Hennessey's Massacre, or even some of the generic attacks on cabins and stagecoaches—could be read as examples of Native opposition and resistance. While Wild West shows were celebrating white society's ultimate victory, Native performers may well have been singing about their own bravery and victories. Native performers relished such humor and irony at Wild West shows. Native visitors to a Wild West show enjoyed seeing a Sioux perform Omaha dances, for example, and understood "a subversive monologue when Kicking Bear recited his deeds in Lakota" (Kasson 2000, 212). Rocky Bear commented on the delight of such private understandings: "Sioux have plenty fun, too. He dance Omaha dance when he feel like fun; white man no understand and say it war dance; no war dance, but dance for fun. . . . White man no understand all of Indian fun; Indian no understand all of white man fun, but understand enough to laugh and see good time" (Kasson 2000, 212).

If warrior identity continued to be honored through recontextualized (modified and new) songs and dances associated with the warrior society, did Wild West shows also provide a context for acknowledging warrior *status*? Greci Green states that the Lakotas recognized participation in *oskate* as an "honorable accomplishment" and a way to gain status, similar to that of a warrior: "The show experience is conceptually related to the older tradition of going on a warrior's expedition, for it parallels the structure of that type of event: The departure for a challenging endeavor, the outcome of which may not be known, and the successful return home, laden with trophies and experiences for which to be celebrated" (2001, 123). She further asserts: "For Lakota headmen, touring in the shows was a validation in the white world of their accomplishments as warriors" (2001, 125). Other scholars have also suggested that there was status associated with performing in Wild West shows. Kasson notes that "performing for the Wild West may have satisfied other purposes, obscure to white observers: preserving their culture, securing leadership and status, even perpetuating spiritual traditions" (2000, 211). Maddra writes that the ghost dance prisoners, through performing in Cody's show, "achieved a certain amount of status and recognition" (2006, 174). Moses (1996, 171, 137–39) likewise suggests that Native participants gained status because they became viewed as professional performers. It appears that, among the performers themselves, there was some status associated with performing. Whether the public recognized this extended and modified form of "warrior" status is another question.

Newspapers consistently referred to some of the Native performers as "famous Indians," but their fame was not due only to their status as "show Indians," as Moses suggests. I posit that their status was also a result of their involvement in significant historical events, battles, and uprisings; that is, their fame was also connected to aspects of their warrior identity.[34] There is some archival evidence to support the idea that the public recognized Native performers' warrior status. Newspaper accounts often included narratives of Native warriors as worthy opponents or as defenders of their land, traditions, and rights. For example, an 1893 article recounting the burial of a performer with Cody's show, Young-Man-Afraid-of-His-Horse, described him as a courageous warrior who defended his people, property, and home.[35] The reporter wrote that friends gathered at the show camp to mourn and recount his valorous deeds. In another example, William Cody stated in an interview that Sitting Bull was a great warrior and knowledgeable about his country.[36] In general, Cody emphasized Native performers' abilities as horsemen and warriors rather than classifying them as savages (Deloria 1981, 53). It is unlikely, however, that the public saw beyond the savage-warrior stereotypes produced in the shows or print media or viewed Native performers as "honorable warriors" in the same way the Lakotas viewed themselves. Then again, the print media represents the public's view to a certain extent; just as discourses of progress and savage Indians in newspaper reports reflected Euro-American ideas at the time, so too could they reflect their views of Native performers' warrior status. Audience perceptions were just as complex and varied as the images produced in the print media and performance (Kasson 2000, 212). Recognizing their warrior status, albeit a romantic understanding, may have been one of the public's perceptions of Native performers.

What is important here is that the evidence presented above of warrior songs modified for new contexts lends support to the argument that Native people also modified or recontextualized their war songs and dances for Wild West show performances. Native people adopting and adapting the performance encounter as an occasion for expressing a warrior identity illustrates transculturation. Native people engaged with dominant society by performing in shows, but their cultural life is also shaped by their own preexisting social relationships and agendas—their cultural projects.[37] Thus, although Wild West shows produced imagery of Native people as exotic noble savages, and Native performers did not necessarily challenge or change this imagery, they nonetheless also constructed meaning and experienced identity in their own ways (even if the public did not recognize these meanings). As a result, representations of a "warrior" are produced and experienced in two different ways at the same time. This "dual signification," or process of coproduction, often occurs in instances of transculturation (Phillips 1998, 19–20). However, rather than being a coproduction or a *blending* of two representations to produce a hybrid expression, the performance of a warrior in Wild West shows consists of two parallel representations: the production of the savage warrior, and personal meanings of a warrior identity. Therefore, rather than "colonial mimicry," the performance of a warrior identity in this context represents cultural projects and transculturation; both are evidence of agency.

To qualify the form and limit of this agency even further, I suggest that Native performers exerted *expressive* agency: they had the ability to express and experience personal meanings of Native identity, in this example expressions of warrior identity, thereby negotiating power. I add this qualification to make clear that performers did not necessarily transform images or perceptions of the audience, or, to the best of my knowledge, publicly resist images produced in Wild West shows. They did, however, modify warrior songs for this new context, demonstrating intention and action, based on their existing warrior traditions. Thus, their agency is limited to their ability to express (and modify) expressions of a warrior identity for a new context.

Dance as Expressive Agency

Dance in general was a feature of Wild West shows and also took place in the associated encampment where performers lived during their tour with the show. Thus far, I have focused on just one possible meaning of the "war dance" performed in Wild West shows—the modification of warrior songs and dances in a new context (and new contexts of status and honor). Lakotas, as with other Native American tribes, had various dances for different purposes with multiple meanings; moreover, dances were creative and adaptive, constantly changing. This perspective was not shared by the federal government or by audiences. Neither the OIA nor the public recognized or distinguished between the "war dance" and the numerous other dances of the various tribes. I do not attempt to decipher the different dances performed in Wild West shows and described in the programs, newspapers, and OIA documents. The archival record does not permit such detailed distinctions. Still, a handful of show programs and newspaper reviews acknowledge that Native participants performed (and engaged in) other dances besides the war dance both inside and outside the Wild West show arena. For example, a program for Buffalo Bill's Wild West show of 1885 indicated that one of the twenty-two acts consisted of "War, Grass, Corn, and Scalp Dances by Pawnee, Wichita, and Sioux Indians."[38] Cody's 1887 and 1889 show programs also listed a series of Native dances. One of the acts was described as "Indian Dances: The War Dance, The Sun Dance, The Love Dance; etc., of the Sioux, Arapahoe, Brules, Ogallala, and the Cheyenne."[39] In another example, the Miller Brothers' 1910 show included an "Indian Snake Dance."[40] Newspapers consistently report that Indian dances were the most interesting and popular part of Wild West shows.[41] The authors of these sources may have muddled the dances, but they did recognize that there was some diversity.

Entrepreneurs did not choreograph these songs and dances, although performers were likely encouraged to yell enthusiastically. We cannot know for certain how Native performers felt or which dances they were actually performing, but an ethnological understanding of the significance of dance more broadly in Native communities allows us to assume that there would have been a certain amount of pride in performing for themselves, regardless of how others perceived the dances. Young Bear and Theisz (1994, 43) point out that music was an important part of Lakota life both in the old days and in the reservation period; singing gave Native peoples "a lift in life"; it gave them an identity and pride. It is not difficult to imagine the importance of this "lift" and sense of pride amid the depressing conditions of the reservation period and the context of assimilation policies. In fact, external political forces such as assimilation often lead to resistance, or at the very least to the assertion of identity (Troutman 2009; Weaver 2001, 244).

Some personal memoirs from Native performers with Wild West shows attest to this sense of pride. Standing Bear recounts he and other Indians dressing in their best and dancing before the king of England: "But when I got down to doing my fancy steps and gave a few Sioux yells, he had to smile in spite of himself. I saw that I had made a hit with him, and was very happy" (Standing Bear 1975, 256). Native performers also took pride in their role as representatives of their people. Black Elk said that after the command performance for the queen she shook hands with the Indians and said they were the best-looking people (DeMallie 1984, 249). At the queen's jubilee celebrations, she further acknowledged them with a bow, and the Native performers responded with a song: "As the Queen passed us, she stopped and stood up back to where the Indians were sitting. All her people bowed to her, but she bowed to us Indians. We sent out the women's and men's tremolo. . . . then we all sang her a song. This was the most happy time!" (DeMallie 1984, 251).

Besides giving the Native performers a sense of pride, their singing and dancing abilities were highlighted and praised by the public. For example, the Miller brothers' program praised the Osage performers in their Wild West show as famous dancers and horse racers.[42] Among the performers themselves, to be a good dancer meant recognition and some status. Greci Green argues that "during the early reservation period social recognition became associated with dancing, so that the best dancers were accorded the honor previously bestowed on warriors. . . . the *oskate* contributed to this focus on dance ability by providing one area of opportunity for young men to prove themselves and earn respect within their communities" (2001, 125). Native performers' dance ability was, then, also recognized through this new context of performing in Wild West shows. This fact is exemplified by Black Elk, who states that, for the performance before Queen Victoria, "we selected the best looking types of the Indians and the best dancers" (DeMallie 1984, 249). Also, when Standing Bear and Cody's show recruiter McCune invited Indians to audition for the show, they chose only the best dancers with the finest clothes (Standing Bear 1975, 270). An *oskate wicasa* ("show man") was respected, and dancers were honored for their ability and courage (Warren 2005, 363). Skilled dancers were highly valued in their home communities, and they continued to be so in the context of Wild West shows.

Young Bear and Theisz assert that music also facilitated survival in new sociocultural and political contexts: "Music helped Lakota people survive a great deal of hardship and endure lots of pain because there was song there. We've proved that in World War I, Korea, Vietnam, Wounded Knee II, and in prisons" (1994, 43). This is a significant observation that also applies to the context of dance at Wild West shows. Native participants used the Wild West show performance encounter to their best advantage. On the reservation, Native people were discouraged, even outlawed, from dancing or participating in ceremonies, but these things were encouraged in the context of the Wild West show and certainly occurred in the associated encampment. This is not to say that the reservation was not a site of resistance as well (see Troutman 2009).[43] But at Wild West shows, they could more easily gather and practice dances under the pretext of performing for the show. Wild West shows may have even played a part in preserving social dances like the Omaha and grass dances (Warren 2005, 363). And outside of the arena performances, Native people traveling with the shows also celebrated traditional ceremonies and partook in social gatherings such weddings, sweat baths, the Dog Feast, and Buffalo Dance Day. On the 1891/92 British tour, Native performers even demonstrated the ghost dance at a special function (Maddra 2006, 131). The fact that Native people had the opportunity (and desire) to maintain dance and ceremonies, facilitated by their employment with Wild West shows, should not be taken lightly, for it is representative of their agency.

Native performers used this performance encounter to suit their new sociopolitical context of assimilation and the prohibition of cultural expressions. Ortner's theoretical explanation of power and agency in the context of Sherpas' involvement in the mountaineering industry once again illuminates the significance of this fact: "People *sustain a culturally meaningful life* in situations of large scale domination by powerful others, including slavery, colonialism, racism" (2006, 142, emphasis added). This view of the negotiation of colonial relationships and power helps makes visible other forms of agency. In this case, Native performers attempted to maintain a culturally meaningful life while performing for Wild West shows. Situated in a new sociopolitical context that prohibited expressive culture and sought to assimilate Native people, Wild West shows were one of the spaces that facilitated Native participants' cultural survival, for they were spaces where they could express, and hence maintain and create, songs and dances.[44] By performing in Wild West shows and maintaining dance, and to a certain degree ceremonies in the associated encampment, Native performers subverted government policies that prohibited dance and encouraged assimilation. The Miller brothers acknowledged this fact in their 1910 program, which states that they had many chiefs with the show who maintained their old customs "in spite of government and in spite of education."[45] In sum, the performance of dance in this context is another example of expressive agency because Native performers could express (and hence maintain) dances and songs in the context of Wild West show performances and in the encampment, even if it was also space where they were asked to perform their exoticism.

Distinctive and Adaptive Dress

Dress is another significant visible marker of identity and form of cultural expression. As Phillips observes, dress is an important site for "the aestheticized expression of group and individual identities" (2004b, 599). Earlier I outlined the range of images of Nativeness, from the exotic and noble to the savage Indian, and these were often judged based on dress or appearance. Dippie argues that the ambiguity found in the variety of Indian images (e.g., the savage, the Indian school student, Indians wearing crucifixes or presidential medals or holding peace pipes) reflects the possibility of progress, civilization, and conversion. These "images of transformation," he states, documented the success of U.S. government policies, schools, or missionaries (Dippie 1992, 134–35). Although this may be the case, Dippie's argument ignores the agency of the Native participants—the fact that Native people selectively appropriated settler/white characteristics, what Pratt (1992) refers to as transculturation. Therefore, the ambiguity of Native images may also reflect the *adaptability* of Native people as they appropriated settler styles and materials to wear with their own styles of dress.

In her study of Iroquois material objects and dress in the nineteenth century, Phillips found that, whereas everyday Native dress took on settler characteristics, formal dress was an important medium for expressing distinctiveness and tradition (2004b, 600). However, formal dress still involved the negotiation of "civilized" and "traditional" clothing. Phillips explains that Dr. Oronhyatekha's clothing, for example, was an "outward marker of 'civilization'" because he eliminated markers of savageness such as the blanket cloak or roach headdress, but at the same time he maintained "traditional" elements such as "older geometric designs that have cosmological references" (2004b, 603).[46] This balance between modern and traditional, she argues, was an expression of both "difference and accommodation" (2004b, 604). His dress marked him as distinct—through its traditional elements—but also as adaptive—as represented by the appropriation of settler characteristics. This seems to be the case for dress in the context of Wild West shows as well.

Native performers dress in Wild West shows was not simply stereotypical exotic garb. Native performers' dress reflected, first, their distinctiveness and, second, their adaptability. Dress for performances involved the negotiation of audience expectations, traditional styles, and clothing influences as a result of contact with settlers. Audiences expected to see exotic, savage warriors. Some photographs show males scantly dressed in breechcloths, holding spears or riding horses in the arena.[47] One such photograph from a scene in Buffalo Bill's Wild West (see figure 4) appears to depict an Indian vignette with horses pulling travoises: a woman is dressed in full regalia and blanket; the men are in breechcloths but wearing full feather headdresses or roach headdresses and bells on their calves and holding spears. This dress corresponds with the popularized image of the (savage) Indian warrior the public expects to see at Wild West shows. Although the performers maintained what Euro-American society considered to be markers of an "uncivilized" society, such as the roach headdress and breechcloth, the headdresses are at the same time regalia used by warriors and hence also represent warrior identity and status. Native performers' dress in the context of Wild West shows was in fact a site for the negotiation of expectations and expression of a distinct Native identity.

Although the images described above are perhaps more stereotypical, feeding into audience expectations, the archival record is filled with other photographs of Buffalo Bill's

Wild West show cast members, depicting Native performers in what I call their "best regalia" (see figures 2 and 3).[48] Native performers were free, in fact encouraged, to wear this traditional style of clothing for the show. Significantly, they also wore their best regalia outside the arena: backstage or on tourist excursions. For tourist outings, Native performers' dress included many more "traditional" elements: cloth dresses decorated with shell or elk teeth for women; beaded vests and leggings, blankets with beaded strips, hair pipe breastplates, and sometimes even full headdress for men, as in a photograph of Iron Tail and an unidentified male Native performer along with John Burke at Cafe Greco in Rome.[49]

Photographs taken backstage, usually in the encampment beside teepees, also show Native performers wearing elements of traditional regalia. Some of the men adorn breastplates of bone and elaborately beaded vests (or quillwork) with geometric four-directions or star, prong, and teepee designs (figure 5).[50] In figure 6, Brave Bird and Flat Iron wear beaded moccasins, cloth shirts and leggings, and a blanket with a beaded strip tied across the waist and hold ceremonial pipes and beaded pipe bags; the boy's vest and leggings are heavily beaded. Women in particular are standouts in their beaded dresses or cloth dresses embellished with cowrie shells or elk teeth; some wear bone necklaces (see figure 3).[51] In one picture postcard of John Nelson's family dated 1886, for example, daughter Julie wears a fully beaded dress adorned with simple four-direction design.[52] Another photograph (figure 7) depicts John's wife Yellow Elk Woman (a.k.a. Jenny Nelson) backstage, standing in front of tepees with other women and children from a Buffalo Bill's Wild West show, in what appears to be the same fully beaded dress her daughter wears in the previously mentioned postcard. The women standing second from the right (probably daughter Julie) wears a hide dress that has a beaded yoke with geometric forked design. This beaded yoke dress makes an appearance in yet another family portrait, ca. 1888, but this

Figure 5. Native performers backstage at Buffalo Bill's Wild West show. Courtesy Denver Public Library Western History Collection, X-33498.

time it is worn by Yellow Elk Woman, with hair braided and looped.[53]

Even though these styles of dress, particularly the men's, became associated with what scholars refer to as the (Wild West show) "Plains stereotype," this best regalia look nonetheless represents traditional styles of Lakotas or Sioux, who made up a large part of the Wild West show cast, and hence it marks their "distinctiveness." In other words, Native performers maintained elements of their traditional dress, and this was also a statement of their "distinct" Native identity.

The context of these photographs needs to be considered. Many of the backstage pictures appear to be posed. It follows that the purpose of some of these pictures, including those of tourist excursions, may have been for promoting the show. Significantly, some of these photographs, such as the ones of John Nelson's family, were also reprinted as postcards, which circulated widely. Another interesting fact about these "backstage" photographs is that, in some cases, Native people are still "performing the Indian"; this is particularly evident in

Figure 6. Brave Bird, Flat Iron, and Little Money at Buffalo Bill's Wild West show. Courtesy Denver Public Library Western History Collection, NS-615.

Figure 7. Yellow Elk Woman (Jenny Nelson), second from left, backstage at Buffalo Bill's Wild West show. The little girl standing next to her is her youngest daughter, Rose. Courtesy Buffalo Bill's Historical Center, Cody, Wyoming, P.6.60.

pictures of tourists posing with Native performers. For these reasons, one might argue that these photographs are more than posed, they are fake or inauthentic representations of Native identity. But his does not contradict the view that Native performers' dress in the Wild West shows marked Native performers as "distinct"; rather, the context supports this premise. If these were in fact more formal (posed or staged) photographs, then they were all the more important mediums for expressing their "distinctiveness and tradition." Therefore, as Phillips found in her study, Native performers tend to wear more traditional regalia for formal occasions, whether for cast pictures or backstage.

There are other backstage photographs that capture men and women going about their daily routines and appear to be more candid. In these more informal occasions, cloth fabric, sometimes lightly decorated with shells, is the material of choice. Everyday dress in the encampment takes on more settler characteristics. In one photograph dated ca. 1904, for instance, a performer with Cody's show in a cloth shirt and vest pokes out of his tepee to hand something to a child wearing cloth leggings, plaid shirt, and cloth vest decorated with what appear to be shells.[54] In another photograph from ca. 1902, a woman standing at the entrance of her tepee is wrapped in a blanket and a little girl is plainly dressed in a cloth dress, a scarf tied around her neck.[55] This type of dress contrasts with the pictures described above, which were also taken backstage but appear to be more posed, portraying Native performers in their best regalia. Still other backstage photographs depict performers in mainly settler dress, but with the addition of some traditional elements. Two photographs of cast members relaxing among teepees are good examples. In one, a woman holding a baby and one child wear cloth while the male performers and another child wear hair pipe breastplates over cloth shirts and leggings.[56] In the other, four men wear cloth leggings and shirts and hold blankets; some wear scarves, one a vest (it is unclear whether the vest is beaded).[57]

What does this all mean? Did Native performers wear stereotypical garb or traditional dress, or did they adopt settler clothing? The answer is yes, yes and yes. Native dress in the context of Wild West shows and performances was multifaceted and hybrid, as was Native people's attire in general back on the reservations. Like Dr. Oronhyatekha, Native performers with Wild West shows incorporated settler materials or styles to varying degrees. In fact, it is difficult to find examples where Native performers do not incorporate settler materials or clothing to some extent. Even photographs of Native performers in their "best regalia" show the influence of contact with settlers. In these examples, Native dress includes settler materials such as cloth dresses, shirts, vests, or leggings, but these are embroidered with beadwork that adheres to traditional designs. For example, the photograph of Brave Bird and Flat Iron (see figure 6) highlights exceptional geometric beadwork on cloth; however, Flat Iron is dressed entirely in unadorned cloth yet holds a ceremonial peace pipe. In another picture ca. 1890 of Cody with some of the Native performers, the men wear either breastplates or beaded vests with geometric designs, but one Native performer appears in cloth shirt, pants, and scarf, wearing a hat; Brave Bird is similarly dressed, but he wears a blanket with beaded strip. A cowboy-like style appears in another photograph from Cody's show ca. 1890, which also illustrates an entire range of styles: "savage warrior," traditional regalia, settler influences (figure 8).[58] It is evident that dress, like culture, is not static; rather, it is creative and adaptive.

Other examples of hybrid dress exist in newspaper descriptions. The reporter in an 1885 newspaper article writes of Sitting Bull wearing a linen shirt and dark flannel Mexican pantaloons, a yellow silk handkerchief with a very dirty gold pin, and a cameo ring; he is braiding his hair and smoking his pipe in the camp.[59] Another article describes him as wearing woollen trousers, a fancy patterned vest, a shirt with "gaudy sleeve-buttons" at the wristband, and a brass chain with crucifix, his copper skin covered with ochre.[60] This clothing consists of materials and styles from settlers in combination with a beaded vest, a "traditional" hair style, and the use of ochre. The crucifix represents the presence (although not necessarily acceptance) of Christianity as well as Sitting Bull's relationship with missionaries. His dress also reflects contact with settler society in terms of economy: the use of silver in the fur trade. Black Heart, another performer with Cody's show, also wore hybrid clothing, including a full headdress and hair pipe breastplate along with a shirt with American stars and stripes underneath. Kasson correctly asserts that his attire suggests "a claim to his own form of cultural synthesis" (2000, 186). In other words, hybrid dress (through the adoption of settler characteristics) was an expression of the wearers' "accommodation" and adaptability.

Figure 8. Native performers with Buffalo Bill's Wild West show, illustrating an array of clothing styles. Courtesy Buffalo Bill's Historical Center, Cody, Wyoming, P6.343b.

These examples show that Native people's dress in the performance encounter was simultaneously an expression of tradition, distinction, and adaptability. Although images and descriptions often referred to Native people's dress as "strange" or "exotic," their dress also indicated their difference from American society—it was a marker of distinctiveness (and survival). It is clear that the Native performers' dress reflected a time of intense cultural contact. The hybrid and multiple nature of their dress is not a question of assimilation or authenticity; rather, it is an example of transculturation. Moreover, the fact that Native people with Wild West shows incorporated settler styles and new materials with traditional clothing and designs may be viewed as a statement of their adaptability instead of their assimilation. These outer signs of "distinction and accommodation" demonstrate that Native people and their culture continued to survive and adapt. It is ironic that, while Wild West shows promoted an opportunity to witness Native people "before they vanished," this context also facilitated the continuation and vitality of Native cultural expressions.

CHAPTER FOUR

Not the Only Show in Town

A Case Study of Mohawk Performers

This chapter adds Native voices to the interpretation of Native performers' experiences in Wild West shows, exhibitions, and other performance spaces historically. In part biographical, it presents the experiences of three Mohawk families who capitalized on opportunities in a variety of spectacles and became successful performers: Jose Akwiranoron Beauvais and family, the Williams-Kelly family, and the Deer family, including Esther Deer (a.k.a. Princess White Deer). My analysis of their experiences through an investigation of the archival collections at the Kanien'kehá:ka Onkwawén:na Raotitióhkwa Language and Cultural Center (KORLCC) in Kahnawake was greatly enhanced by the knowledge and oral histories from descendants of the performers, who offered additional interpretations of the archival record and of their families' experiences. Participation in public performance is also a story of success, identity, and pride, rather than simply a story of exploitation and commercialization.

Kahnawake presents an excellent case where it is possible to link archival textual material, photographs, and oral histories. First, following recent studies that repatriate visual images to the community (e.g., Arid 2003; Brown and Peers 2006), I sought to incorporate Native people's views of the documentary evidence at KORLCC, which led to alternative

interpretations of the photographs. Brown and Peers write
of their project, which explored the different meanings, interests, and discourses of photographs taken by Beatrice
Blackwood and examined by Kainai community members,
"At the theoretical level, we explore the differences and productive tensions between the interpretations assigned to
photographs of First Nations people by non-Native scholars,
and how these same images can be understood quite differently by First Nations peoples themselves."[1] Community
responses offered a "revisionist history" that focused on reclaiming Blackfoot names and on narratives of "disruption
and loss" but also of pride, hard work, and survival (Brown
and Peers 2006, 5, 10).

   Similarly for this project, descendants of performers who
viewed the images focused on different aspects of the photographs and told different stories. It may be that only positive
stories are remembered and told; my goal is not to negate
"official histories" or other studies that have critiqued Wild
West shows as exploitive by highlighting these stories.
Rather, as Cruikshank (1992) argues, I draw on Native oral
histories to build on these studies by offering additional interpretations of the same experience. Engagement with photographs also led to discussions about family histories and
experiences. Photographs encompass more than who, what,
and where. They are relational, "enmeshed in oral stories—
personal, family and community histories" (Edwards 2005,
37). Brown and Peers observe that "photographs . . . can inspire the telling of community and cultural histories which
are otherwise little documented and difficult to retrieve, sub-
merged as they often are by mainstream historical analysis
and by the processes of colonialism" (2006, 7). In this case,
descendants offered an indigenous reading of the visual
record, one that included personal family experiences and
histories and hence provided an alternative history of Native experiences in Wild West shows and other performance
spaces.

The dialogue between oral histories and archival data also allows us to "access different voices and different interpretations of the same historical experience" (Brettell 1998, 528). Although I use oral histories as data in this case study, the goal is not to merge oral histories with archival data or to simply "fill in the gaps" or "write-in Native actors" (Cruikshank 1994a, 147; 1994b, 414; Morantz 2001, 49–50). Rather, oral histories provide insight on how Native people perceive and remember experiences; they offer another perspective, a different story. As Cruikshank maintains in her study of Klondike gold rush narratives, the value of oral histories is not so much for "straightening out facts" as it is for "generating different kinds of social analysis, leading to different interpretations of a given event, one of which is included in official history while the other is relegated to collective memory" (1992, 22). I also addressed concerns about subjectivity by selecting informants with direct knowledge of performers' experiences, conducting multiple and follow-up interviews, cross-checking information, using oral histories in tandem with other sources, and embracing the subjectivity of oral histories, recognizing that they represent one perspective (see Morantz 2001).[2]

Oral histories are "told from the perspectives of people whose views inevitably differ depending on context, social position and level of involvement" (Cruikshank 1994b, 414). In this case, oral histories from the three families differed in the amount and type of detail because of these factors. Also, as elders pass away and memories fade, not all stories are remembered. But then, those stories that are remembered and passed down are the stories that are significant for those families. Therefore, oral histories relate something about significant and important experiences and events for them.[3]

As in the previous chapters, this chapter traces the form and extent of agency Native performers could exert as well as expressions of Native identity. First, in spite of existing stereotypical images and the prevalence of Plains styles in performance spaces, people from Kahnawake incorporated local styles and designs into their regalia. The incorporation of these local identity markers illustrates a limited but identifiable form of agency that I once again qualify as expressive agency—the opportunity, ability, and desire to express their Native identity, in this case, through performance regalia. Second, Mohawks from Kahnawake pursued careers as performers and were quite successful. The narratives of skill and success revealed in their oral histories are also evidence of agency. In some instances, they also consciously employed their Nativeness through their regalia and performances to advance their careers.

MOHAWK PERFORMERS: THREE FAMILIES

Kahnawake provides an exceptional case study for the investigation of Native experiences and perspectives, for Mohawks from Kahnawake and Akwesasne have a long history of participation in a variety of performance spaces, and contemporary community members have preserved memories of these experiences.[4] In the 1860s and again in the 1870s, for example, Kahnawake community members played games of lacrosse for European audiences, and throughout the 1800s some acted as tourist and river guides (Beauvais 1985; Jasen 1993–94).[5] They also traveled across North America and Europe into the early 1900s, performing dances and demonstrating riding, roping, archery, and "everyday life" in a variety of Wild West shows and exhibitions (Blanchard 1984; King 1991; Nicks 1999; Nicks and Phillips 2007). Others performed in vaudeville, films, pageants, commemorative celebrations, and promotional events (Brydon 1993; Nelles 1999).

Mohawk individuals' participation in performance spaces is part of a broader history of their engagement with various industries and economic opportunities as a result of contact. Elder Billy Two-Rivers, who traveled and performed as a wrestler, described in an interview in 2004 the diversity and long history of participation by Kanienkehaka (Mohawk) people from Kahnawake as he knows it:

> We were involved in dealing with the European in terms of money and business, and I guess our adaptability served us to be able to survive in many different circumstances. We went from fur trade to harvesting the great oaken forest in the lower Quebec and Ontario, sending oak panels to England. . . . After that was over, we quickly went into the construction, bridge building, raising high buildings. . . . So anyways, if this opportunity came along . . . such as entertainment, we were ready for it. Our people have already traveled much of the developed United States selling our beadwork, our medicines, and whatnot; they traveled, they went to Chicago and to Atlanta, they traveled to New York, to Toronto, they traveled all over the place selling beadwork, you know, and stuff like that. . . . And, like I said, over here they found quite a number of people ready and experienced to do that type of work; the work . . . to be able to travel, you know, and be able to manage the requirements of traveling.[6]

The entertainment industry provided another way for Native people to make a living, and performing required Native individuals, among other things, to "act Indian." Thus, Native performers often conformed to the public's expectations, performing what Francis (1992) calls an "Imaginary Indian" (see also Deloria 1998). However, these performance spaces are more complex than simply a story of essentialization or exploitation. Scholars have considered the complex relationships of various encounters between Natives and non-Natives (e.g., Comaroff and Comaroff 1991; Lomawaima 1995; Ortner 1999; Phillips 1998). Pratt (1992) has argued that the history of Native–white contact is a two-way process involving transculturation, in which both parties negotiate relationships. In this case, people from Kahnawake engaged with these performance opportunities as impresarios sought

Native performers for profit. As Billy Two-Rivers noted in the interview, many recruiters came to Kahnawake because the people there were well suited to the industry and participated willingly: "And so when they arrived over here to recruit people who might fit into their Wild West show, they found a rich and plentiful number of people who could participate in the shows and what was required of them. To be able to sing, to be able to dance, to be able to ride horse, and had the costumes to go with their different performances." He explained that individuals weighed the prospect of performing in terms of its potential, opportunities, and benefits. Traveling around was part of the fun, and there were monetary benefits as well (Two-Rivers 2004).

Akwiranoron

Jose Akwiranoron Beauvais (1872–ca. 1913) and his wife, Mary (Margaret) Irihwiioston Beauvais, performed in various spaces such as exhibitions, pageants, and film in the early 1900s. In 1908, Akwiranoron participated in one of the grandest Canadian pageants, the Quebec Tercentenary. Held in Quebec City in July, the celebrations consisted of lavish parades, military and naval demonstrations, and eight elaborate historical pageants. It is probable that he also participated in the 1909 Champlain Lake Celebrations that took place in the states of New York and Vermont. Akwiranoron also performed at the Canadian Indian Village at the Naval, Shipping, and Fisheries Exhibition, Earl's Court, in London, England, which opened on May 6, 1905. He traveled there with his wife and three children, Agnus, Margaret, and baby Takariwaben.[7] Pictures at KORLCC captioned "stills from the Edison movie Hiawatha" and variously dated "before 1890?" "about 1900s," and 1905 indicate that Akwiranoron and his wife were also actors in a film about Hiawatha shot at an uncertain date.[8] Conway Jocks (personal communication, 2004),

Akwiranoron's grandson, believes that these photographs
are stills from the Edison film *Hiawatha* shot in New Jersey.[9]

"Scar Face": The Williams-Kelly Family

Thomas Thanenrison Williams (1851–?), also known as Scar
Face, traveled the world as a well-known performer. Scar
Face; his wife, Mary Kwa-to-ra-ni Williams; daughter Margaret Jawitson Tsiohawison (nee Williams) Kelly (1876–1970);
son-in-law Michael Kelly (1877–1957); and their son Paul
Kelly (1907–1986) all participated in various performance
spaces, often working together as a family. They performed
at the Canadian Indian Village at Earl's Court in 1905, the
1908 Quebec Tercentenary pageants, and the Lake Champlain pageant in 1909, to name but a few. Scar Face's great-
great-granddaughter Barbara Koronhienhén:te Little-Bear
Delisle has been researching her family history in an effort to
keep their memories and experiences alive for her children.
In addition, Barbara's great-grandfather Michael and great-
grandmother Jawitson were still living when Barbara was
very young, and they would tell her all about their experiences and adventures. Paul Kelly, Barbara's grandfather, also
told her stories about traveling with a Wild West show and
going to England.

The Deer Family and Princess White Deer

Esther Deer (also known as Princess White Deer); her grandfather Chief Running Deer; her father, James Deer; her
mother, Georgette (nee Osborne) Deer; and her uncles John
Jr. and George performed together as the Deer Family.[10] Esther Deer was born in 1891 (d. 1992) in Akwesasne, but her
family is originally from Kahnawake. In the late 1800s and
into the early 1900s, the Deer family participated in Wild

West shows and exhibitions across North America: Colonel Cummins Wild West show at the Pan-American Exposition in Buffalo in 1901 and the Texas Jack Wild West show in 1904, for example.[11] From 1904 to 1910, the family traveled abroad to perform in countries across Europe and in South Africa, touring with their own Deer Family Wild West show from 1905. Esther then emerged as a solo performer and traveled abroad extensively from 1911 to 1915 to places such as Russia, Poland, Ukraine, England, and France.[12] She enjoyed a successful career in vaudeville into the 1920s, performing at venues in the well-known and highly successful Keith-Albee circuit and in Ziegfeld productions and revues.[13] Later in her career she staged performances as a contribution to the war effort and appeared at special events and commemorations into the 1930s.

PLAINS DRESS FOR THE WILD WEST?
PERFORMANCE REGALIA AND
NATIVE IDENTITY

Performances of Nativeness often incorporate Plains imagery, which for the general public came to signify all Native people. Early explorers' accounts, paintings, books, and popular literature such as dime novels had a role in creating this image of the Plains Indian as quintessential Indian, and Wild West shows popularized it (Ewers 1964; King 1991; Rogers 1983).[14] The Plains image perpetuated in popular media, Wild West shows, exhibitions, and other performance spaces consisted of a warrior dressed in a fringed hide shirt and leggings, wearing a flowing eagle-feather war bonnet, perhaps carrying a shield and spear, and riding a horse; or a woman wearing a beaded buckskin dress with fringe, her hair in braids. The assumption is that performance regalia simply conformed to this popularized Plains image. For this reason, performance regalia worn in spectacles have been thought of as "inauthentic" and not systematically evaluated (Nicks and Phillips 2007, 144; Phillips 1998, xi).[15] There are problems with this assumption. For one thing, the characteristics of "Plains dress" are in fact difficult to pin down in ethnographies.[16] For example, although Wissler argued that the two-hide dress was typical Plains female attire, women wore hide skirts and ponchos, three-skin dresses, and trade-cloth dresses as well (Ewers 1997, 117, 120, 122; Lowie 1963). Hail's book (1993) clearly explains and illustrates Plains styles, materials, and designs but also recognizes that intertribal exchange and contact with settlers resulted in blended styles, which changed through time. Additionally, despite this popular Plains image, performance regalia are diverse, as this section shows.

The Quebec City Tercentenary Pageants, 1908

During our conversations, Conway Jocks, Akwiranoron's grandson, described agents coming to Kahnawake to recruit performers; his mother, Margaret Beauvais, was sought after as a local beauty. He also recalled that his grandfather Akwiranoron was known for his role in the Hiawatha film and participated in the grand Quebec Tercentenary pageants. More research on the Beauvais family is needed, but my investigation into Jose Akwiranoron Beauvais's experiences in performance led me to consider Native participation in the Quebec Tercentenary pageants further.

The Tercentenary pageants depicted the Europeans' arrival and founding of Quebec City.[17] Native people were inserted into this narrative, but their roles were not superficial: five of the eight pageants included substantial Native participation, resulting in multiple, and at times contradictory, productions of Native history. Nonetheless, this participation resulted in an injection of narratives about their role in history, and their very presence at the pageants attested to the fact that they had not vanished.[18] As Nelles (1999, 168, 179, 181) argues, Native participation in these pageants turned a commemoration of two nations—French and English—into a story of three—French, English, and Native. The history of the various First Nations are not, however, clearly presented in the pageant, and different First Nations peoples played various Native roles: Iroquois actors from Kahnawake, Ojibways from Sault St. Marie, and Hurons from Ancien Lorrette played various Native roles. The pageants also provided a space in which to construct and express identity, both Canadian-Quebecois and Native. Multiple images of Native identity were presented, in part because these performers influenced representations of Nativeness by incorporating local styles and iconography into their performance regalia.

According to visual documentation of the pageants, including stereographic cards, newspaper sketches, and souvenir books, it appears that pageant organizers sought to present an overall image of Native people that was based on the well-recognized Plains style described above. In fact, Nelles writes that the Native people participating in the pageants could not present themselves as they were (e.g., as Iroquois, or Ojibway, or Huron) but rather as the public thought Indians should look—that is, as Plains Indians. According to Nelles, Native performers "came as they were," so costumes had to be bought for them (1999, 174). Judging from a stereo card depicting some of the male Native performers, many of the hide shirts were similar in style, suggesting some type of mass-produced generic costume (figure 9). American Horse's dress also calls to mind familiar Plains imagery: he wore a two-piece hide shirt with fringe and geometric and circular beadwork across the chest as well as a feather war bonnet (figure 10).[19] His fringed hide leggings are trimmed in red flannel with an abstract floral and swirl design, which is perhaps more reminiscent of Iroquoian design. A stereo card captioned "Indians Playing Cards in the Pageant Camp—A Modern Development" depicts Native performers relaxing

Figure 9. Regalia at the Quebec Tercentenary, 1908. Courtesy York University Libraries, Clara Thomas Archives and Special Collections, Quebec Tercentenary Photographic Collection, image ASC07029.

Figure 10. American Horse's regalia. Courtesy McCord Museum, M14373-B.

in their performance dress of fringed hide shirts and pants; many wear feather headdresses, although one person has a felt hat (figure 11). These costumes conformed to what the public perceived as being "Indian."

Although the performance regalia at Quebec City drew on the Plains clothing styles common in Wild West shows, they also incorporated local styles and various materials not typically considered "Plains." One of the headdresses pictured in the stereo card of Natives playing cards has an Iroquoian crown-style headband as its base (see figure 11).[20] The stereo card of male performers in generic costumes also depicts a Native person sitting on his heels wearing a shirt with a beaded collar or yoke with an abstract swirly floral design on the bottom, a deer figure in the center, and what appears to be a thunderbird on the very top. This complex iconography might reference the wearer's (mixed?) descent and Iroquoian cosmology (see figure 9, bottom right). A picture of American Horse with women cooking shows the women wearing Iroquois beaded caps and children wearing beaded yokes, both decorated with Iroquois-style floral designs (Nelles 1999, 180). And, as stated above, the beadwork on American Horse's leggings appears to be influenced by Iroquoian designs.

At the Quebec Tercentenary pageants, therefore, Native identity was produced in multiple ways through performance regalia. Despite the pageant organizers' desire to present a Plains image, performance regalia in fact consisted of a more intertribal or pan-Indian expression, indicating that performers also actively constructed identity in this space. Though many scholars view the notion of pan-Indian identity as a generic, Plains-inspired expression that supersedes local diversity, I use it in a more nuanced way here.[21] The idea of pan-Indian is introduced here because it recognizes both intertribal contact and local expressions in addition to contact with non-Natives.

This view of pan-Indian expressions is congruent with the concept of transculturation; Native performers adopted and engaged in these performances, controlled by dominate society, and incorporated non-Native and intertribal influences into regalia. More specifically, performance regalia at the pageants were influenced by non-Natives (new materials as

Figure 11. Stereo card "Indians Playing Cards." Courtesy York University Libraries, Clara Thomas Archives and Special Collections, Quebec Tercentenary Photographic Collection, image ASC07030.

a result of contact and the public's expectations to see Plains imagery) and the Native performers themselves (local expressions) as well as intertribal contact (Plains and other tribes and nations). More examples of these various influences follow in the next section, but it is clear that the production and expression of Nativeness is a process of coproduction (Nicks 1999; Phillips 1998), or, rather, multiproduction. Given this view, it is possible that Native performers remade performance regalia for themselves as active agents in the construction of Nativeness in these performance contexts.

Representing Mohawk through Regalia: The Williams-Kelly Family at Earl's Court, 1905

Taking the analysis of performance regalia from the Quebec Tercentenary pageants one step further, this section provides a closer examination of Plains imagery and styles in performance regalia. We can see in performance regalia worn at Earl's Court and other performance spaces documented in images at KORLCC, in addition to Barbara Delisle's own collection of family regalia, that the influence of Plains dress in performance spaces was present but not all-encompassing. Performance regalia worn by Mohawk performers were in fact diverse and intertribal (as was Plains dress)[22]—part Plains, part Iroquois-inspired. Barbara's oral histories and knowledge of beadwork, as well as her reading of the visual record at KORLCC, highlight the fact that performers also claimed their regalia as statements of identity. This supports Nicks (n.d., 9) suggestion that expressions of Iroquoian identity were visible in public performance regalia. To be clear, Mohawk performers did not necessarily contest Plains imagery; rather, they incorporated local beadwork and regalia styles into performance regalia along with it. I argue, therefore, that Native performers were active agents in the representation of Native identity in public performances, and that regalia are a site of expressive agency and an example of transculturation.

The 1905 Naval, Shipping, and Fisheries Exhibition at Earl's Court in London, England, included Native participants from Canada, some of whom were Barbara Delisle's relatives. According to the program the Indian Village included forty-two "representatives of the Sioux, Ojibbeway, Iroquois, Onondaga, and Abemihi tribes."[23] One of the draws of the exhibition was the "Great Canadian Indian Village," which was advertised as an opportunity to see "Chiefs, Artisans, Squaws and Papooses."[24] King observes that the Indian Village "depended on Cody's type of Wild West Show" (1991, 39).[25] The village was also comparable to Wild West shows in that it had an Indian museum with various "historical curios, war-clubs, tomahawks, idols . . . etc." It was similar to Wild West show encampments in that it offered visitors an opportunity to see Native people going about their daily work.[26] According to a newspaper article about the Indian Village, the public considered the Canadian Native participants to be "subjects of our King" and "genuine Redskins of the old breed."[27] Subsequently, the article stated that the public might see traditional clothing yet noted that Native people had been influenced by civilization. The reporter indicated regret and nostalgia for the traditional: "All may be seen in their historical and traditional garments of leather, beads, and feathers, but, like all the red men of the West, they have fallen in with civilized methods to such an extent that they seem to prefer felt hats of the bowler type to the bonnet of eagles' feathers, sloppy trousers to buckskin leg gear fringed with scalp locks, and cheap brown boots to moccasins; more's the pity."

Based on the photographs and postcards at KORLCC related to Earl's Court, it appears that some Native performers did wear "traditional" clothing, or at least what the public thought was traditional—Plains Indian dress. Performance regalia incorporated Plains elements, as is evident in a group

Figure 12. Williams-Kelly Family and other performers at Earl's Court, 1905. Courtesy KORLCC, Photographic Project—Entertainment, Photograph 055.

photograph from Earl's Court, for example, of males wearing Plains-style large feather headdresses, fringed hide shirts, and moccasins (figure 12). A postcard identified as from Earl's Court depicts Scar Face in a headdress, wearing a tooth and claw necklace, holding a tomahawk, and gazing into the distance (figure 13). Poses and objects in the postcards and newspaper sketches also include recognizable signs of Nativeness associated with the stereotypical Plains imagery. For example, a postcard depicts Akwiranoron in a chiefly warrior pose, looking into the distance and wearing a feather headdress and holding a tomahawk in one hand, a war club in the other.[28] These warrior-chief signs and poses are consistent with colonial images of Native people that were popular at the time, images that had been established by photographers

Figure 13. Scar Face's regalia and bag. Courtesy KORLCC, Photographic Project— Entertainment, Photograph 052.

and painters such as Edward Curtis and George Catlin, who generally reduced Native people to allegorical symbols such as the noble savage (Mydin 1992, 250–51). Audiences longed to see "authentic" traditional Indians, these noble savages, and the reporter mentioned above lamented the influence of civilization and contact with whites on Native dress.

Despite the prevalence of the stereotypical Plains images, evidence from oral histories and other visual images at KORLCC reveals the diversity of performance regalia, which adopted Plains styles but incorporated local styles and designs as well. Barbara Delisle (2004) agrees that Europeans thought everyone looked like the Sioux because they "stereotyped Natives all as one group" and because of the prevalence of the Plains image in Wild West shows. But performers blended styles, she says, "because outside people didn't know the difference," among other reasons. A closer look at the postcard of Scar Face from Earl's Court in fact reveals the influence of local and intertribal styles as well as styles and materials from whites. In this postcard, Scar Face wears a cloth shirt and pants. Although many Native groups, including those from the Plains, had adopted the use of trade cloth, this material is not typically associated with stereotypical Plains imagery; it reflects contact with white society. His beaded cuffs and bag, however, evoke Iroquoian beadwork styles. In addition, although Scar Face wears a feather headdress, it is not the large plumed war bonnet that came to be associated with Plains Indians. Some of the headdresses pictured in the KORLCC photo collection (see also figure 12) appear similar to straight-up headdresses or the Iroquois bonnet-type headdress (*wen-na-so-ton*) worn by the Cayugas and Senecas (Gabor 2001, 2, 4).[29] Thus, they could be eastern-style headdresses, which consist of fewer feathers (often other than eagle) standing straight up rather than flowing over the head and down the back. Scar Face's regalia perfectly illustrate transculturation, resulting in the incorporation of various style and design influences.

Historical documentation indicates that women kept more to their traditional style of dress, with local insignia, rather than conforming to Plains imagery (see also Nicks n.d.). Barbara Delisle (2004) supports this opinion: "Michael Kelly, his outfit was more Sioux style. . . . But the women always had the floral and kept to the more traditional style." Photographs of the Williams-Kelly family show the women in cloth dresses embroidered with Iroquois beadwork designs, and the group photograph from Earl's Court (see figure 12) illustrates women and children wearing Iroquois crown-style beaded headdresses. The floral and bird beadwork designs on Jawitson's (Barbara's great grandmother) skirt, belt, and headband are clear examples of Iroquoian beadwork designs (figure 14); these items are pictured in the photographs from Earl's Court as well, worn by her great-great-grandmother, who passed down this regalia.[30] More on how this beadwork may be viewed as statements of Mohawk identity in a

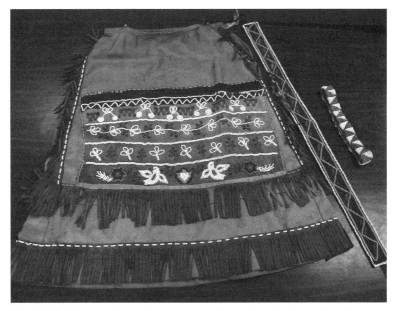

Figure 14. Jawitson's performance regalia—skirt, belt, and headband. Photograph by author.

moment. The critical point here is that performance regalia in fact were diverse rather than simply stereotypical Plains. Women's regalia in particular incorporated local styles, designs, and iconography.

It is important to point out that women's performance regalia were nonetheless variable, cutting across several different styles. Besides Iroquois-inspired clothing, the Plains "Indian maiden" look continued to be popular (figure 15). Women performers such as Esther Deer and Molly Spotted Elk often conformed to the style of fringed hide dress, headband, and braids that the public perceived as authentic Plains.[31] A Native-cowboy look also appears in the photographic record at KORLCC; for example, performers with the Deer Family Wild West Show incorporated both cowgirl styles and materials with Native-style beadwork (figure 16).[32] Many performance outfits did not fit any standard design; indeed, some of the clothing for shows and exhibitions was very flamboyant. Jawitson wore a gold lamé bikini for her riding shows (Delisle 2004), and Esther Deer owned several performance outfits that were quite risqué for the time (figure 17). Clearly, performance regalia were diverse. Notwithstanding this variability, evidence suggests that beadwork in particular was an opportunity to express local identity.

Performance regalia were also inscribed with signs of Mohawk identity. Barbara Delisle (2004) indicated that clothing styles, especially the beadwork, represented local and personal identities (see also Nicks n.d.; Phillips 1998). For example, Scar Face is pictured carrying an Iroquois-style beaded bag with a bear design on the bottom right corner of the bag, referring to his clan affiliation (see figure 13). But because Mohawks are a matrilineal society, Barbara explained, the bear design could also be a reference to the bear in the woods that scratched him on his face, which is how he got his name.[33] Significantly, Barbara noted that, even though some performers wore Plains-style headdresses instead of the small beaded caps typical of the Iroquois, the beadwork and regalia were

Figure 15. Princess White Deer's Plains-inspired regalia. Courtesy KORLCC, Princess White Deer Collection.

ways they represented the Mohawk people to the public in their travels.

Barbara's family made their own regalia, using both geometric and floral designs. For example, the twin flowers used on their dress represent the family. Barbara explained the

Figure 16. Deer Family's Wild West show—riding and regalia. Courtesy KORLCC, Princess White Deer Collection.

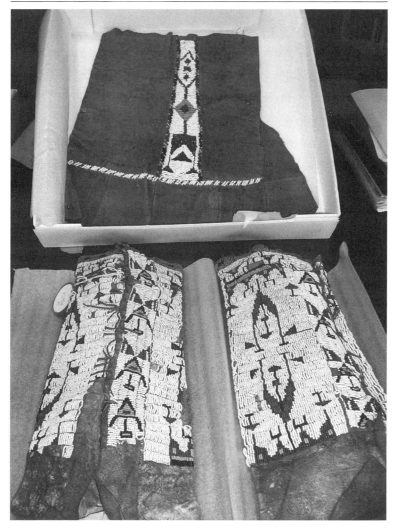

Figure 17. Princess White Deer's beaded skirt and leggings. Courtesy KORLCC, Princess White Deer Collection.

significance of this design and that her son proudly wears the flower Jawitson designed: "I don't have any of her pieces [with the flower], but I have the flower thing [design] that shows me how to make it. She [Jawitson] learned from her mother, my great-great-grandmother. So when I make my children's regalia, I try to incorporate that flower so we carry it on. . . . My grandfather Paul Kelly, his name is Tekatsitsian-eken, which is 'Twin Flowers,' so my son is named after him." Barbara affirms that most of their beadwork was floral but that they also used geometric and celestial designs (see fig-ure 14): "She [Jawitson] has a hummingbird, and most of our beadwork is floral, because we are a Woodland people. . . . Her belt had geometric designs, which I didn't know until I did some research with the Smithsonian, that we did a lot of geometric designs because they did a lot of study with the stars. . . . I thought it was just the Plains that did the geomet-rics, but no."

This comment is interesting because Barbara is claiming geometric designs as "their own" (representative of the Mo-hawks and her family) even though these designs are also associated with Plains Indians. Barbara's explanations of her family's regalia acknowledge locality as well as the owner-ship of designs. On the whole, performance regalia worn by Barbara's family represent Mohawk identity, but it is an in-tertribal expression of local identity markers and Plains styles and designs, illustrating how some Native performers selec-tively incorporated various signs and symbols of Nativeness. Whether the public recognized these distinctions is beside the point; performers viewed their regalia as statements of iden-tity. As in chapter 3, I suggest that, because some performers consciously expressed their Mohawk identity through their regalia, they were active social agents in the construction of Nativeness and hence demonstrate agency. Because agency here is not a question of resisting dominant power structures or stereotypes, I again qualify the extent of agency that per-formers could exert as expressive agency—the opportunity and desire to express local identity (among other existing signs of Nativeness).

As a note, beadwork in general was also a source of in-come. Barbara Delisle says that Kwa-to-ra-ni and Jawitson would bring beadwork with them on their travels to sell at the shows in order to supplement their income. The production of merchandise for the tourism and entertainment industry must have been substantial. Barbara recounts: "They would go to Montreal—a lot of them used to go to the Canadian Exhibition and perform there, on my grandmother's side. They'd fill up their baskets, sell their beadwork. They traveled around Toronto and Ottawa, Philadelphia. They'd sew all winter making their beadwork, and in the spring they'd take off." Sylvia Trudeau, a Kahnawake Mohawk now living in Lachine, Quebec, also mentioned that her grandmother and her mother, Mae (Moonbeam) Splicer, were excellent bead workers and that her mother would go to events such as the Canadian National Exhibition in Toronto to sell her work. She explained further: "My grandmother would make beadworks and my grandfather would travel and sell it. He would send a trunk to Europe and then go down with his one bag to sell it. He went to Europe, Africa, Mexico" (Sylvia Trudeau, personal communication, 2004). Sylvia Trudeau also had other relatives who were very well known and successful performers—the Deer family.

THE DEER FAMILY PERFORMS

At first glance, the archival record appears to support the view that performances by the Deer family, including daughter Esther Deer, conformed to stereotypical constructions of Nativeness typical of Wild West shows. In this section, I question this view and ask how Native people perceive these performances. Recently, scholarly work has demonstrated that oral histories and visual documents may provide access to Native perspectives and alternative readings of history (e.g., Brown and Peers 2006; Dussart 2005; Edwards 2005). As stated earlier, the oral and relational aspects of photographs provide valuable insight into indigenous perspectives (Edwards 2005) and thus enhance our understanding of Native participation in performance spaces. Sylvia Trudeau's oral histories and her reading of the archival record provide insight on Native experiences and perspectives, demonstrating how an indigenous reading of the Deer Family Wild West Show and Esther Deer's career brings to light a story of success and pride rather than of stereotypes. I argue that these narratives of success and pride are indicative of the performers' agency. Moreover, Esther used her Nativeness to her advantage in order to advance her career, illustrating that some performers were able to control their representations, and their careers.

The Deer Family Wild West Show: Beyond the Stereotypes

Mohawk performers actively participated in Wild West shows and other performance spaces on their own initiative as well as forming their own performance troupes and guiding their own careers as performers. The Deer family is a model example. In 1904 the family performed in the Texas Jack Wild West Show in South Africa. Texas Jack followed a standard Wild West show formula, described in chapter 1, complete with historical reenactments, Indian vignettes, cowboy pastimes, circus acts, and a few ethnic Others. Newspaper articles reported that Esther sang "Pocahontas" and "Hiawatha" in addition to performing a war dance for the show.[34] The finale was an Indian vignette presented as a historical sketch; a reporter described the sketch as "very effective and dramatic, and recalls most vividly the awful tragedies perpetrated by their ancestors." The family also performed impressive fancy riding, and some newspapers commented on their skill, declaring that Indians were "the most athletic of all races." An Indian encampment outside the arena provided further opportunity for scrutiny of the Indians. In the menageries at Texas Jack's show, an article announced, one could see the animals and "inspect the cow-boys and Indians" as well as other articles of interest such as a wampum belt, a peace pipe, war clubs, snowshoes, and the scalps that Princess White Deer wore. The combination of the Hiawatha song and the war dance supported the public's contradictory image of Native people as noble savages, and the tone of the historical sketch in particular implied that Indians were savage enemies.

The Deer family also traveled with their own production, the Deer Family Wild West Show, performing in the United Kingdom, Germany, and Eastern Europe from 1905 to 1910 (see figure 16).[35] The show included a sketch called "Indians of the Past," which combined historical reenactment and Indian vignette approaches characteristic of the Wild West show format. Billed as the top act, the sketch was described in an advertisement for their show in Edinburgh in 1908 as a series of tableaux.[36] In the opening scene, Indians sat around a fire while Princess White Deer sang and performed Indian war dances. Next, White Rose and Princess White Deer performed in front of an empty settler's cabin. This romantic picture was interrupted when the settler returned and braves in war paint "attacked an enemy," scalped him, and burned the cabin; the scene included a "sensational knife duel." The seventh and last act was called "Settlers to the Rescue." An article describing their 1910 show at the Zoological Gardens in Dresden gives additional details of this act.[37] The attack by braves was followed by an Indian burial scene with "weird chants" and a medicine man curing sick Indians. The "Indians of the Past" sketch concluded with another stereotype: "the exposition of a genuine American cake-walk."[38] Based on this archival documentation, it appears that the Deer family's production followed a structure similar to the Texas Jack show, in that they presented historical scenes that reproduced stereotypical imagery typical of Wild West shows.

Sylvia Trudeau's memories and discussions of the photographic record bring to light additional interpretations of the

Deer family's show and experiences. As other scholars have argued, photographs elicit memories, connect to family and community histories, and bring forth indigenous perspectives (Arid 2003, 31; Brown and Peers 2006, 4–5, 10; Edwards 2005, 37). For example, when Arid brought photographs back to an Australian Aboriginal community, he found that Aboriginal people "look past the stereotypical way in which their relatives and ancestors have been portrayed, because they are just happy to be able to see photographs of people who play a part in their family history" (2003, 25). On the one hand, the Deer Family Wild West Show Indian sketch was consistent with stereotypical representations of Indian life found in Wild West shows and other spectacles at the time.[39] But Sylvia Trudeau thinks about the show in a different way. While we examined the pictures, I asked her what she knew about the performances in the Deer Family Wild West show, and if she thought they were stereotypical. She responded that Esther and her mother were excellent riders and did amazing tricks on horseback. She recalls with pride: "She [Georgette Deer] was so small, and this white horse would be running . . . and the horse would come by and she'd make a mad dash and jump on him bareback, no saddle or anything, and she's hanging on his mane. And then . . . she's riding with her hands round his neck and she's riding upside down. Or she'll stand up on her hands and her feet are up in the air and this horse is going fifty miles an hour. . . . It was really something" (Trudeau 2004).

What is interesting here is that Sylvia "looked past" the Wild West show stereotypes and saw family members who had demonstrated skill and established successful careers. For her, these were not necessarily pictures of cultural exploitation or commercialization (and certainly not of "savage warriors"). They were pictures of family history, of work ethic, skill, and courage. It seems obvious to state, but the fact that the Deer family produced their own show in itself marks their success and demonstrates that they had their own intentions and goals, as well as control over their career to some extent.

Barbara Delisle's oral histories about her family's experiences at Earl's Court similarly contain narratives of skill and success. Speaking of the variety of skills and acts that her family would perform, she says that they often danced, and that rodeo-like feats and displays of skill and strength were popular as well (Delisle 2004). She recalls that Jawitson was a skilled rider and would do tricks such as jumping off a moving horse or standing on her head in the saddle; Scar Face did tricks with chairs and bow and arrow. The variety of dances and skills that Native performers such as the Deer family and Williams-Kelly family mastered meant that they were able to travel and perform in many different types of spectacles and thus establish successful careers.

Moreover, according to Barbara, Native performers were seen as stars of the show. She remembers her grandfather telling her that people loved seeing Native performers: "My grandfather used to say how people adored having the Native segment in the show as opposed to just, you know, the cowboys, because I guess Native people were glorified at that time, and they really enjoyed the shows, and the people would come up and talk to them and want to touch them and take pictures with them." The idea that Native performers considered themselves celebrities rather than the exploited presents a different perspective on their experiences. "I think at one time they probably thought we were all dead," Barbara jokes, "[but] Custer did not kill us all." "We are like this great mystery," she declares. "They hear about us, read about us, but we are not really out there as much. . . . so when we do appear [they are astonished]." Barbara's comments thus also speak to the status of Native performers and the survival of Native people, which was made evident by their participation in spectacles.

Back to the Deer family. Sylvia Trudeau's perspectives also help clarify the contrasting images of the Deer Family Wild

West Show found in the archival record: newspaper clippings and advertisements for the show appear to tell one story, whereas photographs collected by Esther in the Princess White Deer Collection at KORLCC tell another. Feeding into audience expectations and often used as promotional tools, newspaper articles, reviews, and advertisements emphasized the historical sketches in the show and promoted Natives as noble, savage warriors. Conversely, the photographs collected by Esther showcase the performers' regalia and illustrate their riding skills (e.g., figure 16).[40] The regalia pictured are richly detailed and diverse, a mixture of local beadwork and headdresses and cowgirl style. There are no pictures of war dances or warrior poses among the photographs of the Deer Family Wild West Show in this collection. In an interesting role reversal, one photograph depicts an "Indian" roping a cowboy (likely played by a Native person) on horseback. Both rodeo-type acts and historical sketches were likely part of the show and emphasized to various degrees in America and Europe to meet public demands and tastes. Given the choice, perhaps Native performers preferred to focus on their skills and regalia rather than dramatize their history in these performances. Whereas advertisements and performance reviews were aimed at satisfying audience expectations, the photographs collected by Esther Deer preserve another memory of these experiences, one that highlights their successes, skills, and regalia.

Bearing in mind these contrasts between newspaper clippings and photographs found in the historical record, I offer a cautionary note. There is a tendency to read historical records from a western perspective and to downplay the possibility of gaining access to indigenous voices. On the basis of our knowledge of Wild West shows and what scholars have written about them, world's fairs, and exhibitions, anthropologists often interpret and analyze historical records, including photographs, using a postcolonial approach in order to deconstruct stereotypes. This has contributed much to our understanding of the politics of representation in these spaces. However, Sylvia's oral narratives and her interpretation of the photographs led to other possible meanings and interpretations. The types of perspectives and experiences recollected by Sylvia Trudeau and Barbara Delisle do not always come through clearly in the archives, but their oral histories illuminate alternative interpretations of Native performers' experiences that highlight the performers' skills, adaptability, pride, and successes in the face of dominant society's power to control representations and performances.

Seeing such performance experiences in terms of skill, accomplishment, and success is significant, for it shifts the focus away from externally imposed stereotypical representations of Nativeness in these spaces and toward Native performers' own choices and successes. To use Ortner's term once again, Sylvia's narratives of skill and success and her interpretations underscore the fact that her family had their own intentions, or cultural projects. Similar to my conclusions in chapter 2 that Native performers working in Wild West shows sought employment for their own reasons and benefits, this is an example of agency; narratives of accomplishment, skill, and success represent their cultural projects and reflect Mohawk performers' control over their careers and successes.

Princess White Deer: A Story of Success

Sylvia Trudeau opened up a suitcase filled with memories of her great aunt Esther Deer: photographs, newspaper clippings, and letters, many of them more than a century old.[41] These items—Esther's experiences in tangible form—weave together with Sylvia's memories to tell us the story of the career of Esther Deer. Her extensive performance career, from early childhood into the 1930s, may have been atypical for a Native person. More so, scholars should focus more attention on the many Native performers who were successful in various performance spaces in the mid-nineteenth and twentieth centuries.

Esther's home base was in New York State, but she spent much of her life traveling and performing with her family from as early as 1901 in Wild West shows and exhibitions. She also frequently visited her friends and family in Kahnawake and shared stories about her experiences. Photocopies of newspaper clippings, photographs, and much of Esther's regalia from Sylvia's suitcase form the Princess White Deer Collection at KORLCC. With the aid of this material and Sylvia's oral histories, Esther's career emerges as an example of success and of conscious employment of her Nativeness through regalia and performances, demonstrating significant agency.

Trudeau (2004) speaks with great pride of Esther's success and accomplishments. At that time, Sylvia states, there was little work; Indians were put on reserves and suppressed and could not compete with white society. So performing and selling beadwork were ways to make a living. She recalls that Esther performed with the Ziegfeld Follies, both in the chorus and as a headliner; her illustrious friends included Eddie Cantor, Al Jolson, and Will Rogers. "People she was in show business with would come and visit. And when I was there, I always had to dress up." remembers Sylvia. Esther was successful in the white world: she owned a nightclub, drugstore, and house in Port Chester, New York, with gardens and servants. Sylvia's account speaks to Esther's economic freedom and her ability to enter and succeed in the white world.

Esther was known for her dancing style and ability. Newspapers articles and show reviews recognized her skill as a dancer, which increased her fame and celebrity status. A newspaper clipping about B. F. Keith's bill Tip-Top states: "Princess White Deer is the personification of grace and ability and the manner in which she executes the difficult Indian dances is really wonderful."[42] A review for the Nine O'Clock Frolic production by Ziegfeld reports that Princess White

Deer danced particularly well.[43] Another review of Tip-Top remarks that Esther had appeared in principal theaters and royal palaces abroad and received gifts from royalty, including a gold medal from Grand Duchess Marie of Russia.[44] She even put on a command performance for Czar Nicolas II in Russia.

Esther gained fame and status not only because of her skill as a dancer but also because she was perceived to be a real Native and a real American. In fact, her performances negotiated various subjectivities. Nicks and Phillips argue that Esther played the role of Indian princess but also played with signs of blackness, the exotic, and femininity, thereby "destabilizing tropes of race and ethnicity. . . . She made it impossible for her audiences *not* to know that the Indian stereotypes were as much (dis)guises as the other, more patently fictional images she adopted" (2007, 157–58). These representations of multiple subjectivities or ethnicities were "self conscious and strategic" choices (Nicks and Phillips 2007, 146). Building on this insight, I argue that Esther knew how to use her Nativeness, above all other subjectivities, to obtain success.

Esther created and used both her regalia and performances to her advantage, and her use of regalia and performances were empowering, helping her advance her career. In particular, she drew on her American and Native identities, a combination that appealed to audiences. Sylvia Trudeau says, "She was always proud to represent the country, because she was always asked to do something for the army or navy or whatever. And she liked doing that because 'It's for my country,' she says." Esther was proud to be American, to be North American: "She was very, very patriotic. She'd always say 'our country' or 'my country.'" Sylvia explained further: "Some people don't understand that Canada and the United States are two different countries, but for the Indians, we are North American Indians. So we have—well, we are supposed to have—dual citizenship." Sylvia's statements highlight that Esther acknowledged her identity as an American with pride. Vaudeville producers and event organizers also valued her Americanness. Because of her status as a real Native and a real American, Esther was often asked to participate in the war effort or appear at commemorative events. In a 1925 letter asking Esther to perform her pageant at a tribute to General Pershing at the Hippodrome, for example, Robert Redmond wrote: "It is such a genuine American movement that an added reason for your presence is the fact that you are a REAL American."[45] Thus her status as simultaneously a real Native and an "original American" generated the exotic appeal required to draw in audiences while playing on ideas of patriotism. Esther also highlighted this fact in her performances.

Esther's status as an "authentic Indian" also brought her fame and likewise contributed to her success. Newspapers consistently highlighted her status as a real Native and commented on her famous relations. For instance, they acknowledged her descent, calling her "daughter of the last hereditary Chief" and a "Native American of the truest type."[46] In addition, reviews and articles repeatedly recapped her family's deeds and relations. They noted that James and John Deer were hired by Lord Wolseley to assist in the Nile campaign to rescue General Gordon in 1885 and mentioned their family's connection with Dr. Oronhyatekha and Joseph Brant.[47] That Esther was an "authentic Indian" with such illustrious ancestry undoubtedly enticed audiences.

Drawing on this interest, Esther strategically played up her Nativeness through her performance regalia. Studio photographs in the Princess White Deer Collection depict her in regalia showcasing her Nativeness that played on markers of Plains identity, which the public recognized as authentically Indian—the "Indian princess" role or "Indian maiden" look. Esther's Plains-inspired regalia often consisted of a large feather headdress that trailed down her back and a fringed dress, or shorts (see figure 15). Though feather headdresses of this type were not normally worn by women, they are nonetheless a sign of Plains Indians identity. This is also an example of her playing with signs of gender and femininity, discussed by Nicks and Phillips (2007). She also wore armbands, wrist and ankle bracelets, beaded or bone necklaces, and beaded vests.[48] Her skirt and leggings were beaded with stylized teepees, forks, prongs, and other geometric shapes considered "Plains" (e.g., figure 17).

Some of Princess White Deer's performance regalia also included signs of local identity, such as the Iroquois-inspired beadwork found on a stunning leather vest and short skirt with elaborate floral and bird designs, and a leather bag with a floral design in raised clear beads (figures 18 and 19). These costumes were produced specifically for performance, in order to make an impact, but they used styles and designs inspired by Plains *and* Iroquois designs as well as trade materials that resulted from contact with settlers. As with the Quebec pageants and the Williams-Kelly family examples, this demonstrates the diversity of performance regalia and the process of transculturation. Performers incorporated expression of local identity within the constraints of a performance context that sought to meet audience expectations of Plains Indian imagery. Again, the fact that Esther incorporated local designs and styles in the face of public demand for "authentic Plains style" suggests that she had some control over her representations of Nativeness.

Esther Deer also consciously employed her Nativeness through her performances, which Sylvia Trudeau suggests were from her own imagination. When Sylvia Trudeau asked her uncle Mitchell Williams how Esther started dancing, he replied: "Since she was a little girl like this, she was always making up things. She'd take a dishtowel or something, wrap it around her, and she would dance and sing." Sylvia remembered fondly, "She always liked to be amongst people. She'd put on skits when she was older. . . . we used to do that at home." Sylvia proudly stated that Esther had a "magic" that made her special. Not only were Esther's performances

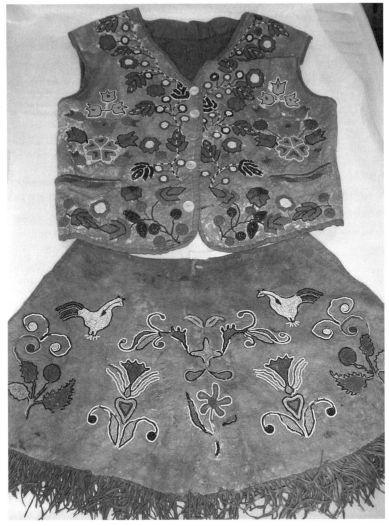

Figure 18. Princess White Deer's beaded vest and skirt. Courtesy KORLCC, Princess White Deer Collection, Regalia box 18.

of her own inspiration, Sylvia claimed that Esther was in control of her own career. I inquired if Esther had an agent; she replied that Esther was her own agent. "She did it her way."

When I asked Sylvia about the type of performances Esther would present, she explained that Esther was what you

Figure 19. Princess White Deer's beaded leather bag. Courtesy
KORLCC, Princess White Deer Collection, Regalia box 14.

would call an interpretive dancer. Esther's range was im-
mense, from Egyptian dancing to ballroom dancing. This
form of "art dancing" reached the zenith of its popularity in
the 1920s and basically consisted of ethnic themes (McBride
1995, 84). Esther's interpretive dancing involved performance

of diverse ethnicities. Notwithstanding this variability, many of the interpretive dances in her repertoire had Native themes—such as the Indian dances she performed in Russia, her "Indian Song and Dance" from 1918, and the "Dance to the Great Spirit" performed at the New Amsterdam Theatre, New York, in 1921—inspired by her personal experiences and cultural background. Indeed, Esther likely had extensive input into her regalia and performances.

In addition, newspaper clippings and revues of the time indicate that many of her productions consistently moved back and forth between dances that represented her Nativeness and those that displayed her Americanness. For example, Esther appeared in two scenes of the production Tip-Top (ca. 1920) with Fred Stone at the Globe Theatre in New York City. In one scene she appeared in "full Indian war dress to do the scalp dance"; in the other she wore modern evening dress and did "a snappy buck and wing dance."[49] Her "Revue of Dances Over Four Centuries" at the Hippodrome in 1925 started with a chief's address by a male performer and Esther in Native costume performing a symbolic solo. The rest of the revue moved from a Native theme to European and American dances; Esther performed a jazz dance and a foxtrot, a novelty waltz in evening dress, and a buck-and-slide routine.[50] For the tribute to General Pershing at the Hippodrome, Esther modified this revue into "American Indian Revue in Three Periods: 1776, 1863, 1918."[51] In this version, a prologue by Chief Eagle Horse was followed by Esther's "Dance of the Great Spirit" from the eighteenth century; her "Pocahontas Dance" represented the nineteenth century. Esther and Peppy De Albrew danced a waltz to represent the twentieth century, and her Americanness. Through performances such as these, Esther oscillated between American and Native identities, which is perhaps representative of her professional and personal journey, which moved between Native and white worlds.

Some scholars may consider these types of performance inauthentic or romantic, but Esther's dances were her artistic creations and interpretations. Esther's promotion of her Nativeness (and Americanness) through her performances and regalia was certainly more complicated than merely essentialist. She adapted her regalia and performances to meet public expectations, drawing on recognizable Plains imagery, but incorporated Iroquois-inspired designs as well. Her use of multiple signs of Native identity and American identity is thus an example of both transculturation and expressive agency. Even though her choices were situated within the constraints of public tastes of the time, she consciously utilized her Nativeness to her advantage. Significantly, Esther's use of her Nativeness, with both Plains and local significations, was empowering and contributed to her success. Esther employed her Nativeness in the pursuit of her own cultural projects. Sylvia Trudeau's words resonate: "She did it her way." Esther's career and her use of Nativeness through regalia and performance provide a telling example of Native performers wielding agency in performance spaces and successfully advancing their careers. Public entertainments may have appropriated Native culture, but Mohawk performers also appropriated performance spaces, and their successes were their own.

CHAPTER FIVE

AN ENCORE PRESENTATION
Euro Disney's Spectacular Wild West Show

As a child, my imagination flourished. I would create stories and adventures. When I was very young, maybe four or six, my father brought home two horses for my sisters. My brother taught me how to ride it, how to be strong. I rode a lot; my riding skills were natural. He showed me how to ride, hunt, and dance. Then from about ten to eighteen years of age, I learned more about my tradition from my father and brother. They took pride in dancing. They would wear bells on their ankles, and it made a sound like thunder or horses galloping when they danced. They would stomp their feet to the beat of the drum and strut proudly, like a rooster and a big warrior. The Crow traditional style of dancing is unique. It is like a rooster: we stand proud, straight, tall. We wear bright colors to show this; we wear our tobacco pouch with a mirror inside. I was taught to dance, and taught my tradition through the powwow lifestyle. These experiences make me who I am today, and make me strong.

The other influence was my mother, who would tell me stories; I learned from her. The elders at the sun dance tell stories like the one about Plays-with-His-Face. He fasted and received many visions and gifts. The Sioux came to get their land, but the Crow stood their ground. Plays-with-His-Face sang a song and kept changing his face; and then when the right song came, he rushed the Sioux camp by himself with one lance. He was brave; he had a powerful vision. These stories give me strength to be who I am—a Crow warrior.

A few weeks after fasting for four days and three nights, I did a reenactment of Custer's battle; I was one of the riders. A man saw us; he wanted ten warriors or chiefs for a show. I was excited, "intoxicated with the possibility." I had never been off the reservation. We would take our own costumes and horses. There was a sun dance in the meantime; I received a vision of going somewhere. There were auditions seeking Crow for Buffalo Bill's Wild West show in 1992. I wasn't sure if I wanted to go, but my friends brought me to the audition. I danced my best; I was a warrior, proud. I was hired!

All this led me to this path. I feel that I have more power, and I am lucky. . . . But I am protected through the medicine man and my strong tradition. I am still here, still proud, and still live. This is my message here. (Dust 2004)[1]

The preceding narrative from Kevin (a.k.a. Kave) Dust describes a journey. When I asked Kave how he came to be a performer at Euro Disney, he replied by describing his experiences growing up, which prepared him and led him along a certain path. His response is significant, because it illustrates how Native performers at Euro Disney in general talk about their experiences—in terms of their traditional background, personal goals, intentions, and successes.

This chapter adds a contemporary analysis of Native perspectives and experiences in Wild West shows. It examines the re-creation of Buffalo Bill's Wild West show at Euro Disney as a spectacular performance encounter that is part of an international market of cultural display and performance. This encounter involves power relationships centering on control of the production and representation of Nativeness. Euro Disney's show perpetuates stereotypical and "Disneyfied"

understandings of Westernness and Nativeness in its reproduction of the American frontier, but Native performers are
also active agents with their own agendas and intentions.
The dynamics of this spectacular encounter become clearer
when Native performers experiences and perspectives are
brought to the forefront. Native performers' agency can be
recognized in terms of the opportunities that employment
at Euro Disney provides and the pride they feel as a result
of their experiences and accomplishments abroad, in spite of
the reproduction of stereotypes in the show.

SETTING THE STAGE: THE SPECTACULARIZATION OF COWBOYS AND INDIANS

Scholars in anthropology and cultural studies have examined how the Disney Corporation produces a metonymic
America, constructing social worlds with its representations
of race, gender, and history in a multitude of media products
(e.g., Bell et al. 1995; Budd and Kirsch 2005; Giroux 1999).
Disney creates a world through simulacrum, reproducing
(essentialized) American ideologies and values (Castaneda
1993; Fernandez 1995; Kratz and Karp 1993). In other words,
it reproduces American life as a spectacle for consumption;
or, as Schwartz (1998) would say, Disney is a "spectacularization" of American life. Disneyland Paris, actually thirty-two
kilometers east of Paris near the French town of Marne la-
Vallée, is no exception.

Owner-operator Euro Disney opened the park to the public in 1992, accompanied by much fanfare.[2] Upon exiting the
train station visitors may enter the enclosed themed areas
of Disneyland Park to the right or Walt Disney Studio Parks
straight ahead. Once through the main gates of Disneyland
Park, one sees Sleeping Beauty's Castle rising beyond Main
Street U.S.A. Town Square and Central Plaza. Disneyland

Park consists of four different themed "lands"—Discovery-
land, Fantasyland, Adventureland, and Frontierland—which
offer rides and reproductions of imaginary and "real" worlds.

Though Disneyland Paris resembles other Disney parks
and follows the standard Disney formula and arrangement,
the "Imagineers" subtly reinvented this park in response to
European expectations and tastes, then promoted it with a
tightly focused marketing strategy and publicity campaign.
For example, marketing research conducted by Euro Disney
revealed that the idea of the frontier resonated with Europeans and that they associated the United States with the Wild
West. Frontierland (originally called Westernland) was designed to satisfy the European appetite for American culture,
and the Phantom Manor was reconceptualized as a mining
town. An indigenous American theme (Native American
and Mexican/Southwest) is also prevalent throughout the
site, from the Pueblo Trading Post and the Legends of the
Wild West self-guided walking tour to the Southwest-style
restaurants and décor and the Pocahontas Indian Village.
These spaces contribute to the construction of what Lainsbury calls "American exoticism" for European consumption.
The French spokesperson for Euro Disney admits that they
are bringing a "naïve, simple view of America" to Europe,
but it is one that reflects European notions of what America
is (Lainsbury 2000, 11, 57–60, 62).

Visitors may also experience American-style entertainment in a free-admission area called Disney Village, which is
located across from Walt Disney Studios, beside the train exit.
The "themeing" strategies of this area similarly contribute to
creating a space for consumption of "American exoticism."[3]
Disney Village brings to visitors the excitement of America
"by evoking the atmosphere of Route 66" (Lainsbury 2000,
79) and by providing American-style entertainment through
themed restaurants such as Annette's Diner, McDonald's,
and Planet Hollywood, as well as live concerts and entertainment, including the Hurricane Discotheque, Billy Bob's

Country Western Saloon, and Buffalo Bill's Wild West dinner show. According to one of the performers, the dinner show is the only entertainment in the Village that is actually making money. Not all the dinner shows I attended were packed with tourists, but they were well attended, especially considering that the end of September (2004) is low tourist season and that Disneyland Paris as a whole was not overly busy. Of course, Euro Disney offers a multitude of entertainment options, such as Ciné Magique and Moteurs . . . Action! (a car stunt show) in the Walt Disney Studios Park, and The Tarzan Encounter and The Legend of the Lion King musical production in Disneyland Park. These take place during the day and are not in direct competition with the dinner show, which plays at 6:30 and 9:30 P.M. Moreover, the dinner show is unique in that visitors can attend without paying for admission to one of the parks, although the price for the dinner show in 2004 and 2005 was €53 for adults and €33 for children (approximately US$62 and $39, respectively). This means that tourists who may have not intended on visiting the park might still go to see the show. Also, for tourists who are staying right at Disneyland Paris, this offers an opportunity to see a show and have dinner.

The Buffalo Bill Wild West show at Disneyland Paris is certainly one of the most spectacular reproductions of a Wild West show (figure 20). The show, which has been in production since the opening of the park, is the product of a team of creative producers, also known as "Imagineers."[4] According to the 2004 press information kit, the show consists of a crew of eighty technicians and a cast of sixty performers.[5] Christel Grevy, the artistic manager of the show when I was conducting this research, maintained that they conducted a good deal of research on America's West, the cowboy lifestyle, Native culture (specifically the Sioux), and the historical Buffalo Bill's Wild West show.[6] In fact, Euro Disney's re-creation of that Wild West show is based on a program from Buffalo Bill's visit to France in 1905. That show had twenty-three acts,

Figure 20. Entrance to Buffalo Bill's Wild West show at Disneyland
Paris, 2004. Photograph by author.

including a grand entry, the famous "Rough Riders of the
World," military displays, historical reenactments (like the
"Battle of Custer"), Indian vignettes, and cowboy pastimes
(which consisted of rodeo-like events).[7] Several acts featured
Indians attacks—on a Pony Express rider, an emigrant train,

a settler's cabin, and the Deadwood stagecoach. Although neither Annie Oakley nor Sitting Bull appeared in the 1905 show, they are featured in the Euro Disney reinvention.[8] The creative team at Euro Disney modified and incorporated acts from the historical show to produce a Wild West show for modern audiences, one that features a grand entry of cowboys and Indians, Annie Oakley and sharpshooting, trick riding and roping, rodeo-type games, a Pony Express race, as well as vignettes of a cattle drive, a buffalo hunt, and the Deadwood stagecoach chase.

Euro Disney's version of the show is laced with Disney flavor and constructs a simulated America that reproduces stereotypical historical constructions—an American Wild West that is full of danger and conflict and inhabited by noble savages. The show begins when four cowboys charge into the arena to the sounds of Western movie music, waving flags representing four ranches: the Gold Star Ranch in Texas, the Red River Ranch in Colorado, the Blue Moon Ranch in Wyoming, and the Green Mountain Ranch in Montana. Buffalo Bill enters and introduces each ranch individually. Audience members, wearing color-coded straw cowboy hats they received upon entry to their seating sections, are encouraged to cheer for their ranch. Next, Annie Oakley demonstrates her sharpshooting skills on horseback. Then the atmosphere changes. As the arena darkens, a backdrop curtain rises to reveal cliffs and a sunrise. Mysterious, mystical Indian flute music floats through the arena. The shadow of an Indian with a spear and shield (which looks like a large dream catcher) moves stealthily along the cliff. Sitting Bull slowly rides out, seated proudly on a pinto horse and carrying his eagle feather staff. He addresses Buffalo Bill in his native language, accompanied by hand gestures. Buffalo Bill replies, "Greetings to you and your tribe, Tatanka-Iyotanka, great medicine chief Sitting Bull. You honor us all with your presence." More Indians arrive; some ride around the arena and others dance to what sounds like something one would hear at a powwow.

Two vignettes, "The Herd" and "Buffalo Hunting," follow the introduction of the main participants and stars of the show. In the herd vignette, chuck wagons pull into the arena accompanied by cowboys on horseback rounding up longhorn cattle to a Western movie–type soundtrack. The cowboys set up camp, sing songs, rope longhorns, and do rope tricks. The light-hearted feeling of this scene is supported by banjo music, upbeat songs, and comic dialogue, complete with a rubber chicken. In contrast, the tone of the buffalo-hunting vignette is serious, mystical, suspenseful, and even dangerous. The music is eerie; the arena is dark, lit only with a blue ultraviolet light. In the distance an Indian rises from the cliffs; he gazes out in search of buffalo. Another Indian, wearing a buffalo headdress, enters the arena with a flaming torch, acknowledges the four directions, lights a campfire, and begins his buffalo dance. Other Indians join in, dancing and singing around the fire to the sound of drumming. Then the buffalo slowly enter the smoke-filled arena (an effect produced by dry ice). After a yell to attack, the Indians chase the buffalo, on horseback and on foot, around and then out of the arena.

Next is the rodeo portion of the show. Cowboys from the different ranches compete to see who can lasso their horse in the fastest time. The Indians, now each associated with a particular ranch for cheering purposes, race in the horse-rescue game. The thrilling action of Indians jumping onto moving horses impresses the audience; spectators cheer loudly. In the Pony Express race, the cowboys vie to deliver the mail in the fastest time—more cheers![9] The Indians are up next, in a lance-throwing competition. Finally, cowboys, Indians, and audience members all participate in the medicine ball game. The audience members for each ranch pass a ball to one another and then throw it into the arena, where the cowboys and Indians try to get their ranch's ball on top of a skeleton teepee.

The excitement does not end yet; there is one last vignette, the attack on the Deadwood stagecoach. Four audience members, along with the announcer, Auguste, are chosen to ride in the stagecoach, which races into the arena. In the blue-lit dark, Indians on horseback and on foot attack the stagecoach and then steal the horses with an incredible display of Roman riding. But it is the James Gang, the comical villains who drop in from above on ropes, who steal the gold. Their plans are thwarted by Buffalo Bill, who arrives with his cavalry just in time to save the day. In the finale, Auguste and Buffalo Bill salute their success in Paris with champagne. All the great legends of the West—Annie Oakley, Sitting Bull, the "true, wise and brave" Native American Indians, Buffalo Bill, and, representing "the West," the cowboys—unite as friends and bid farewell to the audience.[10]

The Euro Disney version of Buffalo Bill's Wild West show carries over much of the discourse of the original show in that it preserves the story of the conquest of the West and heroic cowboy life on the frontier. In fact, the press kit explicitly states that the purpose of the show is to "provide a genuine old-time experience" of the "heroic conquest of the West." Both the herd vignette and rodeo games highlight the heroic feats of cowboys through demonstrations of "western skills" such as shooting, roping, and riding; qualities that made the "conquering of the West" possible, such as a sense of adventure, bravery, hard work, and individualism, are implied. Despite being introduced as the stars of the show and also possessing these skills, the Indians' stardom lies in the action they contribute to the performance; they are not stars as in heroes of the frontier. Moreover, the historical vignettes highlight the relationship between cowboys and Indians as one of conflict. The spectacular action of the Deadwood stagecoach attack in particular perpetuates the idea that the frontier is a dangerous place and that Indians are a threat, an idea enhanced by suspenseful and menacing music. The Indians are not quite the "bad guys," for the bandits take that role, but they are constructed as dangerous rivals on the frontier, a threat in America's West.

In addition, the Euro Disney reproduction inscribes anew many romantic and stereotypical ideologies. The buffalo hunting and herd vignettes are essential for the storyline, for they encapsulate an image of western life (i.e., America) as consisting of cowboys and Indians. Although the aim of the show is to provide a glimpse into "scenes of pioneer life" *and* "Indian rituals," according to the press kit, the representations of Native culture, history, and identity are not contextualized. Whereas the herd vignette includes dialogue, comedic as it may be, the buffalo hunting vignette uses only yells and chants. Thus, the buffalo hunting scene promotes the romantic ideology of a noble savage. The "spectacularization" of Nativeness is hence problematic: it simplifies histories and identities, and the reenactment of Westernness and Nativeness is selective and skewed. As Bryam (2004, 4–9) also observes, the "Disneyfication" of culture and history involves a process of simplification and trivialization. In short, performances do not (and perhaps cannot within the context of entertainment?) deal with complex, subtle, or inclusive representations of histories and identities.

Despite the fact that the reenactment does not represent complex and inclusive histories, Euro Disney claims that its show is authentic.[11] Elsewhere (Scarangella 2010), I consider the issue of stereotypes and analyze discourses of authenticity in terms of power—who has the authority to define Nativeness—and how Native performers attempt to reconcile spectacular representations produced in the show with their own, lived experiences of Native identity. Although performers do not have any control over the representations produced in the show, I found that this spectacular encounter nonetheless provided a space for the evaluation, reflection, and expression of Native identities by the performers, as well as by the managers and creative team at Euro Disney. Performers similarly evoke authenticity discourses in terms of being "real Natives" possessing traditional knowledge (of riding and dancing for example), which is an important aspect of their lived identity; in this way, they challenge Euro Disney's power to define Nativeness, even as Euro Disney also promotes these same traits in other spectacular ways. Related to this complicated issue of authenticity is an obvious question: why would Native people want to perform in such spectacular spaces in the first place?

AGENTS AND AGENCY: THE BUSINESS OF PERFORMING NATIVENESS

The possibility of Native performers challenging stereotypes within the boundaries of the show itself is limited. If Native performers do not control any of the representations produced in and for the show, do they have any agency? And if they are active agents in this spectacular encounter, what does this agency consist of? Native performers' skills and knowledge (e.g., dancing, riding, clothing, and traditional knowledge) are "valuable commodities," as Carter Yellowbird (see below) so eloquently puts it. However, performing Nativeness does not necessarily entail only appropriation and commercialization. I follow other scholars who critique the simplistic view that these spaces are nothing but exploitative commercial enterprises (Mason 2004; Nicks and Phillips 2007; Peers 1999; Tilley 1997; Tuttle 2001; Wiedman 2010). In fact, the Native performers interviewed do not perceive performing Nativeness as selling out (see Myers 1994); rather, they view their accomplishments with pride and see themselves as role models. In addition, Euro Disney has opened up opportunities for some performers to pursue outside what was not available on reservations and reserves.

In the case of Native performers at the Euro Disney show, agency is identified not as resistance to dominant power but as pursuit of one's own goals and intentions, which are nonetheless embedded and enmeshed within a milieu of social relationships (including the power to represent Nativeness by Euro Disney and a global economy of performance). This form of agency is evident in the way Native performers talk about their experiences: in terms of opportunity, accomplishment, pride, and being role models. Specifically, Native performers' agency is evident in the *opportunities* this experience provides—the ability to further their own career goals, control their work life and economic status, as well as a chance to travel—rather than in the control (or lack of) they have over the show's representations. Before I give examples of these narratives of opportunity and pride, a word on what some of the Native performers had to say about the notion of stereotypes and the culture shock they experienced upon moving to France.

Stereotypes and Culture Shock

Most of the Native performers I spoke to tolerate the stereotypes and representations of Nativeness perpetuated by the show as simply part of show business, and of business in general. In fact, Carter Yellowbird, from Hobbema, Alberta, a businessman, past performer, and current Native recruiter for Euro Disney, points out that *stereotype* is not a Native word: "The bottom line is everybody always thinks stereotype and commodification, appropriations.... I never understood what stereotyping meant" (Yellowbird 2005).[12] Concerned about the issue, Carter once asked an elder if his performing for Euro Disney was stereotyping. The elder replied, "Where the heck has everybody been? This is 1900s now [this was in 1998]. Where the heck has everybody been, sleeping?" Carter elaborated on the elder's comments: "You know that's a re-enactment version of a show. Stick by what you believe in and go with that; show people in France who you are. Go show them your dance, go show them your riding." Buffalo Bill's Wild West show is a reenactment of a historical spectacle, and some Native performers are not so critical about the reproduction of historical stereotypes. Rather, the issue for many of these performers is representing themselves as best they can, as professionals and outside the context of the show, and in a positive way.

Ernest Rangel (figure 21), a Navaho from New Mexico who had been employed by Euro Disney for four summers when I interviewed him, noted that everyone has their own opinion about whether or not the show perpetuates stereotypes, but in his opinion it probably continues on with stereotypes (Rangel 2005). Nonetheless, Ernest believes that the show should include real Native Americans rather than hired "intermittents" (French actors), in order to be an authentic representation of the historical show. Then it would truly be a real Indian and cowboy show, he says: "Like the show says, 'real Native Americans.'" Ferlyn Brass (figure 22) from the Key First Nation in Saskatchewan also commented that people want to see the real thing, including real Native people. Having genuine Native performers is important because audience members presume that they *are* real Natives. "[Tourists] ask all kinds of questions," says Ernest, "like, 'What tribe are you from? Are you a real Native American? [Are] you a French or German?' And we've got to explain to them." Ferlyn's and Ernest's comments are important because they hint at the tensions between the reproduction of stereotypes and the issue of inclusion—that Native people themselves have with the chance to perform Nativeness.

The journey from reservations and reserves to France, however, can be a challenging one. Many performers experience culture shock and need an adjustment period; others are not able to adapt to their new environment and ultimately

Figure 21. Ernest Rangel in the pre-show parade, 2005. Photograph by author.

Figure 22. Ferlyn Brass in Euro Disney's Buffalo Bill's Wild West show, 2004. Photograph by author.

return home before their contract is up (Rangel 2005).[13] Some
of the people interviewed mentioned that some performers
do not stay long because they cannot handle the foreign environment, or they get homesick and leave the show. Earnest
Rangel (2005) explained, "You're in the States, and then all
of a sudden you're somewhere else you don't know nothing
about. But its challenging, you know." According to Kevin
(Wiley) Mustus, a musician and performer from Alexis First
Nation in Alberta, some of the Native performers just do
not make it because they fear themselves (Mustus 2004).
Kave Dust and Ernest clarified this statement by noting that
Disneyland Paris is filled with many temptations, and that
working there is a test of one's character, a "test to maintain
oneself."

Carter Yellowbird noted that Euro Disney managers and
recruiters do not realize the extent of the culture shock that
Native performers face when they arrive, which makes it
difficult for them to focus on work (Yellowbird 2005). They
are uprooted from what they know and their families and
communities. Carter explained the many challenges Native
performers in Europe have to deal with: culture shock, the
language issue, loneliness, and depression, all while trying
to be themselves. He has suggested to management that they
consider sending a mentor along with new performers to
ease the transition and provide a link back to the community (personal communication, 2004). A good support system
seems to have helped some Native performers deal with the
culture shock and adapt to their new work environment and
job responsibilities. For example, when Ernest Rangel first arrived, he found it frustrating; however, he learned to work it
out with his friends already there (Rangel 2005). At the time
of our interview (August 2005), William Jim from Carl Point,
New Mexico, had been at the park for only a month and a
half. He said that he enjoyed working there now, but the
first couple of weeks were tough, and it was harder than he
thought it would be (Jim 2005). But William had the support

of his brothers, Lucas, Sean, and Brad, as well as his uncle Ernest to help him through. In short, some performers went home, others adjusted and stayed. Nonetheless, Carter believes that Euro Disney is a good opportunity: "[If they can] stick it out and be positive ambassadors for our people, then I think that's a positive" (Yellowbird 2005).

Narratives of Agency:
Opportunity, Success, and Pride

Despite the challenges that Native performers face upon arrival, all of the performers I talked to recognize that working for Euro Disney offers an once-in-a-lifetime opportunity. Even within the confines of employment and spectacular representations at Disneyland, therefore, Native performers exercise a certain form of agency in this context. To reiterate, their agency is evident in the opportunities this experience provides—their ability to control their work life and their economic status, to travel, and to pursue future career goals—as well as their pride and successes, rather than the degree of control they have over the show's content and representations. Native performers' narratives of opportunity, success, and pride speak volumes about their agency.

All of the performers interviewed acknowledge that working at Euro Disney was a great opportunity. This fact points to the conclusion that, even within the constraints placed on them by Euro Disney scripts and representations, Native performers underline their own intentions and goals (i.e., agency in terms of cultural projects) in this spectacular encounter. Ferlyn Brass (2004) says about his experiences at Disneyland: "[It] is a good place to build confidence and make a few dollars and show yourself and appreciate what you do as an entertainer for the individuals that come out to see you." Tim Bruised Head (2005), who grew up on the Peigan Nation and Blood Nation reserves in Alberta, states that he took the opportunity because it was "a chance of a lifetime." Carter Yellowbird likewise believes that Euro Disney is a good opportunity, as stated above; he says that for people coming from a small community, working for Disney is a big deal and a phenomenal, lucrative prospect, but that it is important to approach it as a business opportunity and be professional. Still, Native performers also make compromises. In reference to contrasting ideas about horsemanship, for example, Ernest Rangel (2005) insightfully notes, "You just got to learn to work with them [Euro Disney]. That's the bottom line."

Although Native performers work under terms set by Euro Disney, Carter Yellowbird emphasizes how different it is from the 1800s. Now there is more control in the participation, he says (Yellowbird 2005; and personal communication, 2004). As a recruiter of Native performers, Carter exercises an even greater degree of agency in his role as a businessman. "Buffalo Bill back then was a businessman. I'm the businessman today," he declares. "Now they're coming to me. I recruit the Natives, I set up the auditions." Carter wields power in this context by being in a position to choose performers for the Euro Disney show and provide these opportunities for Native people. He optimistically points out that Native people are adapting and changing and moving into the business realm. In his opinion, working for Euro Disney reflects the positive changes occurring for some Native people in general.

Performing for Euro Disney has also led to other opportunities for self-representation and for establishing careers, in addition to the economic benefits. Ernest, Ferlyn, and Kave acknowledge that there are many Native North Americans in France and the rest of Europe working in a variety of shows other than Disneyland Paris. According to them, they go there to express their culture and build confidence and to establish careers as performers, entertainers, musicians, and dancers. Kave performs in other "Indian shows," for example, which he clearly differentiates from powwows or trick-riding kinds of shows such as Euro Disney's (Dust 2005). These shows, he explains, involve performances of self-expression as Native people then and now; he wears his regalia and dances, including the hoop dance. While I was there in 2004, Kave performed at a corporate function, and on my second visit, in 2005, he was about to depart for Italy to perform in one of these Indian shows (figure 23). According to Kave, by French law he can freely express his culture outside of his contract obligations to Euro Disney (Dust 2005). He was also involved in film projects about Native culture and Euro Disney with Blu Claire Productions. Some of these ventures "go sour," says Kave, but he is not discouraged from pursuing opportunities that come his way (Dust 2004).[14]

Back home on the Alexis First Nation, Kevin (Wiley) Mustus is first lead singer in a powwow drum circle; now he is pursuing his music career in Europe on the side (figure 23). On my first day at Disneyland in 2004, his CD was playing in the Native performers' change room backstage; Wiley was booked to play at a venue near Paris with his band. Tim Bruised Head (2005) similarly hopes to further his career: "This is kind of a break for me, [a] foot in the door for other opportunities. I can always use this as a tool for other options like movies and other stuff like that." Some performers such as Ferlyn, Wiley, and Kave are also using this opportunity abroad to perform at schools in the hope of educating students, or at least challenging stereotypes. Although they still promote Disney, they have other goals as well. Ferlyn explains the significance of these other performances and encounters: "When we go to schools and different places, [we] show them traditional dance, we show them fancy dancing, we show them the hoop dance, we talk about our ways. . . . And we get to show our culture the way it should be, without the stage. . . . So for me, I feel like I am a teacher at the same time as an artist" (Brass 2004). Kave Dust agrees with Ferlyn, stating that what we see in cinema, television, and books is

Figure 23. Kevin (Kave) Dust, left, and Kevin (Wiley) Mustus, right.
Photograph by author, 2004.

"fabricated by [the] white man" (2005). But when he speaks
in other spaces, he is representing himself: "When I go out
there and do give a talk, it's the truth, [but] I can't always
speak for all of the Indians of North America" (Dust 2005). In
short, Native performers exert agency in this context by taking advantage of performance opportunities. These opportunities are not just about their engagement with dominant
society (power and resistance to stereotypes); they also cor-
respond with their own intentions—to advance their careers
and make something of themselves.

Rather than ruminate about the appropriation of Native
culture for entertainment, the Native performers I interviewed view their experiences with a sense of pride that
stems from their work at Euro Disney and their experiences
abroad, and they see themselves as role models. As Peers
(1999, 44) observed at living history sites that are likewise

controlled by the dominant society, performances in these spaces nonetheless allow Native participants to communicate pride and validate their identity. Tilley similarly argued that, although cultural tourism may be viewed as a space that reduces culture to an "exoticized spectacle" and reproduces colonial relationships, performing may also be a "matter of personal pride and prestige in the presentation of traditional culture" (1997, 82). This pride, and at times a sense of prestige and status, is evident in the statements made by Native performers in interviews.

Many of the performers are proud to represent their tribe or nation in an international context. Kave Dust, for example, declares that it is both his privilege and right to acknowledge his tribe and lineage as a Crow of the Greasemouth clan, from the paint he wears for his performances and his dancing to the crest on his business card. The pride he feels in his accomplishments is unmistakable: "I learned to be a businessman, but this has also opened doors for me. I have traveled lots. I can express my culture, tradition, and ways—I keep my identity intact. I learned how to share, to be brothers and sisters with all the cast and with different tribes. This goes beyond being Native American—we are indigenous. We accept everyone with a good heart. But I am protected through the medicine man and my strong tradition. I am still here, still proud, and still live. This is my message here" (Dust 2004).

Working abroad has been a confidence booster for others as well. Ferlyn Brass explains: "You want to prove to yourself that you can do more for your people—here. This is a trial for us, but it is actually for everybody who comes to Europe to try this. If you can do this . . . then you can basically make it anywhere." His pride became even more evident when he described the best part about working at Disneyland: "The best part [is that] I get to be Ferlyn Brass every time, just the way I am without my regalia on, or with my regular clothes on. [But] when I put on my regalia, and I stand up in front of a bunch of kids, it makes me feel good. I'm gonna show you guys what an Indian is, this is how an Indian dances a traditional dance, you know? And any questions after that that arises after that, well, I try to explain them as best as possible, in the show or outside the show. When I'm here, in the show, I like going into the audience and shaking everybody's hands and say hello" (Brass 2004).

Ernest Rangel affirms that his community is generally supportive of its young members working abroad. Though the Native community's view is not necessarily homogeneous, many of the performers interviewed express a sense of pride in their accomplishments. Leaving home and what you know is difficult, Ernest explains, but the risk also provides opportunities. He believes that to make a better life, he had to move on and try something different (i.e., Euro Disney). "This job here really changed my life," he asserts. "I had to make decisions on my own." Like Ferlyn, Ernest expresses the view that it is important to be yourself at Disneyland, not only for oneself but also for those back in the community: "The best part [about working at Disneyland] would be being who you are. And try to bring back what we do back home, [what] we get to do here. Our cultures are so long[?]. The young generation doesn't know how to speak their own language. That's pretty sad, and you know, I was always raised traditional . . . so this is like to have kind of an opportunity. . . . That's the best part about it—being who you are" (Rangel 2005).

The recognition and attention performers receive in Europe is more positive than that in North America. In Europe they are celebrities; people are interested in who they are and what they are about. Carter Yellowbird explains that Native people performing in Europe speak with pride about themselves because of this recognition and admiration: "In Europe they're so open in talking about being Native. But these people [Europeans], they appreciate who I am, you know, they talk very positively about it. . . . That's the difference. . . . Yes, they're very, very honored, very honored, to be talking to Natives in Europe, you know, because they've never seen Natives. They're [the performers are] big, they feel very powerful. You can't get that here [in Canada]." According to Carter, this experience contrasts with the way the Canadian public views Native people. "But I can't talk like that over here," he says. "I think that a lot of people here see it as . . . there's not too many Natives walking down the road. It's, you know . . . on skid row, and that's how they stereotype Natives." This type of stereotype concerns Carter more than the Hollywood stereotype. But he does not dismiss the reality of the challenges and issues Native people face: poverty, homelessness, land claim issues, and constitutional rights. In Europe the performers do not have these challenges; all they know is that people come to see them, and they are proud. Over here in Canada, Carter says, it is a challenge (Yellowbird 2005)

Some Native performers also see themselves as role models for their relatives and communities back home. Apart from being actors, therefore, these performers are also ambassadors (Peers 1999, 47). Ferlyn Brass states that some Native people on the reserve are "trapped in the cycle" as a result of the reservation system and the turmoil inflicted on them by colonialism, but slowly that cycle is ending. He hopes to have played a role in trying to break that cycle. "We're given the opportunity to come here and try it, build it, see a different part of something and take your experiences back. That's helping . . . especially breaking the cycle. That helps because then they see a difference from what they seen back home [i.e., see what is possible]. They have a new idea. . . . That brings up a lot of people, especially people that have been doing nothing for maybe ten, fifteen years, maybe going to school, but nothing really, just hanging out. At least you have someone like this, to talk about, you know" (Brass 2004).

Wiley Mustus similarly hopes that his successes offer hope and inspiration: "Maybe there are some little kids who are

watching me right now who say, 'Yeah, I want to do something like that.'. . . I want to be a role model for [my kids]."
Wiley hopes that his children follow his example: "Survival!
Ultimately, yeah, [I want my kids] to be able to adapt, look
around and say, 'Okay, I can do this'" (Mustus 2004). Generally, then, Native performers speak in terms of pride, their
accomplishments, and being role models as opposed to
thinking about spectacular spaces as sites for appropriation
and commercialization of Nativeness, even if this is the other
side of the coin.

It is important to point out that these positive narratives
do not negate the fact that challenges, stereotypes, and prejudices still exist and persist. In a follow-up interview in 2005,
for example, Kave Dust divulged more of his feelings about
working abroad and his encounters with racism. After living
in France for more than ten years, Kave has grown weary of
the politics of working with Euro Disney. Granted, "politics"
exist in many workplaces, but he makes some particularly
relevant points about this specific context. For one, managers are in control; they use the Native performers to promote
the show, but performers have no input on Euro Disney's
approach. Though most performers brushed off this issue
in interviews, it still perturbs some of them. Moreover, Kave
feels that prejudices still exist. One day, he recalls, a security
guard would not let him in to work when he forgot his identity card, even though he had been working there for several
years. It appears that after more than ten years of employment at Euro Disney, these "politics" have began to take their
toll on Kave. Though he affirms that performing is fun and
not work but rather "hard play" (personal communication,
2004), the underlying tensions of racism make it "hard work
mentally." He declares: "Mickey Mouse is not a mouse. He's
a rat, I'm telling you." Kave learned to be a businessman as a
result of working for Euro Disney. Despite the status of being
a "Native star" abroad, there are still challenges to being a
modern Native person living and performing in France.

CONCLUSIONS: AGENTS IN TOURISM

There is a tendency to view Native people as living "traditional" lifestyles, not engaged with modernity. Raibmon recounts in the introduction to her excellent book the public's outrage at the Makah's use of modern technology for their whale hunt. The reaction was based on "historically entrenched ideas about Indian authenticity," but for the Makah whalers the hunt was as much about the present as it was about tradition and identity (Raibmon 2005, 2, 3). Similarly for Native performers at Disneyland Paris, engaging in performance in this spectacular encounter is as much about contemporary Nativeness as it is about traditional ideologies. Significantly, Native performers view their experiences with pride and consider themselves to be role models, revealing that there is more to this experience than simply the spectacular.

The performance of Westernness and Nativeness at Euro Disney's Wild West show is both "Disneyfied" and simplified, resulting in the reproduction of romantic stereotypes and historical narratives of the "conquest of the West." Other studies have offered postcolonial critiques and deconstructed these spaces as sites for the production of an exoticized Native. This chapter focuses on Native performers' perspectives of their experiences. Native performers interviewed think about working and performing for Euro Disney as an opportunity to control their work life and pursue their own career goals, which I argue represents their agency. Some scholars may critique Native performers' participation in an international market of cultural performance as evidence of their conversion to capitalism and neoliberal ideals of individual success, but this does not diminish the importance of their goals and accomplishments for them. It is critical to recognize that these performers have their own intentions, which involve negotiating their interests and goals within their contemporary context—in this case, the performance of Nativeness in a spectacular encounter. Thus, the pursuit of opportunities—of their cultural projects—is nonetheless agentive, even though they are also working within the constraints of a capitalistic context established by dominant society. Native performers are strategically engaging in a globalized economy of cultural performance in order to gain control over their careers, and eventually of their lives (see Scarangella 2010). Other Native peoples have similarly embraced tourism as a way to gain economic well-being and, in some cases, sovereignty (Harkin 2003; Wiedman 2010). For example, Weidman describes how the Miccosukee of the southeast United States, through the impetus of Lee Tiger, have engaged with cultural tourism on their own terms with "a form of indigenized capitalism hybridizing their own ways of entrepreneurship, ethnic marketing, and the use of the capitalist business model in order to succeed at the local and global level." Subsequently, the Miccosukee have used their economic success to gain power and control over their lives, separate from the Bureau of Indian Affairs and federal Indian programs (Weidman 2010, 19–20). Though I have not found any evidence in this study that performer's successes have set in motion such change in their communities, performers at Disneyland Paris are on the road to achieving their financial, career, and personal goals; perhaps these successes will eventually effect broader changes within their lives and the community, ultimately "breaking the cycle," as Ferlyn says.

One last comment, since I conducted this research the Euro Disney show has made some additions and changes. After 2006, according to the artistic director, the "cowboys and Indians" competed together as teams in the rodeo events portion of the show rather than competing against each other. What this small change may mean in terms of audience perception of the relationship between cowboys and Native peoples in the West is unknown. But what is really interesting is the most recent, and more substantial change to the Wild West show to include Disney characters such as

Mickey, Minnie, Goofy, and Chip 'n' Dale. In fact, the show is now called "Buffalo Bill's Wild West show, with Mickey and Friends." This addition changes the whole character (no pun intended) of the show. What impact will this have on the perceived authenticity of the show? Is this change meant to attract more children and families? (Most certainly it is to attract a wider audience and increase profits.) What does this mean in terms of how Native performers connect to the performances in the show (see Scarangella 2010)? Now that Disney characters are the "stars" of the show, are the "Indians" simply the sidekicks, like Tonto in Hollywood's Western films? It is unlikely that Disneyland Paris consulted the Native performers about this change. Whether Disney is a mouse or a rat, as Kave claims, one thing is certain: the face of Disney is Mickey Mouse, and he is in the Wild West show.

CHAPTER SIX

COMMEMORATING THE WILD WEST IN AMERICA
Western History, Native Identity

The number of Wild West show recreations and themed events (for various purposes) across the United States is astounding. One could travel across America with the sole purpose of attending these shows or events.[1] This chapter focuses on one such event, Buffalo Bill Days in Sheridan, Wyoming, to investigate how Westernness and Nativeness are constructed through reenactments and performances. As the name implies, this special weekend event is thematically centered on Cody and his Wild West show, but the purpose of Buffalo Bill Days is to commemorate the history and significance of the Sheridan Inn, a national historic landmark and heritage site. This heritage site encounter is another space where Native participants and non-Natives negotiate representations, performances, and narratives.

The production of Westernness and Nativeness at the Wild West show and event reenactments is a complex process of inclusion and exclusion in which representations are constructed and performed, reflecting the negotiation of power (Bruner 2005; Kirshenblatt-Gimblett 1995, 1998). It involves a process of "heritage making" whereby official narratives of history and identity are produced and linked to narratives of

Buffalo Bill and Westernness. However, Buffalo Bill Days is "a site of struggle" over interpretations and meanings, and there are multiple narratives competing at this event (Bruner 2005, 128). Native performers at this Wild West show challenge official narratives of Westernness by presenting a contemporary Native identity based on powwow music, dance, and regalia, which demonstrates agency. Simply put, in this case, Native performers control their performances.

BUFFALO BILL DAYS IN SHERIDAN, WYOMING

Buffalo Bill Days first took place in 2003 to celebrate the 110th anniversary of the Sheridan Inn (figure 24).[2] The Sheridan Heritage Center Inc. (SHC) hired the Great American Wild West Show, a spectacular traveling variety show complete with all the essential western and Native acts. In 2004 the organizers hired a more affordable show from Denver, Colorado, called the Westernaires (a nonprofit group that teaches disadvantaged kids to ride and perform). Their entertaining show included stunts, horse drills, whip cracking, and an "Indian scene." In 2005, the year of this study, SHC decided to take the reins and try something different. Rather than contract a complete Wild West production, it hired individual acts from all over the United States to participate in the Wild West show, finding these acts through contacts established at previous shows in Sheridan and through Wayne Bauman, a former performer at Buffalo Bill Days. SHC did want to hire high-quality acts that incorporated a historical component, but whether these performers knew the history of Buffalo Bill or Sheridan was not important. Buffalo Bill Days is more than just a Wild West show; it is a complete "Western experience." The weekend events include a historical ball, a birthday celebration complete with chuckwagon barbecue and birthday cake, a Pony Express reenactment, a historical parade, and finally, the Wild West show.[3]

Figure 24. The Sheridan Inn, 2005. Photograph by author.

On the first evening of events, locals and tourists alike dress in period costume to join in the reenactment of the grand opening of the Sheridan Inn. In a re-creation of the events of 1893, the participants promenade along a walkway to the entrance of the inn's ballroom, where Buffalo Bill greets his guests individually. A dance in the ballroom follows; guests join in a Virginia reel. The next day, the New Sheridan Band plays festive music from the era, and Buffalo Bill's Cowboy Band entertains as visitors stroll about the inn and eat birthday cake. Pistol Packin' Paula (Paula Saletnik), who during other events also plays Annie Oakley, demonstrates her gun-twirling and whip-cracking skills while Calamity Jane and Wild Bill Hickok exhibit the "spirit of the West," twirling their guns and mingling with guests. Children and adults alike wait expectantly for the Pony Express riders to arrive and take their postcards, stamped at the inn with an official U.S. Buffalo Bill Days stamp, to the post office. Buffalo Bill is there to ensure that the post arrives and leaves safely. Other events in the town square include a Buffalo Bill look-alike contest. The afternoon events culminate in a historical parade featuring Buffalo Bill, Annie Oakley, Wild Bill Hickok, Calamity Jane, Pistol Packin' Paula, horse demonstrations, Kearney's Frontier Regulars and Company I U.S. Volunteers, horse-drawn wagons and stagecoaches, and Native Americans (figure 25).

The climax of Buffalo Bill Days is the Wild West show that evening at the fairgrounds. Although Buffalo Bill visited Sheridan with the Sells-Floto circus in 1914, Sheridan's Wild West show is not based on this appearance or any specific year. Rather, it is inspired by historical Wild West shows and includes various of their features, including a grand entry, trick shooting and roping, gun spinning, Roman riding and other displays of horsemanship, an attack on a Pony Express rider, and an attack on a stagecoach.

Figure 25. Native Spirit Dancers walking in the Buffalo Bill Days parade, 2005. Lane Jenkins, left, and Brian Hammill, right. Photograph by author.

Despite the theme and recurring appearance of Buffalo Bill, the celebrations are not about the man himself. Edre Maier, manager of the Sheridan Inn and SHC executive director, states that the goal of Buffalo Bill Days is to increase interest in the inn and boost support for restoration projects. She says that Buffalo Bill is very marketable, and that his celebrity status combined with heritage tourism brings attention to the inn and more generally to the history of this western town. Though the main goal is to raise the profile of the inn, SHC is also commemorating Westernness through its heritage tourism strategy.

Heritage literally means something that may be inherited; it is something of value related to the past, a tradition or thing that is passed down from previous generations. It may be tangible (natural or manmade) or intangible (cultural), but we often think of heritage in terms of sites or places. Although heritage may be linked to places of significance, their significance or "value" is often produced. In other words, heritage is a mode of cultural production (Kirshenblatt-Gimblett 1995, 370; 1998). In Sheridan, a series of narratives is endorsed to produce the inn as a valuable site. The building is significant in terms of architecture—it is known for its incredible sixty-nine gables—and as a site of many firsts: the first inn built in Sheridan and the first building in town to have electricity, running water, and a telephone (Atkins 1994, 10). In addition, many famous people have stayed at the inn, adding to the value of the site, including Ernest Hemingway; President Herbert Hoover; Vice President Charles Dawes; generals Pershing, Carrington, Howard, and Wood; humorist Will Rogers; artist Charlie Russell; and comedian Bob Hope. That the inn is also designated a national historic landmark further increases its significance.

In addition to constructing the inn as a valuable site, Buffalo Bill Days involves a process of "heritage making" whereby official narratives of history and identity are produced (Bruner 2005; Kirshenblatt-Gimblett 1995). Symbols and representations of history are selected, remade, and performed. In other words, these performances are occasions in which we define ourselves and dramatize our history (MacAloon 1984, 1). Schouten writes about the process of heritage production: "Heritage is history processed through mythology, ideology, nationalism, local pride, romantic ideas or just plain marketing into a commodity" (in Tivers 2002, 188). Rather than simply existing as an important site, narratives about the value and significance of the inn are produced. This heritage site encounter, therefore, is an active space for the construction (and consumption) of histories and identities, which are then enacted through performance. The success of Buffalo Bill Days, then, lies in SHC's ability to connect the inn and local experiences and memories with what Bruner (2005, 3) calls metanarratives, in this case larger conceptual metanarratives of Westernness and Buffalo Bill. These metanarratives "are not only structures of meaning but [also] structures of power" (Bruner 2005, 21). It is usually dominant society that produces "official" narratives of history and social meanings about the site; but as the next section shows, these "official" metanarratives are not totally hegemonic.

Through the cultural production and performance of this heritage site, SHC constructs the inn as a site that is representative of Westernness more broadly and Buffalo Bill more specifically. First, SHC connects the inn with Buffalo Bill and his spectacular Wild West show. Buffalo Bill traveled to many towns across the country, so what is so special about Sheridan? The key to the Sheridan Inn's heritage narrative is to claim Buffalo Bill as one of its own. In this case, Sheridan is linked to Buffalo Bill through the heritage site itself. Buffalo Bill was a part owner of the inn from 1893 to 1902; the inn was one of his many business ventures, and he auditioned acts for his Wild West show there (Atkins 1994, 15, 29). Even though this is but a small aspect of the inn's long history, Buffalo Bill, and his connection to Sheridan's past through the inn, is the heritage produced for commemoration at Buffalo Bill Days.

Second, the myths and narratives associated with Buffalo Bill—frontier life, the West, the Pony Express and horsemanship, the Indian Wars—may be readily incorporated into existing metanarratives promoting Wyoming as *the* state that epitomizes the West (although it is not the only state to make this claim). Sheridan specifically is promoted as a place where one can see and experience Westernness, a very marketable concept. Visitors can experience western living at Eaton's Dude Ranch or purchase western heritage in the tourist shops and western wear and supply stores throughout the town. King Saddlery sells saddles and ropes but is also home to a museum that showcases a collection of cowboy memorabilia, including saddles, spurs, guns, animal trophy heads, historical posters, other western paraphernalia, and Indian artifacts. One can learn about cowboy and ranching history or the history of the Sheridan WYO Rodeo at several county museums and historic houses. The WYO Rodeo in July in itself epitomizes Westernness. Edre Maier identifies this connection between Westernness and the town of Sheridan succinctly. She says about creating the Wild West show for Buffalo Bill Days: "The nice thing about Sheridan is that you got all the pieces here; it's just a matter of contracting people and putting them together and seeing how it works. We've got the buffalo, we've got the longhorn, we've got the Indians, we've got rope—we've got everything here; it's just putting it together. Fort Phil Kearney [site of the Fetterman battle] is also nearby and is something we could re-create in the show."[4] Thus Sheridan as a place is made up of all things (and experiences) western, including the inn, which cumulate in the production of heritage and link to metanarratives of Westernness though Buffalo Bill Days.

Metanarratives of Westernness also connect with personal experiences and social memories. Schouten's definition of heritage does not account for the significance of experiences and memories in the production of heritage, but Tivers argues that "we live in a dramatized, or 'performative,' society, where leafing through experience is given more credence than learning through cognition. . . . people are drawn into an experience of heritage which may have meaning for them . . . and which may contribute to a sense of identity and a better understanding of society." (2002, 199). Handler and Saxton (1988, 251) similarly observe that the goal of living history sites is to allow visitors to reexperience history through holistic historical narratives that provide access to those lives and experiences reenacted. In this case, western life, ranching, and rodeos are all part of local people's lives and memories in Sheridan. Edre Maier declares, "Everything happened within a hundred miles of here and you can touch people whose grandparents were involved, and you can do it right here in history."

Some citizens have more specific connections with and memories of Buffalo Bill and stories of the West. For example, Tammy Burr's grandfather traveled and performed with Buffalo Bill's Wild West show, even going to Europe with it. Tammy also feels a certain affinity for Calamity Jane, who stayed with some of her relatives when she was ill (Burr 2005). This has motivated her to conduct research on Calamity Jane (whom she plays at the Sheridan event), Buffalo Bill, and his show, contributing to the historical narratives of Buffalo Bill Days specifically and to metanarratives of Westernness promoted in tourism more broadly. By participating in Buffalo Bill Days, locals reexperience their history, validate memories, and authenticate their sense of Westernness.

Finally, reenactment is an important aspect of establishing western heritage at Buffalo Bill Days. As Kirshenblatt-Gimblett suggests, "Heritage is created through a process of exhibition," be it a museum display or a performance, in which it is given new meaning and value (1995, 269, 370; see also 1998). In other words, heritage may be further entrenched through exhibition and performance. Though the Sheridan Inn is not an exhibition or "living history" site per se, reenactment is a feature of the event. An article in the

Billings Gazette asks, "Ever wonder what life was like in the 1890s?"[5] This suggests that one can actually experience the 1890s at Buffalo Bill Days, just as living history sites offer historical interpretations through performance. Edre Maier confirms this goal: "Our concern was just having people here having historical experiences during the three days. . . . and we can have that happen during Buffalo Bill Days, and they can get the true feeling of the West and not Hollywood or Euro Disney." The event incorporates a living history component (reenactment) with a heritage site (the inn) as a way of marketing both Sheridan's history and the inn. From the Wild West show and historical ball to the parade and Pony Express reenactment, these performances are forms of exhibition that work to solidify official narratives of Westernness as well as the importance of the inn and the town of Sheridan.

Buffalo Bill Days involves a process of heritage making whereby official narratives of history and identity are produced and performed. The story of Buffalo Bill and his Wild West show, linked to the inn through this heritage-making process, forms part of a larger metanarrative of Westernness. Within this metanarrative of Westernness, is there any room for alternative narratives? Up to this point, this examination of Buffalo Bill Days illuminates the process of constructing Westernness but brings us no closer to better understanding Native participation and experiences. It is this very absence of narratives of Nativeness that requires further consideration.

NATIVES IN THE WEST? NEGOTIATING PARTICIPATION AND PERFORMANCES

The story of the West at Buffalo Bill Days is not about "cowboys and Indians," at least not explicitly. References to the history of Native peoples and their contributions to "the West" are absent and, in contrast to Disneyland Paris, Native participation at Buffalo Bill Days is limited. Why these exclusions? For one, Buffalo Bill Days (and another American site briefly discussed in this chapter) is connected with heritage sites and museums that target educational entertainment, whereas Euro Disney is interested in presenting a spectacular show. Furthermore, whereas both Disneyland Paris and the Sheridan event are driven by the tourism industry, SHC is concerned with commemorating the inn. But what exactly is being commemorated, which histories are being told, and whose identities are valorized?

In the presentation of history, heritage sites and museums often commemorate the dominant group while excluding marginal groups; that is, they give primacy to the dominant society and its views of history (Levy 2006), reflecting the power of dominant society to produce narratives and social meanings. These narratives, however, are not totally hegemonic. As Bruner observes, performance has the capacity to suggest alternative meanings, regardless of the abundance of official narratives (2005, 141). In this example, performances of a contemporary Native identity at the Buffalo Bill Days Wild West show are a form of self-representation and agency that serves to challenge official narratives of Westernness, contest "Indian" stereotypes, and highlight cultural continuity. First, a look at some of the challenges faced by SHC in terms of inclusiveness.

Historically, Native performers were an integral part of Buffalo Bill's Wild West show. When I asked Edre Maier what she thinks about Native participation at Buffalo Bill Days, she admitted that the show is "missing the Indian contingent" and may need to add more of that. Attempts have been made to include Native participation in the past, but this is a complex issue, logistically and also because of the nature of Native participation itself. In 2003, for example, Buffalo Bill Days included a reenactment of auditions for Buffalo Bill's Wild West show in front of the Sheridan Inn. SHC put out a call for auditions, intending to select acts from those auditions to perform in the Wild West show. They received a variety of entries (both Native and non-Native), and about four acts were chosen to participate in the Wild West show, including some Crow dancers. According to Edre, however, many of the acts that auditioned were amateurs and not appropriate; also, though some dances and performances were quite good, others were "sedate and uninteresting." Moreover, dancers worked to their own time schedules, and things often came together just at the last moment. Buffalo Bill Days is a huge undertaking, Edre clarified, and if they want it to be a success they need high-quality acts and reliable performers. She said that logistically it works better for SHC to hire professionals, since amateurs slow the pace: "We need something exciting for a Wild West show," she proclaims, "like hoop dancers" (Maier 2005). In sum, Buffalo Bill Days needs appropriate acts and professional performers to meet its goal of presenting western history as well as providing "something exciting" to entertain audiences.

The types of performances and reenactments Buffalo Bill Days could include are another reason why Native participation is a thorny issue. Buffalo Bill Days draws on metanarratives of Westernness, and implicitly on the story of the frontier, but unlike at Disneyland Paris "Indians" are not essential to the narratives. Consequently, only two Native performers appear in the Wild West show, presenting music and powwow dancing, and two Indians (played by whites) riding bareback chase a Pony Express rider. The omnipresent stagecoach is robbed by bandits rather than Indians and saved by Calamity Jane rather than Buffalo Bill.[6] This is quite different from Euro Disney's Wild West show, which consists of several reenactment vignettes from the historical show and "traditional" Plains imagery. Edre Maier conveyed an interest in presenting a more historically accurate show by incorporating more historical acts. The only problem is that, historically, Native participation in Wild West shows included "war dances" and "savage attacks." Thus, ethical integrity and a concern for political correctness may have curtailed Native inclusion in terms of staging reenactments of Native history, because historical performances perpetuated stereotypical images.

Beyond these two reasons, the question of inclusion reflects the negotiation of power—the control of representations, performances, and narratives. Wild West shows, rodeos, commemorative events, tourist sites, and other spaces of performance are often controlled by the dominant society, and therefore they present the views of dominant society (see, e.g., Furniss 1999; Levy 2006; Mackey 1999). In her study on Native–non-Native relationships, for example, Furniss (1999, 164) argues that events such as the Williams Lake Stampede in Alberta are controlled by non-Natives yet require inclusion of Native people to complete the "frontier complex" script, which is based on a dichotomy of Indianness and western identity.[7] Because the goal of Buffalo Bill Days is to commemorate *western* history, Native history is subsequently downplayed, in part as a result of the process of constructing heritage and official narratives of Westernness, as already discussed. Yet Native participation is essential to complete the story of the Sheridan Inn, to a certain extent, because of the event's references to Buffalo Bill and his Wild West show.

That being said, the inclusion of minority groups, or of peoples excluded from "official" histories, can be controversial due to conflicting interests. Handler and Gable (1997), for instance, outline such tensions at the living history site Colonial Williamsburg between the desire to present a "critical social history" (one that is inclusive and presents "missing" stories such as the history of slavery) in their interpretation programs and a more "celebratory" paradigm commemorating the history of great men and elites favored by the site's founders and sponsors. It is evident that tourist sites are contested spaces where multiple representations and performances of histories and identities exist and are negotiated (Bruner 2005; Chambers 2000; Handler and Gable 1997). Buffalo Bill Days is no exception. Although it does not incorporate performances of Native history, it does include performances by the professional Native troupe Native Spirit Production. This limited inclusion of Nativeness is significant because it demonstrates, first, that Native performers can destabilize official narratives, and second, the agency Native performers exert in this heritage site encounter.

Native performers at the Buffalo Bill Days Wild West show contest metanarratives of Westernness by generating alternative narratives to that of "cowboys and Indians." Contemporary performances by Native Spirit Production provide a sharp contrast to the historical reenactments and costumed characters of Buffalo Bill, Annie Oakley, Wild Bill, and Calamity Jane.[8] Brian Hammill, of the Ho-Chunk Nation in southern Wisconsin, and Navaho Lane Jenkins are professional performers and powwow dancers who challenge stereotypes through their performances of a contemporary Native identity.[9] Dressed in powwow regalia rather than "traditional" deerskin, Brian asks the audience, "Have you heard this song before? 'Heya, heya, heya, heya.' Well, I can guarantee you that an Indian did not write that song." Brian plays his flute and talks about traditional and contemporary music; he also speaks plainly about stereotypes and the fact that Native communities live and thrive today. Lane's performance of the fancy dance and Brian's hoop dance demonstrate their Nativeness and cultural vitality (figure 26). This insertion of contemporary performances in combination with an educational agenda brings Native culture and identity into the twenty-first century. Though Native *history* is absent in these commemorative events, the Native *present* is being celebrated.

Edre Maier (2005) notes this disjuncture between Native past and present identity constructions: "It was definitely a representation of contemporary Native culture, because that's what you see at powwows." She also mentions that she was disappointed at first to hear that Brian and Lane were going to wear their brightly colored powwow regalia. She

Figure 26. Brian Hammill performing a hoop dance at Buffalo Bill Days Wild West Show, 2005. Photograph by author.

was sure this modern regalia would look great at night under fluorescent lights, but it was not "true Indian dress." In other words, it was not "traditional (authentic) Indian" clothing. Thus, even though the hoop dancers are more in tune with what Edre suggests is required for an exciting Wild West show, their inclusion concerned her because she felt that they might disrupt the historical picture SHC was attempting to create. In the end, however, she admits that Native Spirit Production's presentation was exceptional and the audience loved it; they "stole the show," she says. In fact, when I asked Edre to name her favorite part of the Wild West show, she replied, "The hoop dancers!"

The disjuncture between past and present identity constructions reflects the fact that Native Spirit Production is presenting alternative social meanings of Native identity. Performing Nativeness as it is experienced today is certainly one of the troupe's goals. When I asked Brian Hammill how he felt about perhaps playing a "traditional Indian" in this type of venue and possibly reenacting historical Wild West performances, he replied: "The way we do it here [at Buffalo Bill Days], we're not going back to the 1880s. A lot of the other stuff in the show is 1880s; we show who we are today. We are not showing what it was like in the 1800s, we are showing what we are today. So when somebody wants me to throw on a headdress and dance around a fire, I'll tell them no, that's not what they really want, that we can do it another way which would give them the same energy and give them a better effect" (Hammill 2005). Brian's approach to performance illustrates that performances of contemporary Native identity may be included, even at a heritage site. Most important, Brian's statements reveal that it is possible to contest stereotypical representations of Nativeness associated with some Wild West shows without sacrificing entertainment value or spectacular appeal.

The degree of control performers exert appears to be directly related to their ability to challenge stereotypes and tourists' perceptions. Other studies support this conclusion. Mason similarly observed how it is possible for interpreters (performers) at a Canadian tourist site on Victoria Island, Ottawa, to challenge stereotypes; at one point in the "Aboriginal Experiences" program, for example, the interpreter plays his drum to a "rhythm associated with warriors" from Hollywood Westerns, then challenges tourists to reflect on the differences between this fictional music and the music of the welcoming song heard earlier (2004, 844). In another case study, by Peers (2007: xiv), Native interpreters at five living history sites in North America "gaze back" and change stereotypes by offering their own interpretations of history, even within a space that tends to dramatized the myths and identity(s) of dominant society. Her excellent study includes tourists' perspectives in order to explore whether Native interpreters did in fact change some of the preconceived notions of Native people and history; she concluded that Native interpreters' ability to change stereotypes is a measure of their agency.

In the present case, Native Spirit Production destabilizes official narratives of Westernness at Buffalo Bill Days by inserting an alternative vision of Native identity, reflecting Native agency in this heritage site encounter. Tourist perceptions were not the focus of my study, but it is difficult to believe that audiences at the Buffalo Bill Days Wild West show did not notice the disjuncture between past and present identity constructions, as Edre did. Moreover, Native Spirit Production's educational agenda (see below) was clearly evident in their performances. The group's ability to present this type of contemporary performance within the constraints of a heritage site setting that produces dominant narratives of Westernness in its commemorative celebrations reflects their agency. Because these Native performers wield power to control representations and present their own narratives of Nativeness through performance, I qualify the extent of agency they wield as *performative* agency. Essentially, Native Spirit Production is in control of its performances and the nature of its participation at Buffalo Bill Days. These Native performers, like those at Disneyland Paris, have no input into the entire Wild West show itself, but they do have the desire and, unlike in Paris, the ability to present their own representations and narratives of Nativenness in the Wild West show.

Rethinking Pan-Indianism: Intercultural Exchange and Educating the Public through Performance

The significance of employing pan-Indian identity in this heritage site encounter requires some consideration, because performances of pan-Indian identity are occasions for *self*-representation (Buddle 2004; Ellis 1990; Herle 1994; Lerch 1992; Lerch and Bullers 1996). Even though some scholars and Native people prefer the term *intertribal* to *pan-Indian*, I use the latter because this is a book about encounters between Native and non-Native peoples, not only about intertribal contact.[10] I do not subscribe to early definitions of pan-Indianism as "the process by which sociocultural entities . . . are losing their tribal distinctiveness and in its place are developing a non-tribal 'Indian' culture" (Howard 1955, 215; also Kurath 1957). This definition is obviously problematic because it assumes an old evolutionary view of culture as a static and bounded entity and emphasizes the disintegration of some authentic, traditional culture as a result of borrowing; it also presumes that local distinctiveness will inevitably be engulfed by a new "nontribal" entity that is no longer quite Native.

Moving from acculturation and cultural loss, the next generation of scholars viewed pan-Indianism as a form of cultural revitalization (e.g., Fiske 1977; Hertzberg 1971; Lurie 1971; see also Ellis 1990). Although still problematic, these studies are important because they highlight the (re)assertion of "Indian" identity as well as the hybrid or pluralistic nature of identity. For example, Lurie (1971, 419) maintains that pan-Indian identity consists of local traits, traits of white origin reinterpreted in unique ways that become part of Native culture, and traits diffused from tribe to tribe. This conception of pan-Indianism is similar to transculturation (recall the incorporation of white/settler traits discussed in chapter 4), particularly as it was originally conceived by Ortiz (e.g., Ortiz 1995), in that culture is a process of negotiation, (re)incorporation, and (co)production. Rather than view pan-Indianism as strictly a homogenizing process, pan-Indian identity here refers to an intertribal expression that exists in tandem with other local or tribal expressions of identity, involving both intertribal and international (with other nations and with the public) exchange.[11] The term is meant to evoke the multiplicity of expressions of identity as well as the multiplicity of interactions that occur.

Moreover, I suggest that presenting a pan-Indian identity is acceptable in spaces of cultural performance such as tourist sites, because it is a form of self-expression appropriate for *public* performance contact zones. As in powwows (although this is a different type of encounter), pan-Indian dances and regalia cut across tribal affiliations and local tribal expressions and encourage members to imagine themselves as part of a larger community (Herle 1994, 76–79), in this case for the purpose of public performance.[12] Moreover, as Ellis argues, pan-Indian expression does not replace tribal identities; rather, "it serves a particular function in a particular place" (1990, 26).

The Native Spirit Production website uses the word *intertribal* rather than *pan-Indian* to describe its dances, which "represent various nations from all across the United States as well as Canada." Although Native Spirit Production's performance repertoire is intertribal—encompassing dances that meld styles from various tribes, such as powwow dances, in addition to their own local dances and those from other tribes—another important aspect of their performances (alluded to on the website) is intercultural exchange with non-Natives. Because this is an integral part of this heritage site encounter, the theoretical application of the concept of pan-Indian is appropriate here. The powwow dances Native Spirit Production draws on are social dances suitable for public display, but these intertribal dances shared by various Native communities do not replace Brian or Lane's local identities or tribal affiliations. In the case of Native performances at Buffalo Bill Days, therefore, pan-Indian identity is a multiple and inclusive (rather than homogenizing or superseding) expression of Native identity, expressed through powwow dancing, music, and regalia, and it *serves a particular function:* to provide educational entertainment for the public.

Also central to negotiating power—controlling representations, meanings, and preconceptions of Nativeness—in this heritage site encounter is Native Spirit Production's approach

to performances: performances are didactic; they are professional, highlighting performers' skills and reliability; and
they emphasize cultural continuity. This performance approach facilitates agency, which is evident in their ability to
negotiate narratives and meanings of Nativeness in this heritage site encounter.

One of Native Spirit Production's goals is to educate the
public through performance of contemporary Nativeness
(see Bramadat 2001; Mason 2004).[13] Buffalo Bill Days, like
many other tourist sites and spaces of performance, is a productive space for cross-cultural exchange. Brian Hammill
formed Native Spirit Production in 1997 with this intention
in mind: "[It is] a way to share native culture and dances with
various people from all across the United States as well as
overseas."[14] In our interview, Brian clearly stated the organization's didactic priority: "We offer a good dance show
and we also educate. The main thing is education through
dancing, through talking, whatever. We want a show where
people have a better understanding of our culture." Lane
Jenkins echoes this sentiment: "A lot of people . . . think it's
a really big deal to see Native American dancing and Native American singing." Native Spirit Production provides
"educational entertainment" through dances, music, artist
demonstrations, videos, CDs, and lectures at a variety of
venues, ranging from corporate events to rodeos and fairs,
special public events and celebrations, and schools and museums.[15] The educational agenda explicitly aims to increase
cross-cultural understanding, confront stereotypes, and correct misconceptions. Participating in the Wild West show at
Buffalo Bill Days is an opportunity for these Native performers to inform the public about contemporary Native music,
explain the significance of the dances, and present contemporary Nativeness as opposed to some perceived notion of a
"traditional Indian." These performances of a contemporary
pan-Indian identity are thus examples of *performative* agency;

Native Spirit Production controls the performances, which are employed to negotiate representations and social meanings of Nativeness in this heritage site encounter.

Brian Hammill expresses the importance of providing a "professional face" and employees who are reliable. This meets the requirements of clients such as Edre Maier, who are looking for dependable, professional performers. Brian is an all-round performer (hoop dancer, musician, and storyteller) who works with a core group of people whom he can depend on as ambassadors, people, he says, who have "exceptional skill and dance quality." Putting a professional face on Native dancing and performance in general means that the performers' skills are highlighted—their skills as dancers, musicians, storytellers, and artists—underscoring Native Spirit Production's vision of how to represent Nativeness. Besides emphasizing the skills and accomplishments of contemporary Native performers, this professional face also defies such misconceptions as that Native people simply do not work. The group's didactic and professional approach to performing Nativeness is essential to its ability to control representation and wield agency.

Performing pan-Indian identity also provides opportunities to make statements of cultural survival. The point that Native performers at Buffalo Bill Days present contemporary identity rather than representations of Native history requires some qualification. I have indicated that the limited inclusion of Native participants contributes to erasure of Native history. However, the significance of the "past" is not completely disregarded by Native Spirit Production. Brian Hammill and Lane Jenkins emphasize cultural continuity in their performances, linking the past and present. Their website explicitly states that Native culture is adaptive and that their dances have historical roots and modern influences. Brian confirms that the dances we see are not only educational presentations but also representative of dances that "have survived thousands of years." Native culture not only survives, it thrives. He proudly proclaims that "the Native culture is a living culture."

Indeed, passing on knowledge and skills to others, as well as information to the public, is a way of keeping Native culture alive. Lane Jenkins hopes that his performances are an inspiration for youth: "Well, the best part is, I would say for myself, is to see the young generation keep on going and, you know, passing it on, passing it along. And I see a lot of different kids out there that we dance with sometimes; we dance with a couple of school kids and stuff like that. . . . I work with some kids, you know. They really wanted to dance, but they get really into it. I just try to help them along and do the best that I can." Performing in public is not just a way to demonstrate cultural continuity for the public to witness; it is also a way to pass down cultural knowledge. Performing also promotes a sense of personal satisfaction and pride. Lane Jenkins explains: "It makes you feel better, that you're performing for people. I don't know, it's not just performing like show-wise, it's how you feel, how you feel about yourself. And if you're doing something good, you know, keep on doing it."

The performance of a pan-Indian identity in this context is an expression of pride, contemporary Native identity, and cultural continuity; it is simultaneously tribal and intertribal, or, as have I suggested, pan-Indian. Performers use their pan-Indian identity to facilitate cross-cultural exchange and offer alternative narratives of Nativeness to those found in other reenactment Wild West shows. Most important, these performers are in control of their representations and performances of Nativeness. The accomplishments of Native Spirit Production should not be underestimated. Not only is this a group of skilled performers and artists, but the founder, Brian Hammill, is a savvy businessman who has strategically engaged in a global economy of culture via tourism (see Scarangella 2010; Wiedman 2010). Such economic and performative agency represents another vision of what Native participation in Wild West shows, tourism, and heritage sites might entail.

Pawnee Bill Ranch and Museum Wild West Show: Another Case of Exclusion, or Absence?

Many tourist sites and towns in North America promote a Wild West theme; the Pawnee Bill Ranch and Museum is another example. In this case, however, the museum and site are more directly related than SHC to the history of Wild West shows; the ranch (now museum) belonged to show entrepreneur Lillie Gordon, also known as Pawnee Bill. The Pawnee Bill Ranch and Museum (hereafter, the Ranch) in Pawnee, Oklahoma, puts on a three-weekend extravaganza of Wild West entertainment in June complete with a parade, barbecue, and Wild West show.[16] In the Pawnee Bill Wild West Show 2005/6 brochure, visitors are invited to experience the "excitement," the "history," and "the man" of yesteryear, "where the west remains wild." The two-hour reproduction of the Pawnee Bill Wild West Show is packed with excitement: trick roping, pistol shooting, gunfire, whip cracking, a cavalry drill team, a sack race, stagecoach holdups, bad guys attacking settlers, a cabin burning, and, of course, Indian dances.[17] It appears, however, that inclusion of Native participation at historic sites and museums is complicated not only by the form of representations and competing narratives of Westernness and Nativeness, as is the case of Buffalo Bill Days in Sheridan, but also by the various priorities of organizers, producers, and Native performers, including, perhaps, a conscious choice by Native Americans not to participate in this type of heritage site encounter. Native participation at this event has varied throughout the years, even declined.

The priorities and goals of various organizations influence the show's content, emphasis, and purpose (cf. Handler and Gable 1997). The Oklahoma Department of Tourism, the Oklahoma Historical Society, and the Ranch produced the first show in 1988 to celebrate the centennial of Pawnee Bill's Wild West Show. Erin Brown (personal communication, 2005), co-manager and caretaker of the Ranch, says that they are interested in presenting an accurate historical portrayal because that is the goal of the Oklahoma Historical Society, of which the Ranch is part. Co-manager and caretaker Ronny Brown (2005) concurs, stating that he wants tourists not only to be entertained but also to learn about Pawnee Bill and get an idea of what it was like to go to a Wild West show: "It's about his life, his show, Oklahoma State, and business." However, because they are just the "hosts" of the event, Ronny says, they have not had an opportunity for much input. Though the Ranch aims to commemorate Pawnee Bill and western history and to provide an educational experience, overall the advertisements emphasize the show's entertainment value.[18]

The show's script was written by a Wild West show committee along with the Pawnee Chamber of Commerce and the Ranch's friends group, the Pawnee Bill Ranch Association. The show is produced by the Chamber in collaboration with the Oklahoma Historical Society (Brown 2005). Education is not a priority for the Chamber, whose main goal is to promote tourism to Pawnee, but the latter goal is not contrary to the aims of the Ranch, which also wishes to increase tourism to the site.[19] However, the priorities of the various show directors fluctuate from year to year; some are interested in historical accuracy, others are more interested in entertainment value, as with the 2005 show (E. Brown, personal communication, 2005). These competing priorities and goals influence the choice of which histories, whose cultures, and which identities to perform.

At first Native performers had a prominent role in the Wild West show, with a contingent of about thirty actors and performers in 1988. According to Ronny Brown (2005), the large Native component may be explained by the fact that they had more funds for the centennial event because of Oklahoma Tourism's involvement. As it stands now, Ronny says, the Ranch can pay only a small honorarium for specialty acts and depends mainly on volunteers who perform for fun. Jeff Briley (2005), assistant director of the Oklahoma Museum of History and occasional Pawnee Bill actor, confirms that the number of Native participants in the show varies from year to year depending on script, director, interest, and availability of acts and performers. By 2002 only three Native dancers were part of the cast—A. J. Leading Fox, Josh Leading Fox, and Sly Isaac—and in 2003 only one of the twenty acts included Native participation.[20] Advertisements promoted an Indian component in the 2005 Wild West show events, but participation was limited to the Leading Foxes dancing and drumming in two of the three weekend shows.[21] The question is, does this limited participation necessarily signal a problematic issue?

As in Sheridan, the Ranch must deal with the complexity of including Native participation in historical reenactments. Besides the issues of funding and differing priorities, the notion of authenticity may be another factor influencing participation. Both managers and performers at historic sites and museums are concerned about representation. Jeff Briley (2005) says that some actors are really well organized and top performers, such as the fellow who came with his own complete troupe one year. These performers knew what it was about, he says—their regalia and paint, their attention to detail—they looked great and were very convincing in their roles. But one year they had local performers who were not as enthusiastic; Jeff explains that some actors, both Native and non-Native, understand what it is about, while others do not have a clue. He notes astutely that authenticity is important for museums and historic sites when the aim is historical accuracy for educational purposes, but that Native representation must be important for the Native American participants as well, because even though they are reenacting the past they are representing themselves. Taking into account all these factors, one can see that the performance of history and identity is a challenging task for historical sites and museums, consequently leading to the construction of partial histories and selective identities.

Because heritage sites and museums are contested sites of representation involving negotiation of power, I posit that some Native people may consciously have chosen not to play historical roles. For one thing, many Native dancers who would be good candidates for the show are already engaged at other performance venues. The powwow circuit, for instance, is a vibrant and popular series of events, and for many Native people it is a more preferable space for dancing and performing Nativeness than Wild West shows and other such spectacles. Still, the powwow circuit itself is also complicated by politics and critiqued by some as commercial. Furthermore, as outlined in the introductory chapter, scholars have critiqued the appropriation, representation, and commercialization of indigenous peoples in spaces of cultural display and performances, such as tourism, as sites for reproduction of colonial discourses and relationships.

For these reasons, Native people may be contesting power and knowledge construction in this space through their absence, what Phillips calls "disappearing acts"—postcolonial strategies "intended to disable the axis of knowledge and power that was activated during the colonial period through academic and popular projects of representation" (2004a, 78–79). An example is Native peoples' requests to remove sacred items like masks from display in museums or to have them returned; in part, this request represents their contestation of western traditions of production and exhibition of knowledge (Phillips 2004a, 56). The removal of Iroquois false-face masks, Phillips argues, is part of a series of "strategic removals from and insertions into spaces of display that articulate proto-colonial, colonial, and emergent postcolonial phases" in Native–non-Native relations (2004a, 73). Still, museums and heritage sites that engage in historical reenactments are ideal spaces for a critique of historical relationships and stereotypes (Tivers 2002). Whereas the negotiation of power and representations and performances at Sheridan involves *insertion* by presenting alternative narratives and meanings of Nativeness, the reduced and limited Native participation at the Ranch in Pawnee could be a case of *removal*—of "disappearing acts." Either way, both the Buffalo Bill Days at Sheridan and the Wild West show at the Ranch illustrate the negotiation and contestation of representation, power, and colonial relationships in the Wild West contact zone, specifically in a heritage site encounter.

CONCLUSIONS

Native Performers in the Wild West Show

The Wild West contact zone may be conceptualized as another type of colonial relationship; however, negotiations occur among the various social actors. Pratt (1992) calls this process of negotiation and incorporation *transculturation*. In this case, Native performers have actively engaged in encounters, adopting and modifying the Wild West show contact zone for their own reasons, and have expressed multiple notions of Native identity.

Even if agency has been variable in form and extent, Native experiences have been more complex than simply a story of government control, exploitation, and commercialization. Intersecting this story are narratives of opportunity and success. Native performers had to cope with dire conditions in both the United States and Canada as a result of colonization, assimilation policies, and the establishment of the reservation/reserve system. Some Native people in the United States recognized the benefits of working in Wild West shows and actively pursued these opportunities as a viable option to their new living conditions. Some even became professional performers, or "show Indians" (Moses 1996). In fact, Mohawk performers from Kahnawake such as the Williams-Kelly family, the Deer family, and Esther Deer guided their own careers and created their own Wild West shows. Descendants of these Mohawk performers speak about their families' experiences in terms of the variety of skills they possessed and their successes.

Moving through time, the similarities between past and present Native performers' experiences are striking. Given the limited opportunities on reservations/reserves, Native performers view Disneyland Paris as a chance to earn income and pursue their career goals as well as other performance opportunities. Proud of their successes, many speak about this opportunity as a matter of survival and hope that their experiences inspire their children and Native youth in general to be their own agents and pursue available opportunities. Significantly, narratives of opportunity, success, and pride can be traced from the archives, through the oral histories of Mohawk performers' experiences, and finally to the interviews with contemporary performers. In both past and present, these narratives reflect the fact that Native performers have their own intentions, which are at the same time situated in the sociopolitical and economic constraints that structure their lives. This does not diminish their ability to exert agency; in fact, their agency is all the more evident when situated within this context of structure and power relationships with dominant society.

A thread that runs through this story of Native experiences through time is the link between agency and the representation of Native identity through performance, dance, and dress. Regalia and performance are sites for the expression of Native identity, and thus important sites for the investigation of this agency. The representation of Nativeness in this context is part of a dialogical process of construction, negotiation, and incorporation. Thus, although Wild West shows have produced hegemonic (often stereotypical) representations of histories and identities, performers have also created meaning in this context and have expressed Native identity in other ways as well. For me this realization first crept

out of the visual record at Kanien'kehá:ka Onkwawén:na
Raotitióhkwa Language and Cultural Center. Some of the
performance regalia pictured did not conform to the stereotypical Plains style thought to be characteristic of Wild West
shows. Performance regalia, as a site of transculturation,
were diverse and also incorporated local styles and beadwork and thus were statements of Mohawk identity. Esther
Deer knew the value of highlighting her Nativeness in performances and through her Plains-inspired regalia in order to
advance her career, but she also used local beadwork designs
in her costumes. Hence the representation of Native identity through performance regalia emerges as an example of
expressive agency. Moreover, playing with their Nativeness
through performances and regalia, these Native performers
consciously and strategically were their own agents.

Native performers from tribes in the United States similarly adapted, modified, and expressed their Native identities. Wild West shows had the capacity to reflect and form
cultural identities and myths and promote social meanings
such as progress. They reduced Westernness and Nativeness
to archetypical performances that became viewed as authentic representations of history and cultures; they constructed
stereotypical images of Indians as exotic, noble savage warriors. However, Native performers also produced their own
meanings of Nativeness. They adopted the performance encounter as a space in which to maintain and express aspects
of their warrior identity by modifying war songs for this new
context; it was also a space where they could maintain and
express Native culture and identity through other dances
and dress. In fact, we see in the visual and written record a
multiplicity and variability of regalia and dance. That Native
performers used Wild West shows and modified war dances
and songs demonstrates not only the process of transculturation but also the fact that they had their own intentions that
shaped their participation, in addition to responding to this
colonial context.

Whereas performers in the nineteenth century asserted their Native identity in local or adaptive ways, Native performers at the modern Buffalo Bill Days in Sheridan, Wyoming, were in complete control of the nature of their participation and thus able to express their own vision of Native identity based on powwow culture. In doing so, they purposely and strategically contested "traditional" imagery associated with Wild West shows by presenting an alternative view of Nativeness—a contemporary pan-Indian identity. In this case, Native participants wield performative agency, because, unlike the case in most historical Wild West shows, they are in control of their performances. What is significant with this example, therefore, is that, not only do they express their own vision of Native identity, they also used this heritage site encounter to challenge official metanarratives of Westernness, contest stereotypes, and make statements of cultural continuity via their performances, even within the confines of heritage tourism. At the Pawnee Bill Ranch and Museum in the town of Pawnee, however, rather than confront stereotypes and challenge misconceptions, Native performances are limited, or excluded from (or disappear from), participation in the historical reenactments. Yet this absence of Native performers may be a subtle way of contesting representations.

Performances at tourist and heritage sites are dynamic and have the capacity to generate various meanings—the American West and a "traditional" Indian at Disneyland Paris, a western experience in Pawnee, and Westernness and contemporary Nativeness in Sheridan. These meanings are negotiated by the various participants and guided by different priorities and agendas. Though still part of an industry that appropriates and consumes Nativeness, Native performers, past and present, have reflected on, expressed, modified, and sometimes contested representations and performances of Native identity; some have had a choice in how they represent themselves through performance or regalia, even if in small (and different) ways. In this Wild West show contact zone, Native performers from the nineteenth century to the present have found ways to negotiate encounters for their own purposes. In short, they have engaged in this context as active social actors. The effects of colonialism are undeniable, yet Native peoples adapt, survive, and thrive.

Notes

ABBREVIATIONS

BBHC	McCraken Library at the Buffalo Bill Historical Center, Cody, Wyoming
BBMG	Buffalo Bill Museum and Grave, Golden, Colorado
DPL	Denver Public Library, Denver, Colorado
IAF	Indian Agency Files, Oklahoma Historical Society, Oklahoma City, Oklahoma
KORLCC	Kanien'kehá:ka Onkwawén:na Raotitióhkwa Language and Cultural Center, Kahnawake, Mohawk Territory in Quebec
OHS	Oklahoma Historical Society, Oklahoma City, Oklahoma
OIA	Office of Indian Affairs, U.S. Department of the Interior
PWD	Princess White Deer Collection, Kanien'kehá:ka Onkwawén:na Raotitióhkwa Language and Cultural Center, Kahnawake, Mohawk Territory in Quebec
WHC	Western History Collection, University of Oklahoma Libraries, Norman campus

INTRODUCTION

1. *Buffalo Bill's Wild West show 1905–2005 Official Program*, Euro Disney 2005 (abridged).

2. *Tatanga!/Yeeehaaa!* Buffalo Bill's Wild West Show color brochure, Euro Disney 2004.

3. See, for example, Berkhofer (1978), Deloria (1998), Ewers (1964), Francis (1992), and Rogers (1983). Francis (1992) coined the term "Imaginary Indian" to refer to a fictional, romantic, and essentialized conception of

Indianness constructed by white society based on travel literature, dime novels, performances, and popular images, for example.

4. The Provost show operated for three years from 1997 to 1999 (Notzke 2004, 38).

5. "Swedish Pow Wow," *Country Canada* CBC, Season 2005/6.

6. See Ruth Ellen Gruber, "Deep in the Heart of Bavaria," *International Herald Tribune Electronic Edition*, April 16, 2004.

7. Wilmeth (1982, chap. 2) discusses the chronological development of outdoor amusements. Hinsley (1991), Rydell (1984), and Rydell et al. (2000) provide exceptional analyses on world's fairs and exhibitions as nation-building projects and as promoting visions of imperialism and consumerism.

8. In 1908, Buffalo Bill's Wild West merged with Pawnee Bill's Wild West show. See chapter 1 for details.

9. Warren (2005, 39, 41, 214–16, 238) argues that vignettes such as "Attack on the Settler's Cabin" reflected the anxieties caused by threats to the home and family, such as urbanization, increasing slums, labor tensions, and increasing immigration, and suggests that progress toward urbanization was perceived as parallel to the expansion of the frontier.

10. Because I was interested in hearing personal experiences, narratives, and stories rather than gathering quantitative data, I conducted semistructured and open interviews with ten Native performers from the United States and Canada at the two main sites: Buffalo Bill's Wild West Show at Disneyland Paris and Buffalo Bill Days in Sheridan. I also interviewed the artistic director of the Euro Disney show and the organizer of Buffalo Bill Days and director of the Sheridan Heritage Center.

11. I conducted archival research at several depositories: the McCraken Library—Buffalo Bill Historical Center (BBHC) in Cody, Wyoming; the Oklahoma Historical Society in Oklahoma City (OHS); the Western History Collection (WHC) at the University of Oklahoma, Norman campus; the Denver Public Library, Western History Collection (DPL) in Colorado; the Buffalo Bill Museum and Grave (BBMG) in Golden, Colorado; the Pawnee Bill Ranch and Museum near Pawnee, Oklahoma; the Kanien'kehá:ka Onkwawén:na Raotitióhkwa Language and Cultural Center (KORLCC) in Kahnawake, Quebec; the McCord Museum Archives and Documentation Centre in Montreal, Quebec; the Archives Nationale du Quebec and the Bibliothèque Nationale du Quebec in Montreal; the Archives of Ontario in Toronto, Ontario; the York University Archives and Special Collections in Toronto, Ontario; and the Pompineau Library in Paris, France. On average I spent two to three weeks at each location (except Paris, where I spent only one week). I examined diverse visual and textual sources from

approximately 1883 to the 1930s, ranging from scrapbooks, newspaper clippings, and correspondence to show programs and couriers. Visual sources included images in newspapers and programs, posters, postcards, and photographs.

12. Some researchers investigate more broadly Native travels abroad, examining the cross-cultural encounters in a variety of performance spaces as well as performances for a white audience (e.g., Calloway et al. 2002; Feest 1999; Foreman 1943; *Ethnohistory* 50 [2003, no. 3]).

13. See Reddin (1999) and Fiorentino (1999) for specifics on European tours and audience reception, and Gallop (2001) for more on Cody's tours in Britain. Fiorentino (1999) also discusses the public perception of Native performers, and Napier (1999) provides one of the first attempts to examine Native performers' perceptions while on tour in Europe, as reported by the press.

14. See Beauvais (1985), Blanchard (1983, 1984), Nicks (1999, n.d.), and Nicks and Phillips (2007).

15. See also Said (1979) for an analysis of orientalism.

16. Lischke and McNab (2005) explore the (mis)representation of Native people in history, literature, and film.

17. See Troutman (2009) for a comparable examination of the politics of music produced by Native Americans in the late 1800s and early 1900s.

18. The examination of Native people's participation in Wild West shows intersects larger anthropological questions about the construction of Nativeness. It also illuminates social processes of interest to anthropologists, such as the negotiation of power, questions of agency, and the circulation of images in a global world. For examples of studies of power, see Bourdieu (1990), Foucault (1980), and Gramsci (1971); on questions of agency, see Ahearn (2001), Asad (2003), and Ortner (1994, 2006); for studies of the circulation of images in a global world, see Appadurai (1990) and Gupta and Ferguson (1997).

19. *Transculturation* is a term coined by Ortiz (1995) as an alternative to the notion of acculturation.

20. As was the case with the "Into the Heart of Africa" exhibit on display from November 1989 to August 1990 at the Royal Ontario Museum, Toronto.

21. See Gramsci (1971), who argues that power is never totally hegemonic.

22. See Scarangella (2005) for my initial findings and thoughts about multisited fieldwork. For theoretical discussions of problematized notions of place, culture, and nation, see Anderson (1991), Appadurai (1990, 1996,

Gupta and Ferguson (1997), and Kearney (2004). Scholars who have discussed the changing nature of fieldwork and multisited fieldwork include Amit (2000), Appadurai (1990), Hannerz (2002, 2003, 2002), Hendry (2003), and Marcus (1995).

23. Examples of multisited fieldwork that follows the people may be found in diaspora, migration, globalization, and transnationalism studies; that follow the object in studies of material culture; that follow the metaphor in studies of discourse analysis, signs, and symbols; and that follow the story or biography in studies of narrative and social memory.

CHAPTER ONE

1. See Truettner (1979). Catlin exhibited his paintings in the United States in the late 1830s; he sailed for London in 1839.

2. The first exposition, the Crystal Palace Exhibition of 1851, took place in London during the height of industrialization; the first exhibition in the United States was the Centennial International Exhibition in Philadelphia in 1876.

3. According to Benedict, world's fairs derived from smaller exhibitions and expositions and often took place near centers of production and industry, but they did not sell their goods directly. He writes: "World fairs became more than other fairs in that they promulgated a whole view of life" (1983, 3, 5). World fairs are imbued with ideas about race, nature, and progress and created a cohesive "symbolic universe" of corporate, political and scientific ideologies. They reaffirmed national identities and notions of progress, which was equated with material and economic growth (Rydell 1984, 2, 4).

4. I would include parades in this category, although not all Wild West shows had parades. Press agents came to cities in advance to publicize the show. As part of this publicity, parades through the town or city gave audiences a glimpse of what they would see and set a tone of excitement and anticipation.

5. Zouaves are infantry regiments in the French army, but the name was used by other army units, including those from the United States such as Devlin's Zouaves.

6. For more on Cody's early life and career, see Kasson (2000) and Warren (2005).

7. Dime novelist E. Z. C. Judson, also known as Ned Buntline, featured the life and adventures of William Cody in dime novels from 1869. BBHC (Series X) and DPL contain extensive collections of dime novels from the era.

8. Buffalo Bill's Wild West Program 1885, BBHC, MS6, Series VI:A, FF1/4, Microfilm roll 1, Buffalo Bill's Wild West Programs 1883–1903.

9. Buffalo Bill's Wild West Program 1886, DPL, Series 2, Copies box 2, FF22.

10. Ibid. Steel Mackay was a famous actor, playwright, and producer (Reddin 1999, 82).

11. For a description of the show, see Moses (1996, 34).

12. See, for example, "The Wild West Show," *The Era*, April 23, 1887, DPL, Series 2, Copies box 3, FF37.

13. "Buffalo Bill's Show (By one who has seen it)," Court and Society section of newspaper article, source unknown, March 23, 1887, DPL, Series 2, Copies box 3, FF38.

14. "Wild West on the Ocean" *Herald* April 28, 1889, BBHC, MS6, Series IX, 1889 Scrapbook (microfilm).

15. See, for example, *The Graphic*, BBHC, MS6, Series VI:D, Box 1, FF4; "Buffalo Bill's Show (By one who has seen it)"; "The American Exhibition and the WW Show," *Observer*, April 24, 1887, DPL, Series 2, Copies box 3, FF38; "Mr. Gladstone and the United States," *Daily Telegraph*, April 29, 1889, DPL, Series 2, Copies box 3, FF38; "'Red Shirt' on Mr. Gladstone. A Big Indian Battle. The Future of the Red Man," *Sheffield Leader*, May 3, 1889, DPL, Series 2, Copies box 3, FF41; and articles of the time from the *Evening News, Daily News,* and *Globe*.

16. For a detailed description of some of these tour dates and how the different countries received and reacted to the show and the Native performers, see Reddin (1999, chap. 4, esp. 96–117).

17. Buffalo Bill's Wild West Program 1887, DPL, Series 2, Copies box 2, FF22; see also programs from 1893 and 1897 at BBHC, MS6, Series VI:A, Microfilm 1/9 and 1/10.

18. Cody's use of the name *Rough Riders* alludes to Roosevelt's cavalry, which later fought in the Spanish American War in Cuba in 1898.

19. See, for example, the 1897 *Buffalo Bill's Wild West and Congress of Rough Riders of the World Historical Sketches and Programme,* DPL, Series 2, Copies box 2, FF29; *Buffalo Bill's Wild West and Congress of Rough Riders of the World Historical Sketches and Programme,* ca. 1901, WHC, M-360, Box 13, FF4.

20. Cody's show was not part of the Columbian Exhibition. The arena was constructed by the main entrance of the exhibition on land leased by Nate Salsbury (Moses 1996, 134). Moses argues: "To most fair visitors, the Wild West show located near the main entrance appeared as an integral part not to be missed" (1996, 137). Exhibitions and displays of Indians and other ethnic races could also be found in the anthropological exhibits and

the Midway Plaisance section (under the direction of Fredrick Ward Putman) of the fair.

21. The show toured Europe while the Bailey and Barnum circus returned from Europe to cover the North American market (Moses 1996, 169).

22. See, for example, the 1903 *Buffalo Bill's Wild West Historical Sketches and Programme* for London, BBHC, MS62, Series I-G: BBWW, Box 1, FF31; and the 1905 *Buffalo Bill's Wild West and Congress of Rough Riders of the World Historical Sketches Programme Officiel* for France, BBHC, MS6, Box 1, Series VI-A, FF2/6 (Micro roll 2).

23. *Buffalo Bill's Wild West Combined with Pawnee Bill's Far East: Official Program,* 1909, DPL, Series 2, Copies box 2, FF42.

24. The 1909 program of eighteen acts included a Pony Express display, an attack on an emigrant train, a buffalo hunt, the Deadwood stagecoach attack, and a train holdup by bandits. The battle reenactment of choice for that year was the Battle of Summit Springs, complete with an Indian village scene of cooking and dancing followed by an attack on the village in which Tall Bull is killed.

25. *Buffalo Bill's Wild West Combined with Pawnee Bill's Far East: Official Program,* 1909, DPL, Series 2, Copies box 2, FF42.

26. *BB Bids You Good Bye: A Life Story and Book of Brave Deeds. The Farewell Salute. Magazine and Official Review. 1910,* DPL, Series 2, Copies box 2, FF43; and "Buffalo Bill's Farewell Proclamation," BBHC, MS-6, Series I-B, Box 2, FF2, item 3 (1910).

27. "Buffalo Bill and Pawnee Bill Shows Stopped by Attachment," newspaper article, BBHC, MS6, Series I-B, Box 2, FF2, item 17; and "Buffalo Bill-Pawnee Bill Show Closes, the Season Came to an Abrupt and Surprising End at Denver on July 22," *Billboard*, August 2, 1913, OHS, Tompkins 88.07, Box 1, Scrapbook 5.

28. Cody's participation with Sells-Floto was limited to an appearance in the parade and a few acts of horse riding. In addition, only six of the twenty-six acts were "wild west type" acts; see 1914–15 *Sells-Floto Circus Story Book and Program,* BBHC, MS6, Series VI-A, Box 1, FF3/3 (Micro roll 2). He then worked with the Miller brothers; the show's theme urged "military preparedness."

29. For more on Gordon Lillie's early life, see Shirley (1993). See also "Interview of Effie May Judy" (Henryette, Okla.), OHS, Indian Pioneer History, Vol. 32; "Interview with Pawnee Bill," OHS, Oral History Collection, April, no. 117; newspaper article "Pawnee Bill to Be 80 Years Old This Week," *Daily Oklahoman*, no date, OHS, Tompkins 88.07, Box 1, FF Pawnee Bill; and *Souvenir of Buffalo Ranch and Its Owners,* booklet (ca. post-1911), WHC, M360, Box 13, FF16.

30. The 1890 Canadian tour started in Montreal and played in Ontario, Quebec, New Brunswick, and Nova Scotia from June 25 to August 24 in 1893. *Pawnee Bills Historic Wild West and Mexican Hippodrome Official Route Book,* season 1893, DPL, Series 6, Copies box 5, FF1.

31. Lillie exhausted all his resources to perform at the world's fair in Antwerp under the invitation of King Leopold of Belgium but recovered in Holland; however, he left France for the United States without profit (Shirley 1993, 141–44).

32. 1898 *Official Route Book of the Pawnee Bill Wild West Show,* WHC, M360, Box 13, FF1; Shirley (1993, 133).

33. *Pawnee Bill's Historical Wild West and Mexican Hippodrome Official Route Book,* season 1893, DPL, Series 6, Copies box 5, FF1. The "Mountain Meadows Massacre" act is a re-creation of the 1857 attack on a wagon train in Utah (Moses 1996, 183).

34. *Pawnee Bill's Historical Wild West Official Program,* (n.d., ca. 1904–1908), WHC, M360, Box 13, FF6. See also *Pawnee Bill's Historical Wild West and Mexican Hippodrome Official Route Book,* season ca. 1893, DPL, Series 6, Copies box 5, FF1. Lillie also included an act that featured Prince Lucca with his Cossacks and Japanese warriors in a reenactment of the Russo-Japanese War.

35. *Pawnee Bill's Historical Wild West and Mexican Hippodrome Official Route Book,* season ca. 1893, DPL, Series 6, Copies box 5, FF1.

36. 1898 *Official Route Book of the Pawnee Bill Wild West Show,* WHC, M360, Box 13, FF1.

37. 1901 *Program Pawnee Bill's Wild West: America's National Entertainment,* DPL, Series 6, Copies box 5, FF2.

38. Pawnee Bill program 1904, DPL, Series 6, Copies box 5, FF5.

39. Program section "The Owners of the 101 Ranch" in 1911 *Miller Bros. & Arlington 101 Ranch Real Wild West Magazine and Daily Review,* WHC, M-407, Box 95, FF14.

40. *Bulldogging* was the term used for steer wrestling. It was invented by Bill Pickett, who also bulldogged at the 101 Ranch Wild West show in Mexico in 1908.

41. See Gleach (2003) for more on the Wild West show at the 1907 Jamestown Exhibition.

42. Advertisement in *Victoria Daily Times* May 27, 1912, BBHC, MS-6, Series VI:G, Box 1, FF 15.

43. Ibid.

44. *Miller Bros. & Arlington 101 Ranch Real Wild West Magazine and Daily Review,* 1911 program, WHC, M-407, Box 95, FF 14.

45. Advertisement in *Victoria Daily Times,* May 27, 1912, BBHC, MS-6, Series VI:G, Box 1, FF 15.

46. These are rough-riding categories as they appeared in different advertisements and programs. Advertisement in *Victoria Daily Times*.

47. The connection between Wild West shows and the growth of the rodeo requires further investigation; however, I suspect that Wild West shows played a significant part in the development of early rodeos, which combined spectacle, entertainment, and cowboy contests.

48. *Miller Bros. & Arlington 101 Ranch Real Wild West Magazine and Daily Review*, 1911 program, WHC, M-407, Box 95, FF14. The grand entry and introduction acts also included Natives; it is not specified if Indians attacked the Pony Express rider, as was the tradition in most Wild West shows. In this version, the stagecoach was attacked by Mexican bandits.

49. See, for example, the cover of a 1925 newspaper bill that depicts a sketch of an Indian in full headdress holding a tomahawk; WHC, M-407, Box 95, FF11. The predominant image in the center of a 1912 advertisement is a sketch of an Indian on horseback holding a spear; BBHC, MS6, Series VI:G, Box 1, FF15. A 1928 large-size paper program includes pictures of Crazy Bear, White Cloud, Eagle Eye, Julia Little Snake, White Calf, Flying Hawk, Eagle Elk Chief Creeping Bear, Black Wolf, and others; WHC, M470, Outsize, Scrapbooks Box 1, Black Newspaper Clippings—large. The 1926 program contains a story about "Real Primitive Indians of the Wigwam," complete with pictures of Standing Elk, a teepee, Indian women, and the 101 Ranch Indian encampment. In this program, one section describes the Osage people and their land and another describes the "Famous Warriors of the Indian Camp"; WHC, M-407, Box 95, FF16.

50. The Millers and their agents hired more Sioux and Apaches after 1925 (Roth 1965–66, 425).

51. The United Sates considered the possibility of war in Europe (on the brink of World War I) and with Mexico after Francisco "Pancho" Villa raided Columbus, New Mexico.

52. *Miller Brothers 101 Ranch Real Wild West Official Review and History of the Great Wild West*, WHC, M407, Box 95, FF16; *Miller Bros. & Arlington 101 Ranch Real Wild West Magazine and Daily Review*, WHC, M407, Box 95, FF16.

53. *Miller Bros. 101 Ranch Wild West Show Daily Review*, 1929 magazine program, WHC, M407, Box 95, FF 14.

54. Zack Miller took charge of the show after the death of Joe Miller in 1927.

55. See also *Miller Bros. 101 Ranch Real Wild West and Great Far East*, 1925 newspaper bill, WHC, M407, Box 95, FF11.

56. *Miller Bros. & Arlington 101 Ranch Real Wild West Magazine and Daily Review*, 1926/7, WHC, M407, Box 95, FF16. "The Covered Wagon" scene reproduced the Mountain Meadow massacre with an attack by Indians,

and the stagecoach is attacked by Mexican bandits. Only two acts in 1926/7 were Indian vignettes: the buffalo hunt and dancers from Sioux and Cheyenne reservations.

57. See *Miller Bros. 101 Ranch Wild West Show Daily Review,* 1929 magazine program, WHC, M407, Box 95, FF 14. The 1929 program expanded to twenty-two acts and nine "after show" acts.

58. See Moses (1996, 223–51) for a discussion of early films and Cody's motion picture venture, and Wallis (1999) for information on the Miller brothers' film projects.

59. Cody gave a copy of the film to the Department of the Interior and War Department for future education; "Buffalo Bill to Feature in Historical Moving Pictures," BBHC, MS6, Series IX, Box 22, Scrapbooks 1914.

60. The Buffalo Bill and Pawnee Bill Film Company also produced the one-reel film *Life of Buffalo Bill* in 1912, which featured Cody's life and career as a scout and actor (Kasson 2000, 256).

61. The film includes reenactments of the battle of Summit Springs with general Eugene A. Carr on June 11, 1869, which resulting in the death of Tall Bull; the War Bonnet Creek battle on July 17, 1876, with general Wesley Merritt (Custer campaign) and Cody's duel with Yellow Hand ("first scalp" for Custer); the battles of Wounded Knee and the Mission battle of December 1890 with general James Forsyth and the 7th Cavalry; as well as the Ghost Dance War of 1890/91 (Wounded Knee massacre and death of Sitting Bull). Film Program "Last Indian Battles and Final Surrender to Lieutenant-General Nelson A. Miles with Colonel W. F. Cody—Buffalo Bill," Washington, D.C., February 27, 1914, BBHC, MS6, Series I:D, Box 3, FF1. See also newspaper article "Real Soldiers, Real Indians, Real Heroes March, Fight, Die, in Great War Films," BBHC, MS6, Series IX, Box 22 (1914).

62. Cody wrote to Secretary of War Lindley W. Garrison for permission to film at Pine Ridge; letter from Cody to Garrison, August 24, 1913, BBHC, MS6, Series I-A, Box 2, FF24. According to the film program, the last part of the film illustrated Indians at work and adopting the industries of white man.

63. Pawnee Bill's Pioneer Days lithograph and program; film produced by Pawnee Bill's Buffalo Ranch Feature Film Company. The cover of the film program resembles show program covers; WHC, M360, Box 13, FF17.

64. Brochures advertising the films produced by Pawnee Bill's Buffalo Ranch Feature Film Company; WHC, M360, Box 13, FF18.

65. I could not find any record of how audiences received these films, but Lillie declared that his films were a great success and an "innovation in Western Entertainment." Pawnee Bill's Pioneer Days lithograph and program, WHC, M360, Box 13, FF17.

66. Film reels included *Bucking Bronchos; Home Life of 101 Ranch;* and *The Indian Buffalo Hunt;* letter from Turnbull to Millers, October 1, 1912, WCH, M-407, Box 2, FF8. The Millers' also produced three reels of their Wild West show in Europe; see correspondence between P. A. Powers and Joe Miller, September 1915, WHC, M-407, Box 3, FF4. The film *On with the Show* depicted life in the arena and behind the scenes at the Millers' 101 Wild West show, including a scene of mad, runaway steers; 1925 route book *Miller Bros 101 Ranch Real Wild West and Great Far East,* WHC, M-407, Box 91, FF5.

67. Letter, JMC to Kinemacolor Co. of America, October 4, 1913, WHC, M-407, Box 3, FF3. See also Wallis (1999, chap. 32).

68. Although the 101 Ranch did not make a profit in the moving pictures industry, many of its cowboys and cowgirls, such as Tom Mix, Will Rogers, Hoot Gibson, Buck Jones, Ken Maynard, Mabel Normand, and Helen Gibson, made the leap into early Western films (Reddin 1999, 186–87; Wallis 1999, 6).

CHAPTER TWO

1. William McCune in Harriet Quimby, "Engaging Indian Actors and How the Shows Secure Them," *Leslie's Weekly,* July 23, 1908, 87–90, BBHC, MS62, Series I:G, Box 1, FF16.

2. For example, small-time operations hired Natives for local events or short-term exhibitions such as games of lacrosse (letter from J. Basye to "Sir," February 14, 1882, OHS, Indian Agency Files (IAF), Quapaw Agency—Indians, shows and exhibitions microfilm QA-17-151882); travel on lecture tours with exhibits of Indian relics (letter from Mrs. Jason Halloway to Agent J. D. Miles, March 20, 1880, OHS, IAF, Cheyenne and Arapahoe Agency—Indians with shows and exhibitions, March 20, 1880–June 13, 1931, microfilm C&A-46-4); performances in Indian boy music bands (letter June 17, 1891, OHS, IAF, Kiowa Agency—Indians with Shows & Exhibitions 7/30/1879 to 2/9/1923, Microfilm KA-47, 1875–1924); appearances with medicine shows (letter July 28, 1891 to Anadarko Indian agent, OHS, IAF, Kiowa Agency); and appearances in fairs where the public could "study the Red Man as he was" (letter, C. Thornbury to "Sir" November 1894, OHS, IAF, Kiowa Agency) or baseball game exhibitions (letter from D. M. Browning to Baldwin December 24, 1896, in regards to a letter from Henderson to recruit Kiowa Indians, and letter from Browning to Baldwin, February 12, 1897, giving permission for Indians under $5,000 bond and contract and return arrangements; OHS, IAF, Kiowa Agency), to name a few.

3. Quimby, "Engaging Indian Actors."

4. Moses bases this on Standing Bear's comment: "While all the Indians belonged to the Sioux tribe, we were supposed to represent four different tribes, each tribe to ride animals of one color" (Standing Bear 1975, 252). However, Standing Bear later states that "in all my experience in the show business I have met many Indians of various tribes" (1975, 261). Black Elk also recounts that there were Pawnees at the Hippodrome in New York (DeMallie 1984, 246).

5. A letter from the commissioner of the OIA to Myers, Indian agent at Kiowa Agency in May 1889, discusses Thompson's desire to recruit Indians. Another letter from the commissioner to Doc Carver dated May 10, 1889, outlines the conditions for hiring Natives for Doc Carver's European tour; OHS, IAF, Kiowa Agency.

6. "Major Gordon W. Lillie's (Pawnee Bill) Own Story," n.d., 9. WHC, M-360, Box 10, FF1.

7. Letter from Cody to Captain Penny (Agent Pine Ridge), February 25, 1884, DPL, FF6, Series 1, Copies box 1, 91.

8. See "How to Secure Long-Haired Indians," Pawnee Bill program, 1893; DPL, Series 6, Copies box 5, FF1. Also, in a letter from the commissioner of OIA to Myers, the commissioner gives permission to William J. Thompson to have twenty Comanches for exhibition; in subsequent letters the conditions are stated: reasonable pay for time and service; to be fed, clothed, and cared for in case of sickness; and to be returned to reservation; OHS, IAF, Kiowa Agency. See also letter from the Department of the Interior to Doc Carver May 10, 1889, OHS, IAF, Kiowa Agency. The Department granted Doc Carver permission for twenty-five Indians for a European exhibition, dependent on the same type of conditions granted Adam Forepaugh, an American entrepreneur and circus owner from the late 1800s: fair pay; compensation for time and services; fed and clothed; return arranged if sick, disabled, and at end of contract; report of name and pay of each Indian, who must agree and sign contact; bond to be arranged before they leave; and they must hire someone to accompany and look after the welfare of the Indians.

9. Lillie advised that the best and most legitimate way to recruit Indians was to go to Washington D.C. and request a review with the commissioner of the OIA; "How to Secure Long-Haired Indians." Most recruiters, local organizers, and entrepreneurs, however, went directly to Indian agents on reservations. The OIA office in Washington was to make the final decision, but at times recruiters went ahead with the Indian agent's permission.

10. For example, in a letter from Acting Commissioner [Fassabee?] to the superintendent of cantonment school in Oklahoma, April 21, 1906, the

commissioner wrote that the Department of the Interior discouraged Indians from leaving reservations for show purposes unless with a reputable company like Cody's. He further stated that recruiters for the 101 Ranch under "the Parker Amusement Company" were of very low character; OHS, IAF, Cheyenne and Arapahoe Agency.

11. Letter from Commissioner Atkins to Indian agent Jesse Lee Hall, March 28, 1887, OHS, IAF, Kiowa Agency.

12. Memo from Commissioner Thomas Jefferson Morgan to U.S. Indian agent, Kiowa agency, March 8, 1980; OHS, IAF, Kiowa Agency.

13. See, for example, letter from Commissioner Morgan to George [?], June 14, 1892, in which he denies a request for Indians, stating that it is more useful and beneficial for Indians to remain home farming to improve the comfort of his family; OHS, IAF, Kiowa Agency. See also Maddra (2006, 26).

14. "Buffalo Bill Is Home Again," *Herald*, November 19, 1890, BBHC, MS6, Cody 1905 Scrapbook France and BBMG Research Files. For more details about the case, see Moses (1996, 92–105).

15. Letter from Geo. W. H. Stouch, Superintendent to Josefy McIntyre, receiver, Cummins Wild West March 10, 1905, OHS, IAF, Cheyenne and Arapahoe Agency. Other cases included the grievance against the Sells-Floto circus in 1913 initiated by Iron Cloud, who provided a list of performers' names and the amounts they were due (letter from Cody to Col. John Brennan, August 23, 1913, BBMG Research Files), and the "Scapula" case. Cliff Pierce and Frank Charcoal of Scapula, Okalahoma, who previously worked as show agents for the Miller brothers, took Natives from the reservation for a show in Springfield, Missouri, in 1927 and left seven stranded there without pay. An alleged amount of $4,000 was owed and settled upon; see letter from Geo. W. H. Stouch, Superintendent, to Josefy McIntyre, receiver, Cummins Wild West March 10, 1905; letter from L. S. Bonnin (superintendent) to Mr. Cliff Pierce, July 20, 1927; and letter from Bonnin to Mr. Frank Charcoal, August 3, 1927; all from OHS, IAF, Cheyenne and Arapahoe Agency.

16. See, for example, letter to Col. Randlett (attorney), which stated that sixteen Indians with the Mulhall show were dissatisfied and wanted to return home but had no means to do so; OHS, IAF, Kiowa Agency.

17. See letter from Mack Haay, Coyote, Red Cloud, and Frank Hill to Indian agent, November 22, 1910, OHS, Cheyenne and Arapahoe Agency. The Natives wrote that they met with McNeill, who told them that he had met with the Indian agent beforehand and said that he would see that they were returned home. Apparently, this was not the case.

18. Letter from Sam Mayson to Indian agent, Darlington, Oklahoma, November 25, 1910, OHS, IAF, Cheyenne and Arapaho Agency.

19. See, for example, letter from Cody to Capt. G. Leroy Brown, August 30, 1892, DPL, Series 1, Copies box 1, FF6, item 93; and letter from Cody to Major John R. Brennen (Pine Ridge agent), May 27, 1904, DPL, Series 1, Copies box 1, FF7, item 95. In the latter letter, Cody notified Pine Ridge Indian agent John Brennen that he was sending home Sitting Bull Jr. and Jones Specler[?] with lung problems, but that "the rest are well and happy. I will take good care of them." John Long Bull was sent home with consumption; letter from Cody to Brennen, September 3, 1908, DPL, Series 1, Copies box 1, FF7, item 99. In the summer of 1908, Cody sent home at least seven Native people due to health issues; four were not fit for duty and two had sick family members; letter from Cody to Brennen, July 8, 1908, underline original, DPL, Series 1, Copies box 1, FF7, item 99. Lone Bear was similarly sent home in 1907 to take care of his sick wife; letter from Cody to Brennen, June 20, 1907, DPL, Series 1, Copies box 1, FF7, item 97).

20. Illness and infections also spread quickly because people were living in close quarters. A Cheyenne performer at the Jamestown Exhibition wrote that the 101 Ranch Wild West show was too big for the exposition, and that there was much sickness everywhere. Following the death of Cheyenne Nocomiata from typhoid pneumonia, the 101 management split the show and sent all the Cheyennes and part of the Sioux to Coney Island; letter from Richard Davis to Mr. Homer J. Bibb, July 2, 1907, OHS, IAF, Cheyenne and Arapaho Agency.

21. One exception is the letters of Walter Battice, performer with the Millers' 101 show from the Sac and Fox agency, who wrote frequently about his positive experiences; see OHS, IAF, Sac and Fox Agency—Indian history, shows, and exhibitions file 36-6.

22. See, for example, Starita (1995) and Standing Bear (1975), who both discuss these issues.

23. Warren (2005, 376). Warren bases his numbers on the conclusions of the Merriam Report of 1928, cited in Weeks (1988, 240). A missionary record for 1890 also reports drought, crop failure (which may have led to an inadequate diet), measles, and whopping cough (Maddra 2006, 82). In 1894, 285 Native people died on the Pine Ridge reservation of 8,000, a death rate of 3.6 percent (Starita 1995, 161).

24. For example, ceremonies were banned for the Lakota Sioux in 1883, and land allotment was implemented with the Dawes Act of 1887 and the allotment bill of 1889. The Dawes Act attempted to force allotment on the Lakotas, and the allotment bill of 1889 split the reservation into six smaller reservations (Warren 2005, 363, 375).

25. *Indian Helper*, May 25, 1888, BBMG, Research Files.

26. "Iron Tail," *Indian Helper*, August 13, 1897, BBMG Research Files. The article refers to Iron Tail as "a noble red man" yet "weak and helpless

in many ways." In the article, Iron Tail represents the "old Indian" because he has no education, cannot speak English, and has no experience that would fit him for life in the outside (white) world.

27. Ibid.

28. "The Indians and Traveling Shows," *The Arrow*, September 15, 1911.

29. *Indian Helper*, August 6, 1897, BBMG Research Files.

30. Letter from Commissioner Browning to acting Indian agent Capt. F. D. Baldwin, December 24, 1896; OHS, IAF, Kiowa Agency files.

31. See newspaper article "Buffalo Bill Is Home Again," *Herald*, November 19, ca. 1890, BBHC, MS6, Cody 1905 Scrapbook, France, and BBMG Research Files.

32. Letter from Commissioner Browning to acting Indian agent Capt. F. D. Baldwin, December 24, 1896; OHS, IAF, Kiowa Agency files.

33. Quimby, "Engaging Indian Actors." The fact that Cody employed a massive number of Natives is also evident in the visual record; cast pictures such as the ones found in the DPL digital image catalogue depict the size of the Native contingency.

34. The first Wild West show was Buffalo Bill's Wild West in 1884. Col. Tim McCoy's Real Wild West and Rough Riders of the World was one of the last, playing into 1938. The Miller brothers consistently produced shows from 1907 to 1916 and from 1925 to 1931 and also produced shows with various entrepreneurs periodically in 1933, 1945, 1946, and 1949. See Russell (1970, 121–27) for a list of shows.

35. In his 1904 European tour, Cody employed seventy Natives and wished to hire forty more; "Buffalo Bill Is Home Again," *Herald*, November 19, ca. 1890, BBHC, MS6, Cody 1905 Scrapbook, and letter from Cody to Liddiard, July 2, 1904, DPL, Series 6, Copies box 1, FF7, item 70. The Millers claimed that their 1905 show included one thousand Indians (Reddin 1999, 161), but on average they hired about one hundred Native performers every year. However, their Wild West show and Indian Village at the Jamestown Exhibition in 1907 featured "some 500 Indians, cowboys, cowgirls, Mexicans" (Gleach 2003, 425); Native performers numbered in the range of eighty to one hundred; letter from High Chief Cheyenne to Mr. Charles Shell, Superintendent, May 12, 1907, OHS, IAF, Cheyenne and Arapaho Agency. Exact numbers are unclear. In this letter he wrote that the Jamestown Exhibition had forty-six Cheyennes and forty Sioux, but in another letter he said that 110 Sioux and Cheyennes were there. In a letter to Mr. Kohlenburg received May 6, 1907, Walter Battice wrote that the Millers Brothers 101 Ranch Real Wild West Show was making a success of the show with 165 Indians.

36. Warren (2005, 359) states that more than a thousand Native people worked with Buffalo Bill's Wild West shows over the course of thirty-three years.

37. I did not find any letters to Cody requesting employment. One possible explanation is that Cody made his recruitment requests mainly through his Indian agent connections and personal connections with Native performers. On the other hand, Native people lived or worked near or on the Miller and Lillie ranches and therefore had an unusually close connection with them. The Miller brothers leased and purchased land from the Poncas, Otoes, Pawnees, and Osages (Collings 1971, 50; Reddin 1999, 158–59). Similarly, Pawnee Bill's ranch on Blue Hawk Peak was leased from Pawnees. Thus, Native people could inquire directly to them about employment opportunities.

38. Letter from Sells Brothers to D. B. Dryer, December 20, 1880, OHS, Quapaw Agency. See also letter from Commissioner D. M. Browning to acting Indian agent Baldwin from February 13, 1985, which refers to Joseph W. Hunter's ("Apache Indian") desire to take with him twelve Apaches from Kiowa and Comanche reservations for "song and dance"; OHS, IAF, Kiowa Agency.

39. See, for example, letter from Michael Brahm to Millers brothers, December 26, 1912, saying he is a first-class bronco rider (WHC, M-407, Box 1); letter from J. Miller to Miss Hazel, December 7, 1912, from Montreal about joining the show "at the lowest price" (WHC, M-407, Box 2, FF7); and letter from Bear Runs in Wood about employment with the show (WHC, M-407, Box 1, FF4). I counted twenty-one such letters from the 1909–11 files and eleven letters in 1912 alone; WHC, M-407.

40. Letter from Chas. Black Horse Sr. to Mr. Miller, November[?] 15, 1920, WHC, M-407, Box 5, FF1.

41. Letter from Creeping Bear to Joe Miller, March 11, 1926, WHC, M-407, Box 38, FF2 (letter typed by Seger Indian Agency with Creeping Bear's signature).

42. See Scarangella (2008, chap. 4) for a discussion of Native travels abroad.

43. In order listed, BBHC, MS6, P.69.972, P.6.365, P.69.784, P.69.1147, P.69.1004, and P.6.361.

44. Black Elk said that he and three other men got lost in Manchester just before Buffalo Bill's show was to leave in 1887; he found work with Mexican Joe's show to earn his way back (DeMallie 1984, 251–52).

45. Letter from Millers to John R. Brennan, Superintendent Pine Ridge Agency, July 19, 1913, WHC, M-407, Box 3, FF2. He wrote that several of

the Indians got tired of show business and went home. He also said that
they picked up some Indians in Michigan and at Rose Bud.

46. Letter from Henry Papocsul[?] and Henry P. to Col. Blackman, Indian agent, Dallas Texas, April 14, 1906, OHS, IAF, Kiowa Agency.

47. In a letter from the Sells Brothers to Indian agent D. B. Dryer on December 20, 1880, he wrote that an Indian (name illegible) had one month
pay of $20 owing him when he left the show; OHS, IAF, Quapaw Agency.
Indian schools claimed that Native performers made anywhere from $20–
30 to even $50 a month; see "Iron Tail," *Indian Helper*, August 13, 1897,
BBMG, Research Files. In the 1908 article "Engaging Indian Actors and
How the Shows Secure Them," Quimby wrote that the salary was $30 a
month. High Chief Cheyenne made $8 per week (which is about $32 per
month), his wife made $3 per week, and his children $1 and $2 per week;
letter from High Chief Cheyenne to Mr. Charles Shell, Superintendent,
May 12, 1907, OHS, IAF, Cheyenne and Arapaho Agency. Bill Weadick
paid only $15–20 per month plus board and transportation for a show; let-
ter from Cheyenne Bill Weadick to Major Stouw[?], Indian agent, December 26, 1907, OHS, IAF, Cheyenne and Arapaho Agency. Henry Paposcul[?]
wrote in a letter to Indian agent Col. Blackman that Comanche boys got
$1 per day, OHS, IAF, Kiowa Agency. Margaret Horse[?] Road wrote in a
letter, June 16, 1925, that men and women in Canada were paid $3 and $2
instead of $7 and $5.50 (respectively); OHS, IAF, Cheyenne and Arapaho
Agency. But in a letter from Ghost Dog to Mr. J. C. Miller, December 3, 1926,
Ghost Dog wrote that his salary was $70 per month; WHC, M-407, Box 38,
FF2. Later he wrote that his salary was $1.07 per day, his wife's $0.71, older
boy's $0.35, and younger boy's $0.35.

Most contracts stipulated that Native performers be paid from day of
departure to day returned to reservation. At times, the rate was less for
"travel" days than for "show" days.

48. "Small Boys Happy; Wild West Here. Buffalo Bill, Cowboys and In-
dians Gave Realistic Show," *Washington Eve Star*, April 11, 1911, BBHC,
MS6, Series IX, Box 21 (1911). The article notes that President Taft visited
the show with some cabinet members. The story repeated in *Baltimore Star*,
April 19, 1911, and included a picture of Short Boy with caption "A real
Indian brave."

49. There is some evidence that wages varied among Native performers
with Buffalo Bill's shows as well. In a letter to Brennen, Cody compared
the wages received by the Brulés and the Ogallalas: "These Brules haven't
got the get up and go that the Ogalallas have but they do fairly well and
they work for about half the wages. We paid the Ogalallas which accounts

to a big lot of money on the season. Please remember me to Iron Tail or any of my red brothers"; letter from Cody to Brennen, n.d., DPL, Series 1, Copies box 1, FF7, item 101. It is also possible that in this case the Ogallalas were more experienced in show business, which necessitated higher wages, or that they demanded more pay.

50. According to a payroll list, the top-paying cowboy with the Millers brothers was paid $160 and the top cowgirl $100 per month. The "boss cowboy" was also paid $160. The average cowboy pay was about $80, and the rest of the cowgirl troupe was paid $40. Of the seventeen cowboys and twelve cowgirls on this list, four were also husband and wife; "List of cowboys and cowgirls with skills, duties and pay," n.d., WHC, M-407, Box 91, FF3.

51. A payroll report from 1928 reveals that cowboys were paid on average $25, cowgirls $20, and Indians $10. Specialty acts, like the Mexicans and Albert Hodgini Troupe, however, were paid even more than the cowboys; "Wild West & Great Far East Show Co. Inc. Season 1928 analysis of final payroll 23 1928," WHC M-407, Box 91, FF1.

52. Letter to Miller brothers, June 30, 1925, WHC, M-407, Box 36, FF4. Some of the performers who signed the letter were Dan Sitting Bull, Morgan Little Elk, Laura Little Elk, Louse Sutton, Bearhead, Ernest Makes Life, and Noah Blackhorse.

53. *Pawnee Bill's Historical Wild West and Mexican Hippodrome Official Route Book*, Season 1893, DPL, Series 6, Copies box 5, FF1.

54. "Buffalo Bill Is Home Again," *Herald*, November 19, ca. 1890, BBHC, MS6, Cody 1905 Scrapbook.

55. Ibid. Also, in a letter from Cody to Capt. Geo. Le Roy Brown (Pine Ridge), Cody wrote about Indians sending money home and that the Indians should be sure to also write for whom the money is intended; DPL, Series 1, Copies box 1, FF6, item 93.

56. Quimby, "Engaging Indian Actors."

57. See Shirley (1993, 134–35), and *Pawnee Bill's Wild West Route Book and Program*, 1893, DPL, Series 6, Copies box 5, FF1.

58. Letter from High Chief Cheyenne to Mr. Charles Shell, Superintendent, Darlington, Oklahoma, May 12, 1907, OHS, IAF, Cheyenne and Arapaho Agency.

59. Letter from Ghost Dog to Mr. J. C. Miller, December 3, 1926, enclosed with letter from Miller to Jermark (Pine Ridge Indian Agency), December 11, 1926 and check of $115.52 for wages owed and travel expenses incurred for their return trip from New York to Pine Ridge; WHC, M-407, Box 38, FF2.

60. See also "Native Americans behind Scenes in BBWW," BBHC, P.6.93; and "Native Americans from Buffalo Bill's Wild West on Deck of Cliff House San Francisco, California," BBHC, P.69.784.

61. Another example of cast photographs portraying women and children is "Native Americans from BBWW," BBHC, P.69.965.

62. See also "Indian Dancers at Wild West Show," WHC, Miller Brothers 101, Nesbitt/Lenders Collection, item 2317.

63. DPL, NS-749 and NS-750.

64. Letter from Mr. B. Freer to Joseph Miller, March 22, 1911, OHS, IAF, Cheyenne and Arapaho Agency. The letter says that this girl would have opportunities not available to other Indian girls if she stayed in school, and also that he should not employ Julia because she had three children to look after.

65. Letter from Hauke to Mr. Freer, April 24, 1912, OHS, IAF, Cheyenne and Arapaho Agency. These minors stayed to work with Bison Moving Pictures Company even though transport had been arranged to return them to the reservation.

66. Warren (2005, 364, 375) writes that the Sioux became dependent on rations for survival; in addition, a reduction in rations in the 1890s left many in debt. Rations continued to decrease among the Sioux after 1890.

67. Here, I differ slightly with Sewell in terms of control of resources.

68. Thank-you to the reviewer for pointing out that this may have been one of many ways to maintain culture, but not necessarily a better way.

CHAPTER THREE

1. See Mackey (1999) for a comparative look at a contemporary Canadian nation-building project via spectacles and celebrations.

2. "'The Yankeries' and Buffalo Bill," *Gazette* (Thames), April 20, 1889, DPL, Series 2, Copies box 3, FF45. The 1909 Two Bills program advertised the show as an opportunity to see "authenticated, genuine people of different races"; *Buffalo Bill's Wild West combined with Pawnee Bill's Far East: Official Program*, 1909, DPL, Series 2, Copies box 2, FF42. The Millers also declared that all their Indians were "pure bloods"; *Miller Bros. & Arlington 101 Ranch Real Wild West*, 1910 program, BBHC, MS6, Series VI-C, Box 1, FF3.

3. Sitting Bull paraded in the 1885 Buffalo Bill's Wild West show, where audiences could heckle or cheer him for his part in the Battle of Little Big Horn. Charlie-Owns-the-Dog, Standing Cloud, and Long Bull were also witnesses of the Custer massacre; Miller Brothers 1910 program, BBHC, MS6, Series VI:C, Box 1, FF3. For the 1891/2 season in Europe, Cody

engaged a total of twenty-three ghost dance prisoners from Fort Sheridan who could bear testimony to the tragic events at the Battle at Wounded Knee in 1890, the last of the Indian Wars (Kasson 2000, 191). Chief Bull Bear led the reenactment of the Pat Hennesey massacre, the "1876 attack on a wagon train in the Indian Territory" (Moses 1996, 183); see also Roth (1965–66, 425), and "*Official Review and History of the Great Wild West. Miller Bros. 101 Ranch Wild West*" official program, 1926, WHC, M-407, Box 95, FF16.

Veterans of the 6th Regiment of the U.S. Cavalry, for example, were also a mainstay with Cody's show; see, for example, show programs of 1897, 1901, 1902, 1903, 1905, BBHC, MS6, Series VI-A. For other examples, see "Wild West Show Is Here," *Daily Sun* (St. John, N.B.), August 21, 1893, BBHC, Series VI-G, Box 1, FF15, and *Pawnee Bill's Wild West and Great Far East*, courier, ca. 1908/9, WHC, M360, Box 13, FF17.

4. A reporter writes how crucial the knowledge of frontiersmen like Cody was for the conquest of the West: "These are brave hunters, initiated to the customs and the language of the Indians. Only men of that caliber and possessing this knowledge could provide the American army with scouts without which the conquest of this huge territory . . . would have been impossible"; *L'Illustration*, June 8, 1889, 492, Pompineau Library (Paris, France), translated from French.

5. Whissel (2002, 228) refers to this performances strategy as "pictorial realism."

6. Cowboy skills in particular interested French audiences. See, for example, newspaper articles "La Première de Buffalo-Bill," *Le Petite Journal*, May 20, 1889, 2; "Le Gala de Buffalo Bill," *Le Figaro*, April 2, 1905, 1; and "Arrivée au Havre. De Buffalo-Bill," *Le Petite Journal*, May 13, 1889, all in Pompineau Library.

7. *L'Illustration*, June 8, 1889, 492, Pompineau Library, translated from French.

8. For example, in 1893 Buffalo Bill's Wild West show featured the Battle of Little Big Horn or Custer's Last Stand acts, and Pawnee Bill's Wild West show toured with its reproduction of the Mountain Meadows massacre; *Pawnee Bill's Historical Wild West and Mexican Hippodrome Official Route Book*, Season 1893, DPL, Series 6, Copies box 1, FF1; and Moses (1996, 147–48). Pawnee Bill's finale, "Trapper Tom's Cabin," included scenes such as an attack by Indians, a massacre of white settlers, and the burning of the cabin; *Pawnee Bill's Historical Wild West Official Program*, n.d. (ca. 1904–1908), WHC, M-360, Box 13, FF6. See also newspaper article "Pawnee Bill's Show," *Morning Chronicle* (Halifax, Nova Scotia), August 12, 1893, BBHC, MS6, Series VI-G, Box 1, FF15; and 1898[?] route book of the Pawnee Bill show, WHC, M-360, Box 13, FF4.

9. "The American Exhibition," *Morning Post*, May 5 [1887?], DPL, Series 2, Copies box 3, FF40. The Millers likewise invited the public to visit the encampment and talk with Indians through interpreters; 1910 program section "Miller Bros & Edw. Arlington vast and conglomerate array of Indians," BBHC, MS6, Series VI:C, Box 1, FF3.

10. The cowboys also camped in tents outside the arena. Native people, cowboys, and animals were "on display" for visitors before the show.

11. Couriers are magazine-style booklets that served as an elaborate form of advertising. They contained illustrations and stories as well as the program for the show. Their covers were often color lithographs and just as striking as posters and billboards.

12. Cody first developed more elaborate couriers in 1886 (Slotkin 1981, 33); other Wild West shows quickly followed suit.

13. See, for example, *Buffalo Bill's Wild West Courier Program 1885*, DPL, Series 2, Copies box 2, FF19, and the Two Bills courier program for 1909, DPL, Series 2, Copies box 2, FF40 and FF42.

14. See, for example, the more than seventy-page Buffalo Bill 1901 show program, WHC, M360, Box 13, FF4; the sixty-four-page Buffalo Bill 1887 show courier, DPL, Series 2, Copies box 2, FF22; the 1893 Buffalo Bill show program, BBHC, MS6, Series VI-A, microfilm 1/10; and the 1909 Two Bills courier program, DPL, Series 2, Copies box 2, FF40 and FF42.

15. See Goldie (1989) for a discussion of the production of this dichotomy in literature.

16. See, for example, "Redskins at St. Paul's," *Herald* (London), October 25, 1891, BBMG, Research Files.

17. See, for example, "A Touch of Nature," *London Abbertiser*, July 10[?], BBHC, MS6, Series IX, 1897 Scrapbook (microfilm).

18. "Opening of the Wild West Show," *Daily Dispatch*, April 14, 1903, BBHC, MS6, Series IX, 1903 Scrapbook (microfilm).

19. "The Wild West at Beacon Park," *Evening Transcript*, July 28, 1885, DPL, Nate Salsbury Scrapbooks, vol. 1, microfilm 18, reel 1.

20. "Mr. Gladstone and the United States," *Daily Telegraph*, April 29, 1887, DPL, Series 2, Copies box 3, FF8. "Buffalo Bill's Show (By one who has seen it)," Court and Society section of newspaper article, source unknown, March 23, 1887, DPL, Series 2, Copies box 3, F38. See also *Evening News*, April 28, 1887, and other articles from the *Daily News* and the *Globe*.

21. "The Wild West show. Buffalo Bill and his Band of Indians," no source (Montreal, Quebec), [1885?], DPL, Nate Salsbury Scrapbooks, vol. 1, microfilm 18, reel 1.

22. "Buffalo Bill á Paris," *Le Petite Journal*, May 14, 1889, 2, Pompineau Library, translated from French.

23. "Sitting Bull. A Half Hour in the Tent of the Great Sioux Chief—He Talks about the Campaign against His People," *Evening Leader*, September 13, 1885, DPL, Nate Salsbury Scrapbooks, vol. 1, microfilm 18, reel 1.

24. "The Reasons of the Sioux Revolt," *Herald*, January 3, 1891, BBHC, Series VI-E, OS1 Green/Brown Scrapbook, ca. 1890/91. Significantly, this article was written during the Sioux uprisings and revolts of the ghost dance.

25. The number of articles and programs containing these references is numerous, for example, "The Wild West," no source (Brantford, Ontario), July 16, BBHC, MS6, Series IX, 1897 Scrapbook (microfilm); "The Red Indian. A Premier Attraction at the Wild West Show," [*Daily*?] *Dispatch*, April 15, 1903, BBHC, MS6, Series IX, 1903 Scrapbook (microfilm); "Opening of the Wild West Show," *Daily Dispatch*, April 14, 1904, BBHC, MS6, Series IX, 1903 Scrapbook (microfilm).

26. "War dance" became the generic name for all the dances performed; the public could not distinguish one dance from another.

27. See, for example, Buffalo Bill's Wild West 1893 show program/booklet, BBHC, MS6, Series VI-A, microfilm 1/10; and *Buffalo Bill's Wild West combined with Pawnee Bill's Far East Magazine of Wonders and Daily Review*, 1909 program. See also newspaper articles in Canada, the United States, and London: "The 101 Ranch Wild West," *Victoria Daily Times*, May 27, 1912, BBHC, MS6, Series VI-G, Box 1, FF15; "101 Ranch Wild West show," advertisement, *Lethbridge Herald* (Brandon, Alberta), June 24, 1912, BBHC, MS6, Series VI-G, Box 1, FF15.

28. "Pawnee Bill's Show," *Morning Chronicle* (Halifax, Nova Scotia), August 12, 1893, BBHC, MS6, Series VI-G. Box 1, FF15; and 1898[?] route book of the Pawnee Bill show, WHC, M-360, Box 13, FF4.

29. "101 Ranch Wild West show," advertisement, *Lethbridge Herald* (Brandon, Alberta), June 24, 1912, BBHC, MS6, Series VI-G, Box 1, FF15.

30. See *Buffalo Bill's Wild West Courier Program*, 1885, DPL, Series 2, Copies box 2, FF19; and *Buffalo Bill's Wild West Program*, 1887, DPL, Series 2, Copies box 2, FF22, which includes additional illustrations of "Indian Religion" and an "Indians at Home" section that provides a detailed description of setting up camp. This program also includes a "Ghost Dance" section with individual Indian profiles. The *Cummins Indian Congress and Rough Riders* 1904 program includes essays on "Indian Dances" such as the ghost dance, buffalo dance, war dance, and devil dance; DPL, Series 6, Copies box 5, FF14.

31. Buffalo Bill's Wild West show program/booklet, 1893; BBHC, Series VI-A, microfilm 1/10.

32. "Dog Feast at White City," newspaper article, no source, n.d., WHC, M-407, Outsize Scrapbook Box 1, Large Black scrapbook of news clippings.

33. However, both volume 1 and volume 2 (Comaroff and Comaroff 1991, 1997) examine agency in terms of power—the dialogical colonial relationship between missionaries and the Tswanas—where the Tswanas do exert agency of this kind.

34. Some Native performers in this category with the Cody show were Sitting Bull, Crow Eagle, Iron Tail, American Horse, Rocky Bear, Red Shirt, Red Cloud, and Short Bull. The Millers 101 Ranch had their fair share of well-known warriors, such as Crazy Bear, White Cloud, Eagle Elk, and Black Wolf.

35. "A Hereditary Chief. Death of Young-Man-Afraid-of-His-Horse. His Life and Character. How He Came to Be Friendly to the White," July 23, 1893, BBHC, MS6, Series IX, Box 8, 1893 Scrapbook.

36. "Buffalo Bill's Blarney," newspaper article, n.d., BBHC, MS6, Series I:A, Box 1, FF3.

37. As Ortner found in her study of the Sherpas' engagement with mountaineering, cultural life is "shaped less by the mountaineering encounter and more by the Sherpas' own social and political relations, and by their own culturally constituted intentions, desires, and projects" (2006, 142).

38. Buffalo Bill's Wild West 1885 program, BBHC, Series VI:A, FF1/4, microroll 1. See also newspaper clippings in DPL, Nate Salsbury Scrapbooks, vol. 1, according to which Sitting Bull led the war dance and corn dance.

39. Buffalo Bill's Wild West 1887 show program, BBHC, MS62, Series I:G, Box 1, FF27; and *L'Ouest Sauvage de Buffalo Bill* handbill program, 1889, BBHC, MS6, Series VI:A, Box1/FF9 (microroll 1), translated from French.

40. *Miller Bros. & Arlington 101 Ranch Real Wild West* Program, 1910, BBHC, MS6, Series VI:C, Box 1, FF2.

41. See, for example, BBMG Canadian clippings, DPL Nate Salsbury Scrapbooks, and BBHC Series IX: Scrapbooks. See also *Official Review and History of the Great Wild West. Miller Bros. 101 Ranch Wild West,* 1926 program, which stated that dance was the most dominant feature in Indian life and a draw for audiences; WHC, M-407, Box 95, FF16.

42. *Official Review and History of the Great Wild West. Miller Bros. 101 Ranch Wild West,* 1926 program.

43. Thanks to one of the reviewers for reminding me of this fact.

44. Interestingly enough, the use of cultural tourism as a "safe place" to practice traditional activities that are "against the law" still occurs today among the Maasai people, who work (perform) and live for ten months out of the year at Mayers Ranch near Nairobi; in fact, "it is precisely those illegal activities that are most appealing to tourists and that are featured at Mayers" (Bruner and Kirshenblatt-Gimblett 1994, 448).

45. *Miller Brothers and Arlington Program*, 1910, section titled "Miller Bros & Edw. Arlington vast and conglomerate array of Indians," BBHC, MS6, Series VI-C, Box 1, FF3.

46. Dr. Oronhyatekha (also known as Peter Martin) was from Six Nations (near Brantford, Ontario) and was the first aboriginal medical doctor in Canada, as well as an author, office holder, and administrator for the Independent Order of Foresters. In 1860 he was chosen by the chiefs to deliver an address of welcome to the visiting Prince of Wales, after which he became well known for his public life. For more on Dr. Oronhyatekha, see Nicks (1996) and the *Dictionary of Canadian Biography Online,* www.biographica/EN/ShowBio.asp?BioId=41098.

47. See, for example, BBHC, P.69.900; and DPL, Salsbury Collection, Buffalo Bill's Wild West Show, album 5, NS-677.

48. See also BBHC, P.69.965 and P.6.358.

49. See BBHC, P.6.365, P.6.361, and P.69.784.

50. Other examples include "Four Native American men and one child at Wild West show" standing in front of a teepee with a show tent in the background, likely the Two Bills combined Wild West show, BBHC, PN312.3; "Gordon 'Pawnee Bill' Lillie stands with two unknown men" in front of teepees, ca. 1885, BBHC, P.69.2189; and a photograph of a Native performer standing in front of a teepee with two white women at a Buffalo Bill's Wild West show, DPL, X-31728.

51. See also BBHC, P.6.366.

52. "John Nelson with wife and four children," BBHC, P.69.109.

53. BBHC, P.69.1495.

54. BBHC, P.6.188.

55. BBHC, P.69.987. See also BBHC, P.6.93.

56. BBHC, P.6.200.

57. BBHC, MS6, P.6.201.

58. See also "Native American group" of men, women, and children near the encampment at a Buffalo Bill's Wild West show, 1889, DPL, Salsbury Collection, Buffalo Bill's Wild West show, album 1, NS.322

59. "Sitting Bull in Camp. Interview with one of Gen Custer's Murderers." *Evening Journal* (Detroit), September 5 1885, DPL, Nate Salsbury Scrapbooks, microfilm 18, reel 1, vol. 1.

60. "Sitting Bull. A Half Hour in the Tent of the Great Sioux Chief."

CHAPTER FOUR

1. Beatrice Blackwood was a staff member of the Pitt Rivers Museum of the University of Oxford in England in 1925, where the collection is now held; she took these photographs at the Blood Indian Reserve in southern

Alberta (Brown and Peers 2006, 3). Copies of the photographs were taken back to the Blood Kainai Reserve.

2. Specific dates were not a high priority for interviewees, for one, because oral histories can be as much about the present as the past (Cruikshank 1994b, 407). I therefore used other sources to clarify details and chronologies, and then discussed this information with the informants.

3. These oral histories (from the three Kahnawake families) do not necessarily represent the community's collective memory, though there appears to be a strong tradition of involvement in public performances that continues today. Beauvais (1985) has documented some of this history in his book *Kahnawake: A Mohawk look at Canada and Adventures of Big John Canadian, 1840–1919*. Kahnawake community's collective memory of their participation in public performance spaces is at this time a partial history, waiting to be told.

4. See Beauvais (1985) for a summary of the history of Kahnawake's participation in entertainment, including as lacrosse players, river guides, and wrestlers, in vaudeville, and in the tourist industry in general. Nicks (1999 and n.d.) also provide summaries. Blanchard (1984) outlines the participation of Mohawks, in particular the Deer family, in Wild West shows and exhibitions, and King (1991) briefly discusses Mohawk participation in exhibitions at Earl's Court in 1905 and the Coronation Exhibition at White City in 1911. Nicks and Phillips (2007) provide one of the first detailed explorations of Princess White Deer's career in vaudeville and commemorative events. See Nelles (1999) for a discussion of Mohawk participation in pageants at the Quebec Tercentenary and Brydon (1993) for a discussion of Hiawatha pageants. Jasen (1993–94) describes the history of the tourist industry and Native participation in Ontario more broadly. Baillargeon and Tepper (1998) examine Native participation in rodeos. Bara (1996), Lounsberry (2000), and Skidmore (2003) discuss Buffalo Bill's Wild West show in Canada.

5. See also photographs MP-1973.14 of a Mohawk group taken at Kahnawake in 1869, and M2000.21.7.11 "Caugnawaga Indian, European Team, 1876"; McCord Museum Archives and Documentation Centre. Beauvais writes that "fifteen performers went on tour in 1867, including Taiaiake Rice's lacrosse team; and in 1876, fifteen lacrosse players, led by Big John Canadien, completed a tour of the British Isles" (1985, 136).

6. Billy is an elder from Kahnawake; his Mohawk name is Kaientarankwen, which means "where the wood is gathered for the meeting, the council meeting." Billy was immersed in the entertainment industry in the 1950s as a wrestler and traveled extensively.

7. A family portrait can be found at KORLCC, Photographic Project—Entertainment, Photograph 897. The boy standing to the right may be a

stepson or son from another marriage; he is referred to as "brother James/ Jim Beauvais."

8. See Photographs 103B and 104, KORLCC, Photographic Project—Entertainment. According to the accession notes for Photograph 103B, dated "before 1931," Akwiranoron played the uncle of Hiawatha in a play in Philadelphia; the bottom of the photograph reads "Pau-pau-kee-wis."

9. If these photographs are indeed stills from a Hiawatha film, they may be from a 1909 film produced by Carl Laemmle, Independent Motion Pictures, that runs fifteen minutes. A silent film produced in Canada in 1903, directed by Joe Rosthenhal, is another possibility. Also, a third Hiawatha film was produced by the Fort Defiance Film Company in 1913, which included a Native cast of 150 from New York, Canada, and the Dakotas; it was filmed in New York State near Lake Superior. This is the only film for which I was able to confirm a Native cast.

10. Esther's grandfather, Chief (John) Running Deer, was born in 1834 and died at the age of ninety in 1924. Her grandmother, Esther Loft (Kanas-ta-ge), was a descendent of Joseph Brant. Their son and Esther's father, James Deer, was born on the St. Regis Reservation in 1866 and died in 1939 at the age of seventy-nine. His Native name Ar-ha-ken-kia-ka means "cutting of the forest." His wife, Esther's mother, was Georgette Osborne. James, John Jr. Ta-ka-lo-lus Deer (b. 1834?), and George A-na-ta-kari-as Deer (1884–1913) were cousins of Dr. Oronhyatekha. Esther's aunt Mary (Wari-sa-ta-yiu-kio) Williams (sister of James, John, and George) married George W. Williams and had a son Mitchell, Sylvia Trudeau's uncle.

11. Newspaper articles note the daring and skillful trick riding of James Deer, who injured his hand in a performance at Colonel Cummins Wild West show at the exposition in Buffalo, 1901. Esther is billed as Princess Esteeda; the family traveled with special regalia and prized possessions, which were reportedly stolen. Cummins offered a $200 reward for a stolen wampum necklace and $100 for a parchment and other articles stolen from Princess Esteeda's trunk. According to the article, the necklace was more than one hundred years old and was first given to the Navajo people by Jesuit fathers; "Reward Offered by Manager Cummins. $300 will be paid for return of stolen articles of value," no source, n.d., KORLCC, Princess White Deer (PWD) collection.

In addition, newspaper articles state that Chief Running Deer exhibited with P. T. Barnum and toured with Buffalo Bill's Wild West; "John Running Deer Dies," n.d., KORLCC, PWD collection. See also typed document by Princess White Deer, "An Explanation of the Wampum Belt," KORLCC, PWD collection. James Deer also reportedly worked with a variety of Wild West shows and circuses, such as Forepaugh Barnum and Bailey, Colonel Cummings Wild West show, Oklahoma Wild West, Texas Jack Circus, and their own Deer Family show; "The Final Curtain," *Obituaries*, April 20, 1940, KORLCC, PWD collection.

12. For a more detailed biography of Princess White Deer, see Nicks and Phillips (2007).

13. Esther played at upscale vaudeville venues such as the Palace Theatre, The Grand, Liberty Theatre, Bijou Theatre, New York City's New Amsterdam Theatre, the Hippodrome, and the Majestic Theatre in Buffalo. Vaudeville is an American form of variety entertainment that appealed to a broader middle-class audience, including women and children; it consisted of a variety of acts such as acrobats and jugglers, song and dance, music, and comedy that tended to present racial stereotypes (Kennedy 2003). For more on women in vaudeville and issues of gender and cultural reproduction, see Alison (1999).

14. Doxtator (1992) and Berkhofer (1978) also provide a discussion of Indian stereotypes and images.

15. With the exception of Phillips's (1998) examination of tourist arts, including beadwork.

16. See Greci Green (2001), who begins to address this issue in chapter 7 with a review of Lakota dress, and see her chapter 8 for an analysis on the use of trade goods.

17. For more details on the pageant contents, see Nelles (1999). For a colorful detailed account of the pageants, see "Most Impressive Will Be the Pageant: Description of the Different Scenes," *Quebec Chronicle*, July 5, 1908. See also NBC (1908), a historical souvenir book; newspaper article "Performers Were Chosen in Pageants. The Indians," *Quebec Chronicle*, July 29, 1908, Archives of Ontario, F1068 Mu2365, Scrapbook, Tercentenary of Quebec, 1908; and newspaper article "The Meaning of the Pageant," July, 1908, *Canadian Pictorial*, Archives of Ontario, F1068 MU2356.

18. In fact, Native people were the only paid actors in the pageant (Nelles 1999, 174).

19. See also M14372 and M14373, McCord Museum Archives and Documentation Centre. American Horse also appears in full regalia, including headdress, on the magazine cover of *Canadian Courier*, 1908. American Horse's Indian name was Té-wa-ni-ta-né-ke (meaning "two moons"); his English name was Angus Montour (b. 1850–d. 1928). He was from Kahnawake.

20. Consisting of feathers standing up on end rather than abundant cascading feathers, the headdress could be of eastern origin. Also, different types of feathers were used, not necessarily eagle. Some Plains groups, such as the Blackfoot people, similarly wore this type of headdress; this style is also associated with older Plains headdresses used for ceremonial purposes. But the fact remains that the public does not associate this style

with Plains Indians; it is not the typical eagle feather war bonnet with cascading feathers.

21. For critiques of pan-Indianism, see Ellis et al. (2005), Powers (1990), and Jackson and Levin (2002). Jackson and Levine (2002, 301–302) opine that pan-Indianism presupposes a "primordial boundedness" of Nativeness and assumes that participation in intertribal social gatherings results in a loss of cultural distinctiveness. The notion that pan-Indian expressions lead to a generic Indian identity is thus problematic, given the persistence of tribal variation (Ellis et al. 2005, x, xii; Powers 1990, 108). In chapter 6, I delve further into the notion of pan-Indian expressions.

22. The exchange of design elements occurred intertribally outside of the performance context as well (Hail 1993).

23. "Redskins at Earl's Court," BBHC, MS6, VI:D, Box 1, FF4; and the *Naval, Shipping and Fisheries Exhibition, 1905, Earl's Court: Daily Programme* (London: Gale and Polden, 1905), Smithsonian Institution, National Museum of American History, microform 003107.163.5. The Abemihi tribe listed in the article is probably the Abenakis, as listed in other parts of the program.

24. *Illustrated London News*, May 6, 1905, 635, York University Library and Archives. See also *Naval, Shipping and Fisheries Exhibition, 1905, Earl's Court: Official Guide and Catalogue* (London: Gale and Polden, 1905), Smithsonian Institution, National Museum of American History, microform 003107.163.5.

25. Scarangella (2008) shows that the scope and content of Native participation at Earl's Court were more diverse.

26. *Naval, Shipping and Fisheries Exhibition, 1905, Earl's Court: Official Guide and Catalogue*, 142.

27. "Redskins at Earl's Court," BBHC, MS6, VI:D, Box 1, FF4.

28. KORLCC, Photographic Project—Entertainment, Photograph 056a; see also Photographs 108 and 896.

29. Iroquoian style headdresses consisted of a cap with some feathers; see Gabor (2001, 2) for illustration and other styles of eastern headdresses. See also note 20.

30. Barbara also has Jawitson's gold lamé bikini and dress that she wore in performances when she went to England, as well as Scar Face's pouch, hat, and a necklace.

31. For a fascinating and comprehensive discussion of the life and career of Molly Spotted Elk, see McBride (1995).

32. A male counterpart to this style consisting of cowboy styles and beaded vests exists in the record, influenced in part from their involvement with ranching and rodeo.

33. Barbara jokingly added that the bear probably scared him and he fell and scratched his face.

34. For the Texas Jack discussion provided here, see "Texas Jack's Circus," "Texas Jack Show," and "Texas Jack's Great Combined Shows," newspaper clippings, no source, n.d., KORLCC, PWD collection.

35. Information about their tour dates and places are not fully known. On the basis of newspaper articles and performance programs, bills, and advertisements found in the PWD collection, it appears that some of the tours included the United Kingdom in 1905, Germany in 1906, Germany and England in 1907, and a broader tour of the United Kingdom in 1908 followed by a return trip to Germany in 1909 and 1910. Esther also traveled to Russia, the Ukraine, and Poland in 1911 and Paris in 1928.

36. "Alhambra—Theatre of Varieties," advertisement (Edinburgh, Scotland), April 20, 1908, and newspaper clipping, source unknown, 1910; KORLCC, PWD collection.

37. Newspaper clipping, source unknown, 1910, KORLCC, PWD collection.

38. The cakewalk is an African America dance that emerged during slavery. The dance is meant to be a satirical parody of formal European ballroom dances.

39. It is difficult to know for certain whether the tone of the Deer Family show was different than that of the Texas Jack show or whether the newspaper accounts of the show represented the public's perception and expectations instead.

40. It is not known who took these photographs, but we do know that most of them were collected by Esther herself and then donated (photocopies were made) by her great-niece Sylvia Trudeau, who received Esther's collection upon her passing. Although the KORLCC PWD collection is perhaps partial, it is a representative corpus that contains a large mass of materials, which record her career and significant experiences in her life. Some photographs in the collection have been donated by other community members from Kahnawake.

41. Photocopies of newspaper clippings and photographs along with some of Esther's regalia have been donated to KORLCC and form the PWD collection. This research depends on a review of the collection at KORLCC, an examination of the original photographs and clippings together with Sylvia in her home in Lachine, Quebec, and my interview with Trudeau (2004); see also Sylvia's interview in "Princes White Deer Today," *The Papoose*, May 1981, KORLCC, PWD collection.

42. "B.F. Keith's Bill and Grand Scores Heavily," no source, n.d. (ca. 1920), KORLCC, PWD collection.

43. "A New 9 o'Clock Revue," n.d., KORLCC, PWD collection.

44. "'Tip Top' Has Just About Everything Anybody Needs," *New York Tribune*, October 6, 1920, KORLCC, PWD collection.

45. Letter from Robert Redmond for James Drain to Esther Deer, March 26, 1925, KORLCC, PWD collection.

46. "Princes White Deer Says Fred Stone Would Have Made Mighty War Chief," *New York Tribune*, ca. 1920, KORLCC, PWD collection. Sylvia also said in our interview that they were always referring to her as daughter of the last hereditary chief, and so forth.

47. "Princes White Deer Says Fred Stone Would Have Made Mighty War Chief"; "To Enact Historic Role" *Daily Item* (Port Chester), August 8, 1933; and "Chief Deer Will Take Part in White Plains Celebration," n.d., all clippings from KORLCC, PWD collection.

Joseph Brant (b. 1743–d. 1807) was a Mohawk leader known for his role in 1776 in the American Revolution but better known for establishing the Western Confederacy and traveling to London to request compensation for their loses as a result of the war and protection from the Americans in the 1780s.

48. KORLCC, PWD collection, Regalia box 32, contains a wide array of performance regalia accessories including headbands, beaded cap, leather armbands, knee jingles, bags, and beaded yoke.

49. "'Tip Top' Has Just About Everything Anybody Needs." The buck and wing dance is a style of tap dancing that combines steps of the Irish jig and British clogging; it was popularized first by African Americans.

50. "Princess White Deer (2) Dancing. 17 mins.: One and Full State Special. Hippodrome," *New York Variety*, January 21, 1925, KORLCC, PWD collection.

51. *National Tribute to General John J. Pershing by The American Legion, April 25th 1925 11:30 pm*, program, KORLCC, PWD collection. According to the program, this revue was conceived by Mark Leuscher.

CHAPTER FIVE

1. This interview was recorded by handwritten notes; Kave received a copy of the interview for verification and feedback.

2. Lainsbury (2000) discusses how Disneyland Paris became a reality despite economic instability and the controversy surrounding its construction.

3. Bryam defines themeing as the "clothing of institutions or objects in a narrative that is largely unrelated . . . such as a casino or restaurant with a Wild West narrative" (2004, 2).

4. The show's director, Robert Carsen, worked with many people to create the show: Jean Luc Choplin (producer), Ian Burton (script), George Fendel (music), Mario Luraschi (animal coordinator), Andrew Bridge (special effects), and Christel Grevy (lighting), to name a few; *Press Information*,

Euro Disney press kit, Buffalo Bill's Wild West Show, 2004, Press Relations, Karine Moral, and personal communication with Grevy. As explained by Grevy, Carsen continues to direct the show, Grevy is now the artistic director, and Nick Rodgers is currently the head of the show and supervises all technical aspects of the show, from horse coordination to reservations, kitchen, service, and marketing; Christel Grevy, 2004, personal communication. Buffalo Bill's Wild West show was one of the original attractions of Disney Village when Euro Disney opened the park to the public in 1992.

5. *Press Information*, Euro Disney press kit, Buffalo Bill's Wild West Show, 2004, Press Relations, Karine Moral.

6. Euro Disney conducted historical research with the assistance of the Buffalo Bill Historical Center and later with the Buffalo Bill Museum and Grave.

7. My description of the 1905 show in this chapter is based on the historical program, BBHC, MS6, Series VI-A, micro roll 2.

8. Sitting Bull performed with the Cody show only in 1885. According to the 1905 program (France), Indians that year included Brulés, Cheyennes, Ogallalas, and Arapahoes. Johnny Baker was also with the show in 1905.

9. The "Attack on a Pony Express Rider" from the historical show has been transformed into a Pony Express race. This selective censorship suggests that the Euro Disney creative team recognized the force of such performances to perpetuate stereotypes. Christel Grevy (personal communication, 2004, 2005) said that these acts were removed for "obvious reasons" but did not elaborate. It is safe to say that presenting these vignettes would be controversial for the stereotypes and selective view of history they imply and might also bring bad publicity.

10. Euro Disney refers to its reenactment as a stagecoach race; however, the vignette is simply referred to as "The Deadwood Stagecoach" in the new historical reproduction program for 2005. *Buffalo Bill's Wild West*, 2005 program, Euro Disney. In the historical Buffalo Bill's Wild West shows, audience members were also sometimes selected to ride in the stagecoach. At the American Exhibition in London in 1887, Buffalo Bill, the Prince of Wales, and the kings of Denmark, Greece, Belgium, and Saxony rode around the arena together in the Deadwood stagecoach, which was then attacked by Indians. In "Roman riding," the rider stands on the saddle of the galloping horse, usually two horses side by side, rather than sit.

11. It is authentic according to the creative director of the show (Christel Grevy, personal communication, 2004, 2005). Claims of authenticity are also made in the press kit, *Press Information*, 5, in a section called "Authenticity, the Recipe for Success."

12. Carter Yellowbird is also a talent scout for movies and has a base of performer contacts who have rodeo and dancing skills, for example.

13. One reason the show sometimes depended more on French actors to play Native roles was a shortage of Native performers.

14. Kave was referring to his collaboration with Blu Claire Productions for another film, one that went bad.

CHAPTER SIX

1. Once I received approval from Euro Disney, my selection of additional contemporary Wild West shows and reenactments was based on the opportunity for comparison and access to historical materials. Oklahoma, Wyoming, and Colorado, being the "home" of Wild West entrepreneurs such as the Miller brothers, Major Gordon Lillie, and Colonel William F. Cody, held large collections of archival materials, and, being places of historical significance, these states also had contemporary reenactments and museums related to Wild West shows. I observed the Buffalo Bill funeral reenactment at the Buffalo Bill Museum and Grave, but the resulting information is not reflected in this book. I could not stay to see Pawnee Bill's Wild West show in Pawnee in person because it conflicted with my trip to Sheridan, which had already been arranged; however, I viewed a tape of the show, received copies of two scripts, and conducted interviews. Budget, distance, and time constraints limited the number of sites I could visit.

2. My discussion of the establishment of Buffalo Bill Days is based on my fieldnotes and discussions with Edre Maier (Maier 2005, and Maier, personal communication, 2005).

3. Although "Buffalo Bill" is present, the birthday celebration at this event is for the opening of the Sheridan Inn.

4. In 2005, the Fort Kearney's Frontier Regulars and Volunteers were in the parade and ended the Wild West show with a bang, literally, with their canon demonstration.

5. "Celebrate 112 Years," *A Special Advertising Section of the Billings Gazette,* June 19, 2005, 2.

6. The announcer carefully explains the historical context of the Pony Express and stagecoach attacks. The announcer is also crucial in linking Wild West reenactments the audience witnesses with historical Wild West shows.

7. She further writes that Native peoples' responses to these events vary from participation to ambivalence.

8. Native Spirit Production is based in Phoenix, Arizona. For a description of its services and products, see www.nativespiritproduction.com. Since I conducted this research in 2004/5, the website has been reorganized and some text revised. Quotations in the rest of this section that are not otherwise documented are from the earlier version of that website.

9. See Arndt (2005) for a discussion of the public performance history of the Ho-Chunck powwow.

10. Ellis and Lassiter write that the term *intertribal* is "widely preferred by powwow participants . . . and more accurately describes the common negotiated ground of powwow culture"; however, the authors also recognize that dropping the term *pan-Indian* for *intertribal* does not necessarily result in a more intuitive understanding that powwows are simultaneously "community-specific and a cross-cultural institution" (Ellis et al. 2005: xiii). I do not claim to solve this dilemma either with my reconceptualization of pan-Indian.

11. The term *pan-Indianism* refers to processes of social, cultural, economic, and political intertribal and international exchange. Powers (1990, 97, 107) argues that original models of pan-Indianism dealt almost exclusively with music, dance, and material culture and suggests that political, economic, and social spheres should be addressed differently. Perhaps different "types" of pan-Indianism may be distinguished as analytical categories and reviewed in unique ways (following Hetzberg 1971), but it would be erroneous to conclude that these spheres are not connected.

12. For more on the diverse forms and contexts of powwows, see Ellis et al. (2005).

13. Bramadat (2001) examines cultural spectacles in Canada as spaces for "dialogical self-definition," where participants attempt to construct representations of themselves; these representations often involve education about their ethnic identity.

14. My description of Native Spirit Production and its guiding principles is founded on information from the website and interviews with Hammill (2005) and Lane Jenkins (2005).

15. Native Spirit Production provides a variety of dances as part of its presentation, such as the hoop dance, eagle dance, traditional dance, grass dance, fancy dance, jingle dress dance, and fancy shawl dance. At the Wild West show in Sheridan, Lane performed a fancy dance and Brian the hoop dance. See their website for more on their presentations and products.

16. The Ranch presents its Wild West show events on three consecutive Saturdays in June.

17. *Pawnee Oklahoma Visitor Guide 2005* and *Pawnee Bill Wild West Show 2005–06*, brochure. In the past, Pawnee Bill's Wild West show reenactment consisted of an assortment of characters and thrilling acts, such as trick shooting, trick roping and riding, drill team, fancy drill (like square dancing on horses), whip acts, chariot races, a reenactment of a longhorn cattle drive, a stagecoach robbery, Native American dancing, Cossacks (Ivan the Terrible does trick riding), lance target throwing, sword tricks, Annie Oakley, the Pony Express, and, of course, Pawnee Bill and Mae Lillie;

sometimes there was even a hanging of the horse thief (Erin Brown, personal communication, 2005).

18. However, the brochure does state that a visit to the Ranch and show is a chance to "celebrate the American spirit."

19. Nevertheless, Ronny and Erin affirm that the script is based on historical programs of Pawnee Bill's Wild West show.

20. *The Original Pawnee Bill's Wild West Show 2002 Souvenir Program* and *Pawnee Bill Wild West Show 2003 (Final Show) Script;* Pawnee Bill Ranch and Museum. In 2003, Native dancers performed for seven minutes of a two-hour show while Miss Ponca, curator of the White Hair Memorial in Osage County, explained each costume and dance.

21. I did not have an opportunity to interview the Native performers.

References

PUBLICATIONS

Abu-Lughod, Lila. 1990. "The Romance of Resistance: Tracing Transformations of Power through Bedouin Women." *American Ethnologist* 17, no. 1:41–55.

Ahearn, Laura M. 2001. "Language and Agency." *Annual Review of Anthropology* 30:109–37.

Alison, Kibler M. 1999. *Rank Ladies: Gender and Cultural Hierarchy in American Vaudeville*. Chapel Hill: University of North Carolina Press.

Amit, Vered, ed. 2000. *Constructing the Field: Ethnographic Fieldwork in the Contemporary World*. London and New York: Routledge.

Anderson, Benedict. 1991. *Imagined Communities: Reflections on the Origin and Spread of Nationalism*. New York: Verso.

Appadurai, Arjun. 1990. "Disjuncture and Difference in the Global Cultural Economy." *Theory, Culture, and Society* 7, nos. 2–3:295–310.

———. 1996. *Modernity at Large: Cultural Dimensions of Globalization*. Minneapolis: University of Minnesota Press.

Arid, Michael. 2003. "Growing Up with Aborigines." In *Photography's Other Histories*, ed. Christopher Pinney and Nicholas Peterson, 23–39. Durham, N.C: Duke University Press.

Arndt, G. 2005. "Ho-Chuck 'Indian Powwows' of the Early Twentieth Century." In *Powwow,* eds. C. Ellis, E. L. Lassiter, and G. H. Dunham, 46–67. Lincoln: University of Nebraska Press.

Asad, Talal. 2003. "Thinking about Agency and Pain." In *Formations of the Secular: Christianity, Islam, Modernity*, ed. Talal Asad, 67–99. Stanford, Calif.: Stanford University Press.

Atkins, Patty. 1994. *Reflections of the Inn: Historic Sheridan Inn, House of 69 Gables*. Sheridan, Wyoming: Hawks Press.

Baillargeon, Morgan, and Leslie Tepper, eds. 1998. *Legends of Our Times: Native Cowboy Life.* Vancouver, B.C.: UBC Press in association with Canadian Museum of Civilization.

Bank, Rosemarie K. 2002. "Representing History: Performing the Columbian Exposition." *Theatre Journal* 54, no. 4:589–606.

Bara, Jana L. 1996. "Cody's Wild West Show in Canada." *History of Photography,* Summer 1996:153–55.

Bataille, Gretchen M., ed. 2001. *Native American Representations: First Encounters, Distorted Images, and Literary Appropriations.* Lincoln: University of Nebraska Press.

Beauvais, Johnny. 1985. *Kahnawake: A Mohawk Look at Canada and Adventures of Big John Canadian, 1840–1919.* Kahnawake, Mohawk Territory: Khanata Industries Registered.

Becker, Howard S. 1998. "Categories and Comparisons: How We Find Meaning in Photographs." *Visual Anthropology Review* 14, no. 2:3–10.

Bell, Elizabeth, Lynda Haas, and Laura Sells, eds. 1995. *From Mouse to Mermaid: The Politics of Film Gender, and Culture.* Bloomington: Indiana University Press.

Benedict, Burton. 1983. "The Anthropology of World's Fairs." In *The Anthropology of World's Fairs: San Francisco's Panama Pacific International Exposition of 1915,* ed. Burton Benedict, 1–65. Berkeley, Calif.: Lowie Museum of Anthropology with Scholar Press.

Berkhofer, Robert F. 1978. *The White Man's Indian: Images of the American Indian from Columbus to the Present.* New York: Vintage Books.

Bhabha, Homi K. 1994. *The Location of Culture.* New York: Routledge.

Bird, Elizabeth S., ed. 1996. *Dressing in Feathers: The Construction of the Indian in American Popular Culture.* Boulder, Colo.: Westview Press.

Blackman, Margaret. 1986. "Visual Ethnohistory: Photographs in the Study of Culture History. In *Ethnohistory: A Researcher's Guide,* ed. Dennis Wiedman, 137–66. Williamsburg, Va.: College of William and Mary, Department of Anthropology.

Blackstone, Sarah J. 1986. *Buckskins, Bullets, and Business: A History of Buffalo Bill's Wild West.* New York: Greenwood Press.

Blanchard, David S. 1983. "Entertainment, Dance, and Northern Mohawk Showmanship." *American Indian Quarterly* 7:2–26.

———. 1984. "For Your Entertainment Pleasure—Princess White Deer and Chief Running Deer—Last 'Hereditary' Chief of the Mohawk: Northern Mohawk Rodeos and Showmanship." *Journal of Canadian Studies* 1, no. 2:99–116.

Blundell, Valda. 1993. "'Echoes of a Proud Nation': Reading Kahnawake's Powwow as a Post-Oka Text." *Canadian Journal of Communication* 18, no. 3.

Bourdieu, Pierre. 1977. *Outline of a Theory of Practice*. Translated by Richard Nice. Cambridge: Cambridge University Press.

——. 1990. *The Logic of Practice*. Translated by Richard Nice. Stanford, Calif.: Stanford University Press.

Bramadat, Paul A. 2001. "Shows, Selves, and Solidarity: Ethnic Identity and Cultural Spectacles in Canada." *Canadian Ethnic Studies* 33, no. 3:78–98.

Brettell, Caroline B. 1998. "Fieldwork in the Archives: Methods and Sources in Historical Anthropology." In *Handbook of Methods in Cultural Anthropology*, ed. H. Russell Bernard, 513–46. London: Altamira Press.

Brooklyn Museum, ed. 1981. *Buffalo Bill and the Wild West*. New York: Brooklyn Museum.

Brown, Alison K, and Laura Peers. 2006. *Pictures Bring Us Messages / Sinaakssiiksi Aohtsimaahpihkookiyaawa Photographs and Histories from the Kainai Nation*. Toronto: University of Toronto Press.

Bruner, Edward M. 2001. "The Maasia and the Lion King: Authenticity, Nationalism, and Globalization in African Tourism." *American Ethnologist* 28, no. 4: 881–908.

——. 2005. *Culture on Tour: Ethnographies of Travel*. Chicago: University of Chicago Press.

Bruner, Edward M., and Barbara Kirshenblatt-Gimblett. 1994. "Maasai on the Lawn: Tourist Realism in East Africa." *Cultural Anthropology* 9, no. 4:435–70.

Bryam, Alan. 2004. *The Disneyization of Society*. Thousand Oaks, Calif.: Sage.

Brydon, Sherry. 1993. "Hiawatha Meets the Gitche Gumee Indians." M.A. thesis, Carleton University.

Budd, Mike, and Max H. Kirsch, eds. 2005. *Rethinking Disney: Private Control, Public Dimensions*. Middletown, Conn.: Wesleyan University Press.

Buddle, Kathleen. 2004. "Media, Markets, and Powwows." *Cultural Dynamics* 16, no. 1:29–69.

Calloway, Colin G., Gerd Gemunden, and Susanne Zantop, eds. 2002. *Germans and Indians: Fantasies, Encounters, Projections*. Lincoln: University of Nebraska Press.

Castaneda, Terri. 1993. "Beyond the Trocadero: Mickey's Wild West Show and More." *Public Culture* 5:607–13.

Chambers, E. 2000. *Native Tours: The Anthropology of Travel and Tourism*. Prospect Heights, Ill.: Waveland Press.

Clifford, James. 1997. *Routes: Travel & Translation in the Late Twentieth Century*. Cambridge, Mass.: Harvard University Press.

Collings, Ellsworth. 1971 [1937]. *The 101 Ranch*. Norman: University of Oklahoma Press.

Comaroff, Jean, and John L. Comaroff. 1991. *Of Revelation and Revolution*, Vol. 1: *Christianity, Colonialism, and Consciousness in South Africa*. Chicago: University of Chicago Press.

———. 1997. *Of Revelation and Revolution*, Vol. 2: *The Dialectics of Modernity on a South African Frontier*. Chicago: University of Chicago Press.

Conquergood, Dwight. 1991. "Rethinking Ethnography: Towards a Critical Cultural Politics." *Communication Monographs* 59:179–94.

Crosby, Marcia. 1991. "Construction of the imaginary Indian." In *Vancouver Anthology: The Institutional Politics of Art*, ed. Stan Douglas. Vancouver, B.C.: Talonbooks.

Cruikshank, Julie. 1992. "Images of Society in Klondike Gold Rush Narratives: Skookum Jim and the Discovery of Gold. *Ethnohistory* 39, no. 1:20–41.

———. 1994a. "Claiming Legitimacy: Prophecy Narratives from Northern Aboriginal Women." *American Indian Quarterly* 18, no. 2:147–67.

———. 1994b. "Oral Tradition and Oral History: Reviewing Some Issues." *Canadian Historical Review* 75, no. 3:403–18.

Deahl, William, Jr. 1975. "Buffalo Bill's Wild West Show, 1885." *Annals of Wyoming* 47, no. 2:139–51.

Deloria, Philip Joseph. 1998. *Playing Indian*. New Haven, Conn.: Yale University Press.

Deloria, Vine, Jr. 1981. "The Indians." In *Buffalo Bill and the Wild West*, ed. Brooklyn Museum, 45–56. New York: Brooklyn Museum.

DeMallie, Raymond J., ed. 1984. *The Sixth Grandfather: Black Elk's Teachings Given to John G. Neihardt*. Lincoln: University of Nebraska Press.

Dippie, Brian W. 1992. "Representing the Other: The North American Indian." In *Anthropology and Photography, 1860–1920*, ed. Elizabeth Edwards, 132–36. New Haven, Conn.: Yale University Press.

Doxtator, Deborah. 1992. *Fluff & Feathers: An Exhibit on the Symbols of Indianness*. Brantford, Ont.: Woodland Cultural Center.

Dussart, Francoise. 2005. "Media Matters: Visual Representations of Aboriginal Australia." *Visual Anthropology Review* 21, nos. 1/2:5–10.

Edwards, Elizabeth. 1992. "Introduction." In *Anthropology and Photography, 1860–1920*, ed. Elizabeth Edwards, 3–17. New Haven, Conn.: Yale University Press.

———. 2005. "Photographs and the Sound of History." *Visual Anthropology Review* 21, nos. 1/2:27–46.

Ellis, Clyde. 1990. "'Truly Dancing Their Own Way': Modern Revival and Diffusion of the Gourd Dance." *American Indian Quarterly* 14, no. 1:19–33.

———. 1999. "'We Don't Want Your Rations, We Want This Dance': The Changing Use of Song and Dance on the Southern Plains." *Western Historical Quarterly* 30, Summer: 133–54.

Ellis, Clyde, Eric Luke Lassiter, and Gary H. Dunham, eds. 2005. *Powwow.* Lincoln: University of Nebraska Press.

Ewers, John C. 1964. "The Emergence of the Plains Indian as the Symbol of the North American Indian." In *Annual Report of the Smithsonian Institution*: 531–45.

———. 1997. *Plains Indian History and Culture: Essays on Continuity and Change.* Norman: University of Oklahoma Press.

Feest, Christian F., ed. 1999. *Indians and Europe: An Interdisciplinary Collection of Essays.* Lincoln: University of Nebraska Press.

Fernandez, Ramona. 1995. "Pachuco Mickey." In *From Mouse to Mermaid: The Politics of Film, Gender, and Culture*, ed. Elizabeth Bell, Lynda Haas, and Laura Sells, 236–54. Bloomington: Indiana University Press.

Fiorentino, Daniele. 1999. "'Those Red-Brick Faces': European Press Reactions to the Indians in Buffalo Bill's Wild West Show." In *Indians and Europe: An Interdisciplinary Collection of Essays*, ed. Christian F. Feest, 403–13. Lincoln: University of Nebraska Press.

Fiske, Shirley. 1977. "Intertribal Perceptions: Navajo and Pan-Indianism." *Ethos* 5, no. 3:358–75.

Foreman, C. T. 1943. *"Indians Abroad, 1493–1938."* Norman: University of Oklahoma Press.

Foucault, Michel. 1980. *Power/Knowledge: Selected Interviews and Other Writings, 1972–1977.* Translated and edited by Colin Gordon. New York: Pantheon Books.

Francis, Daniel. 1992. *The Imaginary Indian.* Vancouver, B.C.: Arsenal Pulp Press.

Furniss, Elizabeth Mary. 1999. *The Burden of History: Colonialism and the Frontier Myth in a Rural Canadian Community.* Vancouver, B.C.: UBC Press.

Gabor, R. 2001. *Costume of the Iroquois.* Ohsweken, Ont.: Iroqrafts [orig. ed., Akwesasne Mohawk].

Gallop, Allan. 2001. *Buffalo Bill's British Wild West.* Phoenix Mill, Thrupp, Stroud, Gloucestershire: Sutton.

Germunden, Gerd. 2002. "Between Karl May and Karl Marck: The DEFA Indianerfilme." In *Germans and Indians: Fantasies, Encounters, Projections*, ed. C. G. Calloway, G. Germunden, and S. Zantop, 243–58. Lincoln: University of Nebraska Press.

Ginsburg, Faye D. 2002. "Mediating Culture: Indigenous Media, Ethnographic Film, and the Production of Identity. In *Anthropology of Media: A Reader*, ed. Kelly Askew and Richard R. Wilk, 210–35. Oxford: Blackwell.

Giroux, Henry A. 1999. *The Mouse That Roared: Disney and the End of Innocence.* Lanham, Md.: Rowman and Littlefield.

Glassberg, David. 1990. *American Historical Pageantry: The Uses of Tradition in the Early Twentieth Century.* Chapel Hill: University of North Carolina Press.

Gleach, Frederic W. 2003. "Pocahontas at the Fair: Crafting Identities at the 1907 Jamestown Exposition. *Ethnohistory* 50, no. 3:419–45.

Goldie, Terry. 1989. *Fear and Temptation: The Image of the Indigene in Canadian, Australian, and New Zealand Literatures.* Kingston, Quebec: McGill-Queen's University Press.

Gramsci, Antonio. 1971. *Selections from the Prison Notebooks.* Edited and translated by Quintin Hoare and Geoffrey Nowell Smith. New York: International.

Greci Green, Adriana. 2001. "Performances and Celebrations: Displaying Lakota Identity, 1880–1915." Ph.D. dissertation, Rutgers University.

Gupta, Akhil, and James Ferguson. 1997. "Beyond 'Culture': Space, Identity, and the Politics of Difference." In *Culture, Power, Place: Explorations in Critical Anthropology,* ed. Akhil Gupta and James Ferguson, 33–51. Durham, N.C.: Duke University Press.

Gusterson, Hugh. 1997. "Studying Up Revisited." *Political and Legal Anthropology Review* 21, no. 1:114–19.

Hail, Barbara A. 1993. *Hau, Kola! The Plains Indian Collection of the Haffenreffer Museum of Anthropology.* Bristol, R.I.: Haffenreffer Museum of Anthropology, Brown University.

Handler, Richard, and Eric Gable. 1997. *The New History in an Old Museum: Creating the Past at Colonial Williamsburg.* Durham: Duke University Press.

Handler, Richard, and William Saxton. 1988. "Dyssimulation: Reflexivity, Narrative, and the Quest for Authenticity in 'Living History.'" *Cultural Anthropology* 3, no. 3:242–60.

Hannerz, Ulf. 2002. "Notes on the Global Ecumene." In *The Anthropology of Globalization: A Reader,* ed. J.X. Inda and R. Rosaldo, 37–45. Oxford: Blackwell.

Hannerz, Ulf. 2003. "Being There . . . and There . . . and There! Reflections on Multi-site Ethnography." *Ethnography* 4, no. 2:201–16.

Harkin, Michael. 2003. "Staged Encounters: Indians and Tourism." *Ethnohistory* 50, no. 3:573–58.

Hendry, Joy. 2003. "An Ethnographer in the Global Arena: Globography Perhaps?" *Global Networks* 3, no. 4:497–512.

———. 2005. *Reclaiming Culture: Indigenous People and Self-Representation.* Basingstoke, Hampshire: Palgrave Macmillan.

Herle, Anita. 1994. "Dancing Community: Powwow and Pan-Indianism in North America." *Cambridge Anthropology* 17, no. 2:57–83.

Hertzberg, Hazel. 1971. *The Search for an American Indian Identity: Modern Pan-Indian Movements.* Syracuse, N.Y.: Syracuse University Press.

Hinsley, Curtis M. 1991. "The World as Marketplace: Commodification of the Exotic at the World's Columbian Exposition, Chicago, 1893." In *Exhibiting Cultures: The Poetics and Politics of Museum Display,* ed. Ivan Karp and Steven Lavine, 344–65. Washington, D.C.: Smithsonian Institution Press.

Howard, James H. 1955. "Pan-Indian Culture of Oklahoma." *Scientific Monthly* 81, no. 5:215–20.

Jackson, Jason Baird, and Victoria Lindsay Levine. 2002. "Singing for Garfish: Music and Woodland Communities in Eastern Oklahoma." *Ethnomusicology* 46, no. 2:284–305.

Jasen, Patricia. 1993–94. "Native People and the Tourist Industry in Nineteenth Century Ontario." *Journal of Canadian Studies* 28, no. 4:5–27.

Johnson, Katie N., and Tamara Underiner. 2001. "Command Performances: Staging Native Americans at Tillicum Village." In *Selling the Indian: Commercializing & Appropriating American Indian cultures,"* ed. Carter Jones Meyer and Diana Royer, 44–61. Tucson: University of Arizona Press.

Karp, Ivan, and Steven Lavine, eds. 1991. *Exhibiting Cultures: The Poetics and Politics of Museum Display.* Washington, D.C.: Smithsonian Institution Press.

Kasson, Joy S. 2000. *Buffalo Bill's Wild West: Celebrity, Memory, and Popular History.* New York: Hill and Wang.

Kearney, Michael. 2004. *Changing Fields of Anthropology: From Local to Global.* Toronto: Rowman and Littlefield.

Kennedy, Dennis. 2003. "Vaudeville." In *The Oxford Encyclopedia of Theatre and Performance,* ed. Dennis Kennedy, 1400–401. Oxford: Oxford University Press.

King, J.C.H. 1991. "A Century of Indian Shows: Canadian and United States Exhibitions in London, 1825–1925." *European Review of Native American Studies* 5, no. 1:35–42.

Kirshenblatt-Gimblett, Barbara. 1995. "Theorizing Heritage." *Ethnomusicology* 39, no. 3:367–79.

———. 1998. *Destination Culture: Tourism, Museums, and Heritage.* Berkeley: University of California Press.

Kratz, Corinne A., and Ivan Karp. 1993. "Wonder and Worth: Disney Museums in World Showcase." *Museum Anthropology* 17, no. 3:32–42.

Kurath, Gertrude Prokosch. 1957. "Pan-Indianism in Great Lakes Tribal Festivals." *Journal of American Folklore* 70, no. 276:179–82.

Kurotani, Sawa. 2004. "Multi-sited Transnational Ethnography and the Shifting Construction of Fieldwork." In *Anthropologists in the Field: Cases in Participant Observation*, ed. Lynne Hume and Jane Mulcock, 201–15. New York: Columbia University Press.

Lainsbury, Andrew. 2000. *Once Upon an American Dream: The Story of Euro Disneyland*. Lawrence: University of Kansas Press.

Lerch, Patricia B. 1992. "Pageantry, Parade, and Indian Dancing: The Staging of Identity among the Waccamaw Sioux." *Museum Anthropology* 16, no. 2:27–34.

Lerch, Patricia B., and Susan Bullers. 1996. "Powwows as Identity Markers: Traditional or Pan-Indian?" *Human Organization* 55, no. 4:390–95.

Levy, Janet E. 2006. "Prehistory, Identity, and Archaeological Representation in Nordic Museums." *American Anthropologist* 108, no. 1:135–47.

Lischke, Ute, and David T. McNab, eds. 2005. *Walking a Tightrope: Aboriginal People and Their Representations*. Waterloo, Ont.: Wilfrid Laurier University Press.

Lomawaima, Tsianina K. 1995. *They Called It Prairie Light: The Story of Chilocco Indian School*. Lincoln: University of Nebraska Press.

Lounsberry, Lorain. 2000. "Wild West Shows and the Canadian West." In *Cowboys, Ranchers and the Cattle Business: Cross-Border Perspectives on Ranching History*, ed. Simon M. Evans, Sarah Carter, and Bill Yeo. Calgary: University of Calgary Press.

Lowie, Robert H. 1963 [1954]. *Indians of the Plains*. New York: McGraw-Hill.

Lurie, Nancy Oestreich. 1971. "The Contemporary American Indian Scene." In *North American Indians in Historical Perspective*," ed. Eleanor Burke Leacock and Nancy Oestreich Lurie, 418–80. New York: Random House.

MacAloon, John J., ed. 1984. *Rite, Drama, Festival, Spectacle: Rehearsals toward a Theory of Cultural Performance*. Philadelphia: Institute for the Study of Human Issues.

Mackey, Eva. 1999. *The House of Difference: Cultural Politics and National Identity in Canada*. New York: Routledge.

Maddox, Lucy. 2002. "Politics, Performance and Indian Identity." *American Studies International* 40, no. 2:7–36.

Maddra, Sam. 2006. *Hostiles? The Lakota Ghost Dance and Buffalo Bill's Wild West*. Norman: University of Oklahoma Press.

Mahon, Maureen. 2000. "The Visible Evidence of Cultural Producers." *Annual Review of Anthropology* 29:467–92.

Manning, Frank E. 1992. "Spectacle." In *Folklore, Cultural Performances, and Popular Entertainments*, ed. Richard Bauman, 291–99. Oxford: Oxford University Press.

Marcus, George E. 1995. "Ethnography in/of the World System: The Emergence of Multi-sited Ethnography." *Annual Review of Anthropology* 24:95–117.

Martin, Jonathan D. 1996. "'The Grandest and Most Cosmopolitan Object Teacher': Buffalo Bill's Wild West and the Politics of American Identity, 1883–1899." *Radical History Review* 66:92–123.

Mason, K. 2004. "Sound and Meaning in Aboriginal Tourism." *Annals of Tourism Research* 31, 4:837–53.

Mathur, Saloni. 2000. "Living Ethnological Exhibits: The Case of 1886." *Cultural Anthropology* 15, no. 4:492–524.

McBride, Bunny. 1995. *Molly Spotted Elk: A Penobscot in Paris*. Norman: University of Oklahoma Press.

Meyer, Carter Jones, and Diana Royer, eds. 2001. *Selling the Indian: Commercializing and Appropriating American Indian Cultures*. Tucson: University of Arizona Press.

Mitchell, Timothy. 1992. "Orientalism and the Exhibitionary Order." In *Colonialism and Culture*, ed. Nicholas B. Dirks, 289–317. Ann Arbor: University of Michigan Press.

Morantz, Toby. 2001. "Plunder or Harmony? On Merging European and Native Views of Early Contact." In *Decentering the Renaissance. Canada and Europe in Multidisciplinary Perspective 1500–1700*, ed. Germaine Warkentin and Carolyn Podruchny, 48–67. Toronto: University of Toronto Press.

Moses, L.G. 1996. *Wild West Shows and the Images of American Indians, 1883–1933*. Albuquerque: University of New Mexico Press.

Mydin, Iskander. 1992. Historical Images—Changing Audiences. In *Anthropology and Photography, 1860–1920*, ed. Elizabeth Edwards, 249–52. New Haven, Conn.: Yale University Press.

Myers, Fred R. 1994. "Culture Making: Performing Aboriginality at the Asia Society Gallery." *American Ethnologist* 21, no. 4:679–99.

Napier, Rita G. 1999. "Across the Big Water: American Indians' Perceptions of Europe and Europeans, 1887–1906." In *Indians and Europe: An Interdisciplinary Collection of Essays*," ed. Christian F. Feest, 383–403. Lincoln: University of Nebraska Press.

Nash, Dennison. 1989. "Tourism as a Form of Imperialism." In *Hosts and Guests: The Anthropology of Tourism*," ed. Valene L. Smith, 37–52. Philadelphia: University of Pennsylvania Press.

NBC (National Battlefields Commission). 1908. *Historical Souvenir and Book of the Pageants of the 300th Anniversary of the Founding of Quebec, the Ancient Capital of Canada*. Montreal: National Battlefields Commission.

Nelles, Henry V. 1999. *The Art of Nation Building: Pageantry and Spectacle at Quebec's Tercentenary*. Toronto: University of Toronto Press.

Nicks, Trudy. 1996. "Dr. Oronhyatekha's History Lessons: Reading Museum Collections as Texts." In *Reading beyond Words: Contexts for Native History*, ed. Jennifer S. H. Brown and Elizabeth Vibert, 482–508. Peterborough, Ont.: Broadview Press.

———. 1999. "Indian Villages and Entertainments: Setting the Stage for Tourist Souvenir Sales." In *Unpacking Culture: Art and Commodity in Colonial and Postcolonial Worlds*, ed. Ruth B. Phillips and Christopher B. Steiner, 301–15. Berkeley: University of California Press.

———. n.d. "Travelling and Performing, 1850–1950: A Century of Native Entertainments." Unpublished manscript, held by author.

Nicks, Trudy, and Ruth B. Phillips. 2007. "'From Wigwam to White Lights.' Princess White Deer's Indian Acts." In *Three Centuries of Woodlands Indian Art*, ed. J. C. H. King and Christian F. Feest, 144–60. Altenstadt, Germany: ZKF Publishers.

Notzke, Claudia. 2004. "Indigenous Tourism Development in Southern Alberta, Canada: Tentative Engagement." *Journal of Sustainable Tourism* 12, no. 1:29–54.

Ortiz, Fernando. 1995. *Cuban Counterpoint: Tabacco and Sugar*. Translated by Harriet de Onis. Durham, N.C.: Duke University Press.

Ortner, Sherry B. 1994. "Theory in Anthropology since the Sixties." In *Culture / Power / History*, ed. Nicholas B. Dirks, Geoff Eley, and Sherry B. Ortner, 372–411. Princeton, N.J.: Princeton University Press.

———. 1999. *Life and Death on Mount Everest: Sherpas and Himalayan Mountaineering*. Princeton, N.J.: Princeton University Press.

———. 2001. "Specifying Agency: The Comaroffs and Their Critics." *Interventions* 3, no. 1:76–84.

———. 2006. *Anthropology and Social Theory: Culture, Power, and the Acting Subject*. Durham, N.C.: Duke University Press.

Parezo, Nancy J., and John W. Troutman. 2001. "The 'Shy' Cocoa Go to the Fair." In *Selling the Indian: Commercializing and Appropriating American Indian Cultures*, ed. Carter Jones Meyer and Diana Royer, 3–43. Tucson: University of Arizona Press.

Patterson, Micelle Wick. 2002. "'Real' Indian Songs: The Society of American Indians and the Use of Native American Culture as a Means of Reform." *American Indian Quarterly* 26, no. 1:44–66.

Peers, Laura. 1999. "'Playing Ourselves': First Nations and Native American Interpreters at Living History Sites." *Public Historian* 21, no. 4:39–59.

———. 2007. *Playing Ourselves: Interpreting Native Histories at Historic Reconstructions*. Plymouth, U.K.: Altamira Press.

Phillips, Ruth B. 1998. *Trading Identities: The Souvenir in Native North American Art from the Northeast, 1700–1900*. Seattle: University of Washington Press.

———. 2004a. "Disappearing Acts: Traditions of Exposure, Traditions of Enclosure and Iroquois Masks." In *Questions of Tradition*, ed. Mark Phillips, 56–87. Toronto: University of Toronto Press.

———. 2004b. "Making Sense out/of the Visual: Aboriginal Presentations and Representations in Nineteenth-Century Canada." *Art History* 27, no. 4:593–615.

Powers, William K. 1990. *War Dance: Plains Indian Musical Performance*. Tucson: University of Arizona Press.

Pratt, Mary Louise. 1992. *Imperial Eyes: Travel Writing and Transculturation*. New York: Routledge.

Raibmon, Paige. 2000. "Theatres of Contact: The Kwakwaka'wakw Meet Colonialism in British Columbia and at the Chicago World's Fair." *Canadian Historical Review* 81, no. 2:157–90.

———. 2005. *Authentic Indians: Episodes of Encounter from the Late-Nineteenth-Century Northwest Coast*. Durham, N.C.: Duke University Press.

Reddin, Paul. 1999. *Wild West Shows*. Urbana: University of Illinois Press.

Rogers, Phyllis. 1983. "'Buffalo Bill' and the Siouan Image." *American Indian Culture and Research Journal* 7, no. 3:43–53.

Roth, Barbara Williams. 1965–66. "The 101 Ranch Wild West Show, 1904–1932." *Chronicles of Oklahoma* 43, no. 4:416–31.

Russell, Don. 1970. *The Wild West or, a History of the Wild West Shows*. Fort Worth, Tex.: Amon Carter Museum of Western Art.

Rydell, Robert W. 1984. *All the World's a Fair: Visions of Empire at American International Expositions, 1876–1916*. Chicago: University of Chicago Press.

Rydell, Robert W., John E. Findling, and Kimberly D. Pelle, eds. 2000. *Fair America: World's Fairs in the United States*. Washington D.C.: Smithsonian Institution Press.

Said, Edward W. 1979. *Orientalism*. London: Routledge and Kegan Paul.

Scarangella, Linda. 2005. "Fieldwork at Buffalo Bill's Wild West show." *Anthropology News* 46, no. 5:17, 19.

———. 2008. "Spectacular Native Performances: From the Wild West to the Tourist Site, Nineteenth Century to the Present. Ph.D. dissertation, McMaster University.

———. 2010. "Indigeneity in Tourism: Transnational Spaces, Pan-Indian Identity and Cosmopolitanism." In *Indigenous Cosmopolitans: Transnational and Transcultural Indigeneity in the 21st Century*, ed. Maximilian C. Forte, 163–88. Peter Lang.

Scherer, Joanna C. 1992. "The Photographic Document: Photographs as Primary Data in Anthropological Enquiry. In *Anthropology and Photography, 1860–1920*, ed. Elizabeth Edwards, 32–41. New Haven, Conn.: Yale University Press.

Schwartz, Vanessa R. 1998. *Spectacular Realities: Early Mass Culture in Fin-de-Siècle Paris.* Berkeley: University of California Press.

Sewell, William H., Jr. 1992. "A Theory of Structure: Duality, Agency, and Transformation." *American Journal of Sociology* 98, no. 1:1–29.

Shirley, Glenn. 1993. *Pawnee Bill: A Biography of Major Gordon W. Lillie.* Stillwater, Okla.: Western Publications.

Skidmore, Colleen. 2003. "Imagining the 'Wild West': Hugo Vieweger and the Autochrome in Canada." *History of Photography* 27, no. 4:342–48.

Slotkin, Richard. 1981. "The 'Wild West.'" In *Buffalo Bill and the Wild West,* ed. Brooklyn Museum, 27–44. New York: Brooklyn Museum.

———. 1992. *Gunfighter Nation: The Myth of the Frontier in Twentieth Century America.* New York: Antheneum.

Standing Bear, Luther. 1975. *My People the Sioux.* Edited by A. Brininstool with an Introduction by Richard N. Ellis. Lincoln: University of Nebraska Press.

Stanley, Nick. 1998. *Being Ourselves for You: The Global Display of Cultures.* London: Middlesex University Press.

Starita, Joe. 1995. *The Dull Knifes of Pine Ridge: A Lakota Odyssey.* New York: G.P. Putman's Sons.

Tilley, Christopher. 1997. "Performing Culture in the Global Village." *Critique of Anthropology* 17, no. 1:67–89.

Tivers, Jacqueline. 2002. "Performing Heritage: The Use of Live 'Actors' in Heritage Presentations." *Leisure Studies* 21:187–200.

Trigger, Bruce G. 1986. "Ethnohistory: The Unfinished Edifice." *Ethnohistory* 33, no. 3:253–67.

Troutman, John W. 2009. *Indian Blues: American Indians and the Politics of Music, 1879–1934.* Norman: University of Oklahoma Press.

Truettner, William H. 1979. *The Natural Man Observed: A Study of Catlin's Indian Gallery.* Washington, D.C.: Smithsonian Institution Press.

Tuttle, Pauline. 2001. "'Beyond Feathers and Beads': Interlocking Narratives in the Music and Dance of Tokeya Inajin (Kevin Locke)." In *Selling the Indian: Commercializing and Appropriating American Indian Cultures,* ed. Carter Jones Meyer and Diana Royer, 99–156. Tucson: University of Arizona Press.

Wallis, Michael. 1999. *The Real Wild West: The 101 Ranch and the Creation of the American West.* New York: St. Martin's Griffin.

Warren, Louis S. 2005. *Buffalo Bill's America: William Cody and the Wild West Show.* New York: Alfred A. Knopf.

Weaver, Hilary N. 2001. "Indigenous Identity: What Is It, and Who Really Has It?" *American Indian Quarterly* 25, no. 2:240–55.

Weeks, Philip, ed. 1988. *The American Indian Experience: A Profile, 1524 to the Present.* Arlington Heights, Ill.: Forum Press.

Whissel, Kristen. 2002. "Placing the Spectator on the Scene of History: The Battle Re-enactment at the Turn of the Century, from Buffalo Bill's Wild West to the Early Cinema." *Historical Journal of Film, Radio and Television* 22, no. 3:225–43.

White, Richard. 1994. "Frederick Jackson Turner and Buffalo Bill." In *The Frontier in American Culture: An Exhibition at the Newberry Library*, ed. James R Grossman, 7–65. Berkeley: University of California Press.

Wiedman, D. 2010. "Global Marketing of Indigenous Culture: Discovering Native America with Lee Tiger and the Florida Miccosukee." *American Indian Culture and Research Journal* 34, no. 4:1–26.

Wilmeth, Don B. 1982. *Variety Entertainment and Outdoor Amusements: A Reference Guide*. Westport, Conn.: Greenwood Press.

Wilson, R.L., and Greg Martin. 1998. *Buffalo Bill's Wild West: An American Legend*. New York: Random House.

Yellow Robe, Chauncey. 1914. "The Menace of the Wild West Show." *Quarterly Journal of the Society of the American Indians* 2 (July/Sept.): 224–25.

Young Bear, Severt, and R.D. Theisz. 1994. *Standing in the Light: A Lakota Way of Seeing*. Lincoln: University of Nebraska Press.

INTERVIEWS CITED

Brass, Ferlyn. 2004. Interview by author, September 29, 2004, Euro Disney, France.

Briley, Jeff. 2005. Interview by author, May 28, 2005, Oklahoma City, Oklahoma.

Brown, Ronny. 2005. Interview by author, May 29, 2005, Pawnee, Oklahoma.

Bruised Head, Tim. 2005. Interview by author, August 16, 2005, Euro Disney, France.

Burr, Tammy. 2005. Interview by author, June 27, 2005, Sheridan, Wyoming.

Delisle, Barbara Little Bear. 2004. Interview by author, Kahnawake, Quebec.

Dust, Kevin (Kave). 2004. Interview by author, September 28, 2004, Euro Disney, France.

———. 2005. Interview by author, August 12, 2005, Euro Disney, France.

Grevy, Christel. 2005. Interview by author, August 23, 2005, Euro Disney, France.

Hammill, Brian. 2005. Interview by author, June 25, 2005, Sheridan, Wyoming.

Jenkins, Lane. 2005. Interview by author, June 25, 2005, Sheridan, Wyoming.

Jim, William. 2005. Interview by author, August 11, 2005, Euro Disney, France.

Maier, Edre. 2005. Interview by author, June 27, 2005, Sheridan, Wyoming.

Mustus, Kevin (Wiley). 2004. Interview by author, September 28, 2004, Euro Disney, France.

Rangel, Ernest. 2005. Interview by author, August 16, 2005, Euro Disney, France.

Trudeau, Sylvia. 2004. Interview by author, October 26, 2004, Lachine, Quebec.

Two-Rivers, Billy. 2004. Interview by author, August 17, 2004, Kahnawake, Quebec.

Yellowbird, Carter. 2005. Interview by author, January 10, 2005, Edmonton, Alberta.

INDEX